Hearts and Minds

Hearts and Minds

Israel and the Battle for Public Opinion

NACHMAN SHAI

Translated by Ira Moskowitz

Published by State University of New York Press, Albany

For information, contact State University of New York Press, Albany, NY
www.sunypress.edu

Library of Congress Cataloging-in-Publication Data

Names: Shai, Nachman, author. | Moskowitz, Ira (Translator), translator.
Title: Hearts and minds : Israel and the battle for public opinion / Nachman
  Shai ; translated by Ira Moskowitz
Description: Albany : State University of New York Press, 2018. | Includes
  bibliographical references and index.
Identifiers: LCCN 2017019636 (print) | LCCN 2017025549 (ebook) | ISBN
  9781438469072 (ebook) | ISBN 9781438469058 | ISBN 9781438469058
  (hardcover : alk. paper)
Subjects: LCSH: Israel—Foreign public opinion. | Arab-Israeli conflict—Mass
  media and the conflict. | Mass media and public opinion—Israel. | Mass
  media and international relations—Israel. | Mass media and war—Israel.
Classification: LCC DS102.95 (ebook) | LCC DS102.95 .S525 2018 (print) | DDC
  956.94—dc23
LC record available at https://lccn.loc.gov/2017019636

10 9 8 7 6 5 4 3 2 1

This book is dedicated to my parents,
Hava and Eliezer Shaikevitch
of blessed memory, who showed me the way.
To my wife, Rivka, who encouraged and supported me,
and to our children—Noa and her husband Eran,
Iddo and his wife Suzanna, and Dana and her husband Dan—
and to our grandchildren, Mika, Alma, Laila, Yahli, Alex and Leo.
In hope that this book will strengthen our hope and faith
in a future of peace.

Contents

Figures

Abbreviations

ADL	Anti-Defamation League
AICE	American-Israeli Cooperative Enterprise
AIPAC	American Israel Public Affairs Committee
AJC	American Jewish Committee
BDS	Boycott, Divestment, Sanctions
BICOM	Britain Israel Communications and Research Centre
BNC	BDS National Committee
CAMERA	Committee for Accuracy in Middle East Reporting in America
GC4I	Global Coalition for Israel
GOC	General Officer Commanding
GPO	Government Press Office
GSS	General Security Service (the Shin Bet)
ECCP	European Coordination of Committees and Associations for Palestine
IAF	Israeli Air Force
IBA	Israel Broadcasting Authority
ICC	International Criminal Court
IDC	Interdisciplinary Center
IDF	Israel Defense Forces
INFO	Israel Newsmakers Forum

JFNA	Jewish Federations of North America
JCPA	Jewish Council for Public Affairs
JCRC	Jewish Community Relations Council
JDC	Joint Distribution Committee
JNF	Jewish National Fund
JLTV	Jewish Life Television Network
MALMAB	Defense Ministry Security Authority
MALAT	Center for Consciousness Operations
MASHAV	Agency for International Development Cooperation
MEMRI	Middle East Media Research Institute
MK	Member of Knesset
NSC	National Security Council
PMO	Prime Minister's Office
PMW	Palestinian Media Watch
OECD	Organisation for Economic Co-operation and Development
UNRWA	United Nations Relief and Works Agency
WSI	World Standing Index
WZO	World Zionist Organization

Acknowledgments

This book was published with the help and support of hundreds of people in Israel and abroad, who assisted me from the moment of its conception through its concluding words. I am very grateful to all of them.

My thanks to Bar-Ilan University's administrative and academic team, especially Eytan Gilboa, Shmuel Sandler, and Shmuel Lehman-Wilzig.

The book is based on over 250 interviews with key figures in Israeli society, politics, the defense establishment, the media, diplomacy in general, and public diplomacy in particular. A full list of interviewees appears following the acknowledgments, and I owe many thanks to each of them.

The original materials I received were of great importance in light of the limited access to official archives and documentary literature of this period. In this context, I would like to thank former cabinet secretary Israel Maimon and his assistant Tzahi Gavrieli. A number of (retired) IDF officers provided valuable assistance, including Maj. Gen. Mendy Orr, Brig. Gen. Ruth Yaron, Brig. Gen. Miri Regev, Col. Eyal Efrati, and Maj. Limor Gross, as well as present and past Shin Bet personnel, including Lior Akerman and Michal Yaniv. In addition, from the Foreign Ministry, thanks to Nissim Ben-Sheetrit, Gideon Meir, Aryeh Mekel, Shlomo Meir, Ido Aharoni, Ilan Sztulman, and Adi Sheinman, and from Israel Police: Brig. Gen. Nitza Friedman and Maj. Gen. Amichai Shai. And from the Government Press Office, thanks go to Danny Seaman, and from the National Security Council—to all of its former directors, especially Maj. Gen. (ret.) Giora Eiland and Brig. Gen. (ret.) Israela Oron.

Elad Peled, Moshe Yegar, Dr. Dina Goren, Dr. Meron Medzini, Aloph Hareven, and Yaakov Schatz provided primary materials on the history of Israel's public diplomacy.

Unique material on various events discussed in the book were contributed by Nahum Shahaf, Richard Landes, Philippe Karsenty, Charles

Enderlin, Yarden Vatikai, Maj. Gen. (ret.) Yom-Tov Samia, Dr. Sharon Pardo, Ze'ev Schiff, and Hirsch Goodman.

I was assisted in obtaining archival material by Lt. Col. Nava Aloni of the National Defense College; Aviva Karton of the IDF Archives; Col. (ret.) Reuven Erlich, who heads the Meir Amit Intelligence and Terrorism Information Center; and the IT staff at the Prime Minister's Office.

Amy Lev, Meirav Bar-Lev, Racheli Kaplan, Gali Yahav Attias, Naomi Kessler-Feinstein, David Vaknin, and Roni Ezuz helped to prepare and organize the materials. Ruth Pragayi edited and proofread the Hebrew text, and Avi Katzman later helped in this effort. I am very grateful to the journalist Amir Oren.

Above all, I would like to note the unique contribution of Eran Ben-Ari.

The English edition was published with the assistance of Dov Eichenwald, CEO of Yedioth Books, and the contributions of Ariel Roth and the Israel Institute, Bruce Arbit, Richard M. Pachulski, Michael L. Tuchin, and Harold Neumann.

Special thanks to my friends Peter and Amy Bernstein for their encouragement and support.

Thank you to Ira Moskowitz for translating the original Hebrew text. And, finally, I would like to thank State University of New York Press for publishing this book.

I hope that everyone is satisfied with the final product of this collective effort and believes, as I do, that the book will indeed deepen our understanding of public diplomacy and lead decision makers to accord it the weight it deserves at the highest national echelon.

Interviewees

Adler, Reuven—Owner of advertising firm

Agmon, David—Special Aide to the IDF Chief of Staff, Head of Prime Minister's Bureau, Brigadier General

Aharoni, Ido—Consul for Media and Public Affairs in New York and Los Angeles

Akerman, Lior—Head of the Shin Bet Director's Bureau

Almog, Doron—GOC Southern Command, Major General

Alon, Gal—Consultant on Developing Strategic Processes in the Prime Minister's Office

Aloni, Yair—Deputy Director-General for Planning and Development at Broadcast Authority, Director of Israel Television

Amir, Menashe—Commentator and Broadcaster in Persian, Israel Radio

Arad, Eyal—Strategic Consultant

Arens, Moshe—Minister of Defense, Ambassador in Washington, Chairman of the Knesset Foreign Affairs and Defense Committee

Arussi, Eitan—Head of the Arab Media Department at the IDF Spokesperson's Office, Major

Atzmon, Irit—Deputy IDF Spokesperson, NGO Director, Colonel

Avital, Colette—Deputy Director-General of the Foreign Ministry, Ambassador, MK

Avnon, Arthur—Deputy Director-General of the Foreign Ministry (Cultural and Scientific Affairs), Ambassador

Ayalon, Ami—Commander of Israel Navy, Shin Bet Director, Minister, Major General

Baker, Alan—Legal Advisor at the Foreign Ministry, Ambassador

Baker, David—Assistant to the Foreign Media Advisor in the Prime Minister's Office

Baltiansky, Gadi—Media Advisor to the Prime Minister, Media Advisor at the Israeli Embassy in Washington

Barak, Ehud—Prime Minister, Defense Minister, IDF Chief of Staff, Lieutenant General

Bar-Lev, Uri—Commander of Israel Police Southern District, Major General

Be'er, Yizhar—CEO of Keshev, Executive Director of B'Tselem

Beilin, Yossi—Minister of Justice, Deputy Foreign Minister, MK

Ben-Ami, Oded—Journalist, Channel 2; IDF Spokesperson, Brigadier General

Ben-Ami, Shlomo—Foreign Minister, Ambassador, Professor

Ben-David, Alon—Military Reporter, Channel 1; Military Commentator, Channel 10

Ben-David, Calev—Journalist, Managing Editor at the *Jerusalem Post*

Ben-David, Lenny—Deputy Chief of Mission at the Israeli Embassy in Washington, Director of AIPAC's Israel Office

Ben-Eliezer, Binyamin—Minister of Defense, Minister of National Infrastructure, Coordinator of Government Activity in the Territories, Brigadier General

Bentsur, Eytan—Director-General of the Foreign Ministry, Ambassador, Consul General in Los Angeles

Ben-Yishai, Ron—Journalist, Commander of Army Radio, Military Commentator for Israel Television, *Yedioth Ahronoth*, *Ynet*, Lieutenant Colonel

Biran, Yoav—Director-General of the Foreign Ministry, Ambassador, Deputy Director of the National Security Council

Carmon, Yigal—CEO of MEMRI, Colonel

Cohen, Ran—Minister of Trade and Industry, MK, Colonel

Cotler, Irwin—Professor, Canadian Minister of Justice

Dahuh-Halevi, Yoni—Head of the Information and Public Diplomacy Branch at the IDF Spokesperson's Office, Policy Planning Advisor at the Foreign Ministry

Daniel, Roni—Military Commentator, Channel 2

Dayan, Uzi—Head of the National Security Council, GOC Central Command, Major General

Dekel, Ofer—Shin Bet Deputy Director, Coordinator of Government Activities for POWs and MIAs

Dichter, Avi—Shin Bet Director, Minister of Public Security

Diskin, Yuval—Shin Bet Director

Divon, Haim—Deputy Director-General of MASHAV at the Foreign Ministry, Ambassador

Dotan, Amira—Chairperson of the Knesset Foreign Affairs and Defense Committee's Subcommittee on Foreign Affairs and Public Diplomacy,

MK, Head of the Jewish Agency's Office in the United States, Chief Officer of the IDF Women's Corps, Brigadier General

Edri, Yaakov—Minister of Immigrant Absorption, Mayor

Eiland, Giora—Head of IDF Operations Branch, National Security Council Director, Major General

Eisen, Miri—Department Head in IDF Military Intelligence, Prime Minister's Foreign Media Advisor, Colonel

Eizenkot, Gadi—Military Secretary to the Prime Minister (Ehud Barak and Ariel Sharon), GOC Northern Command, IDF Chief of Staff, Lieutenant General

Eitan, Yitzhak—GOC Central Command, Major General

Eldar, Shlomi—Journalist, Channel 1

Enderlin, Charles—Reporter for France 2

Erlich, Reuven—Head of the Intelligence and Terrorism Information Center at the Israel Intelligence Heritage & Commemoration Center, Colonel

Even-Chen, Moshe—Head of IDF Behavioral Science Department, Colonel

Ezra, Gideon—Deputy Director of the Shin Bet, Ministry of Public Security, Minister of Environmental Protection

Fastman, Eli—Producer for Fox Network in Israel

Feingold, Sharon—Head of the International Department at the IDF Spokesperson's Office (2001–2005), Major

Finn, Helena—Counselor for Public Affairs at the U.S. Embassy in Israel

Foxman, Abe—ADL Director

Friedman, Nitza—Director of Public Affairs at Israel Police, Brigadier General

Gal, Orly—Deputy IDF Spokesperson, Colonel

Gal, Yossi—Deputy Director-General of the Foreign Ministry, Head of Public Diplomacy in the Prime Minister's Office, Ambassador

Ganor, Boaz—Dean of the Lauder School of Government and Executive Director of the International Institute for Counter-Terrorism at the Interdisciplinary Center (IDC), Herzliya

Ganor, Shlomo—Director of Israel Television in Arabic

Gavrieli, Tzahi—Assistant to the Cabinet Secretary, Attorney

Gazit, Shlomo—Head of Military Intelligence, Director-General of the Jewish Agency, Major General

Gellert, Alon—Head of the Study Committee on Spokesmanship, Public Diplomacy, and Military Media Relations in the Second Lebanon War; Legal Advisor in the Prime Minister's Office, Colonel

Gil, Avi—Director-General of the Foreign Ministry

Gil, Orly—Head of the NGO Department in the Foreign Ministry's International Organizations Division

Gilad, Amos—IDF Spokesperson, Coordinator of Government Activity in the Territories, Major General

Gilady, Eival—Head of the IDF Planning Division, Responsible for Public Diplomacy during the Disengagement, Brigadier General

Gillon, Carmi—Shin Bet Director, Ambassador

Gissin, Amir—Director of the Foreign Ministry's Public Diplomacy Department, Consul General

Gissin, Raanan—Deputy IDF Spokesperson, Foreign Media Advisor to the Prime Minister, Colonel

Gordin, Arik—Head of the Public Diplomacy Branch at Army Radio, Colonel

Gracier, Ofra—Researcher at the IDF Operational Theory Research Institute

Green, Aryeh—CEO of Media Central

Griffin, Jennifer—Reporter for Fox Network in Israel

Grinstein, Gidi—Secretary of the Negotiating Team with the Palestinians, Head of the Reut Institute

Gross, Arnon—Assistant to the Director of Israel Radio in Arabic

Haber, Eitan—Journalist at *Yedioth Ahronoth*, Bureau Chief for Prime Minister Yitzhak Rabin

Hacham, David—Arab Affairs Advisor to the Defense Minister

Hacohen, Eli—Journalist at Israel Radio, Professional Director of the Netvision Institute for Internet Studies at Tel Aviv University

Hacohen, Gershon—Corps Commander, Military Colleges Commander, Major General

Hadas, Yossi—Director-General of the Foreign Ministry, Ambassador

Halabi, Rafik—Director of the News Division of Channel 1, Editor of *Mabat* News Broadcast

Halevy, Efraim—Head of the Mossad, Head of the National Security Council

Harel, Amos—Journalist, *Haaretz* Military Commentator

Harel, Dan—Head of the IDF Operations Division, Head of the Planning Division, GOC Southern Command, Deputy Chief of Staff, Major General

Hareven, Alouph—Division Head in the Ministry of Public Diplomacy

Hasson, Yisrael—Deputy Director of the Shin Bet, MK

Herzl, Tova—Ambassador of Israel in South Africa

Herzog, Isaac—Cabinet Secretary, Minister of Tourism, Minister of Social Welfare

Hoenlein, Malcolm—CEO of the Conference of Presidents of Major American Jewish Organizations

Horev, Yehiel—Head of the Security Department (MALMAB) in the Defense Ministry

Horowitz, Shaike—Head of Israel Police Bomb Disposal Division, Brigadier General

Kalo, Hezi—Senior Shin Bet Official

Kamir, Eli—Media Advisor to the Defense Minister, Bureau Chief of the Minister of Transportation

Katz, Noam—Spokesperson for the Israeli Delegation to the Durban Conference, Ambassador, Head of the Foreign Ministry's Public Diplomacy Department

Kaye, Yehuda—Director of the Jewish Federation in Johannesburg

Kitri, Ron—IDF Spokesperson, Principal of the Reali School, Brigadier General

Klifi, Meir—Head of IDF Doctrine and Training Division, Military Secretary to the Prime Minister, Major General

Kober, Avi—Physician, Researcher at Bar-Ilan University

Kott, Elam—Deputy IDF Spokesperson, Public Relations Director at Tel Aviv University

Kuperwasser, Yossi—Head of the Research Division of IDF Military Intelligence, Brigadier General

Landes, Richard—Professor, Boston University

Lapid, Efraim—IDF Spokesperson, Commander of Army Radio, Jewish Agency Spokesperson, Brigadier General

Lapid, Yosef—Journalist at *Maariv*, MK, Minister of Justice

Leon, Micha—Senior Shin Bet Official

Lerman, Eran—Assistant to the Head of the Research Division of IDF Military Intelligence, Director of the Israel Office of the American Jewish Committee, Colonel

Leshno-Yaar, Roni—Deputy Director-General for the United Nations and International Organizations at the Foreign Ministry, Ambassador

Levy, David—Minister of Housing and Construction, Deputy Prime Minister and Foreign Minister

Levy, Yaakov—Deputy Director-General for Media and Public Diplomacy at the Foreign Ministry, Ambassador, Head of the Public Diplomacy Branch at the Foreign Ministry

Liel, Alon—Director-General of the Foreign Ministry, Ambassador

Livni, Amit—Head of the Strategy Department at the IDF Spokesperson's Office, Director of Marketing at El Al, Colonel

Nirenstein, Fiamma—Journalist, Writer, Member of Italy's Parliament

Nitzan, Chen—Deputy State Attorney

Olster, Joni—Reservist in Battalion 8110, Brigade 5

Oren, Amir—Military Commentator, *Haaretz*

Orkabi, Amichai—Assistant to the Cabinet Secretary, Attorney, Businessman

Oron, Amira—Director of the Foreign Ministry's Arabic Media and Public Affairs Department

Oron, Israela—Deputy National Security Advisor at the National Security Council, Brigadier General

Orr, Mendy—Coordinator of Government Activities in the Territories; State Comptroller's Office (responsible for auditing defense establishment), Major General

Ostfeld, Ilan—Military Reporter at Army Radio, Lieutenant Colonel

Parsi-Zadok, Merav—Media Advisor to the Prime Minister

Pazner, Avi—Media Advisor to the Prime Minister, Ambassador, Keren Hayesod Chairman

Peled, Elad—GOC Central Command, Chairman of the Peled Committee, Major General

Pentik, Yitzhak—Head of the Shin Bet's Jewish Division

Peres, Shimon—President of Israel, Prime Minister, Foreign Minister, Defense Minister, MK

Peri, Yaakov—Shin Bet Director, Businessman, MK

Perlman, Arnon—Director of Media and Public Affairs at the Prime Minister's Office

Pinkas, Alon—Foreign Minister's Chief of Staff, Consul General in New York

Pogrund, Benjamin—Journalist, Writer on South Africa

Porat, Dina—Professor, Researcher, Member of the Israeli Delegation to the Durban Conference

Prosor, Ron—Director-General of the Foreign Ministry, Ambassador

Rabin, Dalia—Deputy Defense Minister, MK, Attorney, Chairperson of Rabin Center

Raffel, Martin—Senior Vice President of JCPA

Rafowicz, Olivier—Head of the International Media Department at the IDF Spokesperson's Office, CEO of Infolive TV

Regev, Miri—IDF Spokesperson, Chief Military Censor, Brigadier General

Reshef, Eran—Founder and CEO of the Giyus Network

Reshef, Peleg—Chairman of World Union of Jewish Students

Rivkind, Linda—Senior Official at Government Press Office, Deputy Director of Jerusalem Press Club

Ron-Tal, Yiftah—Commander of IDF Ground Forces, Businessman, Major General

Samia, Yom-Tov—GOC Southern Command, Businessman, PhD, Major General

Samuels, Shimon—Director for International Relations at the Wiesenthal Center

Schiff, Ze'ev—*Haaretz* Military Commentator

Seaman, Danny—Director of the Government Press Office

Shahaf, Nahum—Physicist, Researcher

Shai, Amichai—Director of Public Diplomacy at Israel Police during the Disengagement, Head of Human Resources at Israel Police, Major General

Shai, Shaul—Head of the IDF History Department, Deputy Director of the National Security Council, Researcher, PhD, Colonel

Shaked, Roni—Palestinian Territories Reporter at *Yedioth Ahronoth*, Field Coordinator at the Shin Bet

Shalom, Avraham—Shin Bet Director, Businessman

Shalom, Silvan—Foreign Minister, Finance Minister, Deputy Defense Minister, MK, Journalist at *Hadashot*

Shani, Uri—Prime Minister's Bureau Chief, Businessman

Shariv, Asaf—Director of Public Diplomacy at the Prime Minister's Office, Consul General in New York

Shein, Ralph—Head of the IDF Special Means Department, Colonel

Sheinman, Adi—Legal Advisor to Israel's Delegation to the Durban Conference, Attorney

Shek, Danny—BICOM Director, Ambassador

Sher, Gilead—Prime Minister's Bureau Chief, Head of Negotiating Team with the Palestinians, Attorney

Shlein, Eyal—Commander of an IDF Reserve Division, Brigadier General

Shlomo, Meir—Director of the Public Diplomacy Department and Acting Deputy Director-General for Media and Public Diplomacy at the Foreign Ministry, Consul General

Shoval, Zalman—Ambassador, MK, Businessman

Sneh, Efraim—Deputy Defense Minister, MK, Physician, Brigadier General

Sofer, Mark—Foreign Ministry Spokesperson during Second Intifada, Ambassador, Deputy Director-General of the Foreign Ministry

Steinberg, Gerald—Professor at Bar-Ilan University, Founder and President of NGO Monitor

Steinitz, Yuval—Chairman of the Knesset Foreign Affairs and Defense Committee, MK, PhD

Sztulman, Ilan—Head of the Internet Department at the Foreign Ministry, Reservist at the IDF Spokesperson's Office

Tadhar, Rafi—Senior Shin Bet Official, Businessman

Tal, Ilan—IDF Spokesperson, Major General

Tal, Israel—Head of the IAF Communications Branch, Lieutenant Colonel

Tal, Nachman—Senior Shin Bet Official

Tamir, Moshe—Commander of Golani Brigade, Division Commander, Brigadier General

Taub, Danny—Senior Deputy to the Legal Advisor, Foreign Ministry

Teomim, Moshe—Owner of Advertising Firm, Media Consultant

Tov, Kobi—CEO Israel Advocacy Initiative

Tzur, David—Minister of Public Security's Chief of Operations, Commander of the Tel Aviv District of Israel Police, Brigadier General

Tzur, Sharon—Director of Honest Reporting

Vatikai, Yarden—Head of the International Media Branch at the IDF Spokesperson's Office, Media Advisor to the Defense Minister, Director of the National Information Directorate

Weinberg, Larry—CEO of the Israel 21C Organization

Weissglass, Dov—Director of the Prime Minister's Bureau, Advisor to the Prime Minister, Attorney

Wieseltier, Eti—Television Editor and Producer

Wilson, Simon—Head of the BBC's Office in Israel

Yaalon, Moshe—Defense Minister, IDF Chief of Staff, Lieutenant General

Yadid, Mordechai—Head of the Foreign Ministry's Division for the United Nations and International Organizations, Ambassador

Yaniv, Michal—Head of the Shin Bet's Media Department

Yaron, Ruth—IDF Spokesperson, Diplomat, Senior Fellow at the Jewish People Policy Planning Institute, Brigadier General

Yatom, Danny—Head of the Political-Security Staff in Prime Minister Ehud Barak's Bureau, Head of the Mossad, MK

Yatom, Ehud—Head of Shin Bet's Operations Branch, MK

Yegar, Moshe—Head of the Foreign Ministry's Public Diplomacy Division, Ambassador

Zahavi, Shachar—CEO IsraAID

Zakai, Shmuel—Commander of the Gaza Division, Brigadier General

Zangen, David—Brigade Physician, Brigade 5

Ziso, David—Media Advisor to the Defense Minister, Attorney

Ziv, Israel—Head of IDF Operations Division, Major General

Introduction

> We will make our reckoning with ourselves today; we are a generation that settles the land and without the steel helmet and the cannon's maw, we will not be able to plant a tree and build a home. Let us not be deterred from seeing the loathing that is inflaming and filling the lives of the hundreds of thousands of Arabs who live around us. Let us not avert our eyes lest our arms weaken. This is the fate of our generation. This is our life's choice—to be prepared and armed, strong and determined, lest the sword be stricken from our fist and our lives cut down.
>
> —Moshe Dayan, eulogy for Roi Rotberg, May 1, 1956

On May 1, 1956, IDF chief of staff Moshe Dayan came to Kibbutz Nahal Oz, on the border with the Gaza Strip, to eulogize Roi Rotberg, a member of the kibbutz murdered several days before by infiltrators from Gaza. Dayan declared that the fate of Roi Rotberg and his comrades—and perhaps the fate of the young State of Israel—was to fight again and again for their existence. Shortly after, the Sinai War broke out, with many wars to follow. Indeed, since its establishment, Israel has enjoyed only short periods of quiet in a continuous series of military conflicts. The peace agreements with Egypt and Jordan removed these countries from the sphere of military threats but did not weaken the hostility between Israel and most of its neighbors. Slowly, the primary weapon against Israel changed from all-out, high-intensity conflict to low-intensity terrorism backed by political, public diplomacy and media campaigns.

Israel's unique situation requires it to continually develop and improve its weapons, public diplomacy among them, and adjust itself to constantly changing circumstances. *Hasbara*—the Hebrew term for public diplomacy—has been employed by Israel, and before it the Zionist movement, from the beginning of the struggle to establish a Jewish homeland. But it was also clear from the beginning that a political struggle was not enough, and the Jewish people would have to fight for their independence. Israeli public diplomacy grew in parallel with political and military institutions as an essential aspect of this struggle.

From its establishment, Israel was conflicted as to the type of *hasbara* organizations it should establish. The state's leaders tended to look down on *hasbara* and sometimes ignored it completely. In the struggles of war and peace, public diplomacy did not receive appropriate consideration and was mainly used for internal political purposes. In the realm of foreign policy, *hasbara* was the "black sheep" of the family, often a scapegoat for the failures of the political echelon.

As the need arose, several organized attempts were made to coordinate between institutions of public diplomacy. Over time, every action taken by these organizations had to consider revolutions in technology and changes in the world of diplomacy, most recently those caused by globalization. Israel's needs and changes in its diplomatic standing accelerated a shift toward a centralized system of public diplomacy. Since the year 2000, events like the second and third intifadas, the Second Lebanon War, and a series of small-scale wars between Israel and Hamas in Gaza reinforced the need for such a system, leading to a "new public diplomacy."

This book is based on a doctoral dissertation on the new public diplomacy. It includes documentation and extensive interviews with 250 decision makers, elected officials, experts, observers, and participants in the arena of public diplomacy. The book examines the different ways and means that Israel—and, before it, the pre-state Jewish community in Palestine—used public diplomacy in response to challenges on the political and military fronts, until the state established an up-to-date and unique model suited to its needs and abilities. This model is built on a foundation of both the "old" and "new" public diplomacy. The Hebrew title of the book borrows a term coined by *Haaretz* journalist Amir Oren. *Milchamedia* (media war)—a portmanteau of the Hebrew term for war, *milchama*, and the English word "media."

In this book, I will sketch the changes that took place in two arenas—diplomacy and war—both of which have been strongly influenced by globalization and the media revolution. There are strong similarities between the changes that have taken place in these two different arenas, and the point at which they meet is in the battle for "hearts and minds," which brings together the new public diplomacy and the challenges of low-intensity conflict.

In the world today, dozens of such conflicts are underway, often involving battles between liberal democratic states and nonsovereign entities such as guerrilla organizations and terrorist groups. These entities, whose power is inferior to the states they are fighting, wage continuous war based on the use of the media to shape the realm of consciousness.

The second intifada (2000–2006) is a paradigmatic example of such a conflict, in which both military and diplomatic weapons were tested. Once again, the Middle East became a type of laboratory, this time in regard to an asymmetrical war between a Western liberal state and terrorist organizations. The Israeli experience is thus of immense importance and will likely contribute a great deal to the conduct of similar conflicts by other countries.

In conclusion, this book will make several recommendations for an optimal and up-to-date model of the New Public Diplomacy and present a variety of tools that can be utilized in this new media war.

Chapter 1

"Why Are the Jews Shooting at Us?"

Before Israel's 2005 disengagement from the Gaza Strip, Netzarim—a small Jewish settlement amid densely populated Arab areas in central Gaza—was a flashpoint between Palestinians and the Israel Defense Forces for many years. As a result, an IDF post was set up near Netzarim Junction, overlooking the main roads and manned by about 30 soldiers.

On the morning of Saturday, September 30, 2000, near the beginning of what would become the second intifada, hundreds of local residents, many of them teenage boys, streamed into Netzarim Junction, hurling rocks and Molotov cocktails at the army post. Journalist Ron Ben-Yishai, who was at the post, stated that it came under fire from several directions.[1] The soldiers at the post returned fire, aiming at Palestinians who were carrying weapons.[2]

That morning, Jamal al-Dura and his 12-year-old son Muhammad left their home in the Al-Bureij refugee camp to buy a car. "We got in a taxi and drove toward Gaza," the father later recounted. "When we reached Netzarim Junction, the driver stopped and said there was a riot going on and asked us to get out; he said he couldn't continue . . . I got out with Muhammad and tried to cross the street, and then we got caught in a hail of gunfire coming from both sides."[3]

A video of the incident shows the two pressed against a wall of concrete blocks, cowering behind a barrel. The gunfire continued for 45 minutes.[4] "They started shooting at us and there was nowhere for us to go and no place to take cover. The only thing we saw was the concrete wall, so we hid there. Muhammad started asking me: 'Why are the Jews shooting at us?' I couldn't answer because I was busy looking for a way to protect him. After 15 minutes of shooting, Muhammad was wounded in the right leg. He said: 'The dogs got me, the dogs got me.' I told him: 'Don't be afraid. An ambulance will come soon and get us out of here.' But the ambulance didn't come. It came too late, only when everything was over and my son was dead."[5] Pictures of the incident show what appears to be a burst of gunfire sending puffs of dust from the wall, followed by Muhammad lying dead in his father's lap as the father's head lolls helplessly.

The fighting at Netzarim Junction only subsided as evening approached.

•

There were many journalists and photographers present at the Netzarim Junction that day, but strangely, there was only a single report on the death of Muhammad al-Dura: The incident was filmed exclusively by France 2 cameraman Talal Abu Rahma.

France 2's Israel bureau chief, Charles Enderlin, was in his Jerusalem office when Abu Rahma phoned and told him about the exchange of gunfire at the junction. He also stated that he was filming a father and son who were under fire. "I receive the footage and can see that it's very powerful," Enderlin recalled. "I have no choice—all of Gaza knows that I have this footage and I must air it. The question is how to do so. Does it meet the network's rules? They won't show dead bodies or images that are too graphic. In consultation with the editor on duty in Paris, we decided that it complied with the rules and could be aired."[6]

Enderlin contacted Maj. Yarden Vatikai, head of the International Media Branch of the IDF Spokesperson's Unit. "I have some very tough footage," he said, "and I want the IDF's response." Enderlin even suggested one: "The IDF is investigating and apologizes for the shooting." Vatikai replied that he hadn't seen the report, so he couldn't respond to it. He also stated that he did not intend to apologize: "I gave him a response that said the matter has been reported in the media and we will check into it. Within an hour, the footage was on [Israeli] Channel 1 and Channel 2."[7]

Later, in the wake of information gathered from the field, the IDF Spokesperson's Unit issued the following statement: "The Palestinians make cynical use of women and children by bringing them to points of conflict in the territories. The incident filmed in the Gaza Strip began with deliberate live fire, the hurling of explosives and firebombs by Palestinians, including police officers, at IDF forces, and with hundreds of rioters charging toward IDF posts. Heavy exchanges of gunfire ensued and the picture focused exclusively on the injury to the boy and his father who were caught in the crossfire, with no way to identify the source of the gunfire, and thus no way to ascertain who struck the boy and his father. The IDF always regrets the loss of life, particularly of children, but it is clear that given the situation that arose at this location, any-one—Palestinian or Israeli—who came there could have been wounded by gunfire. The responsibility for this falls on the Palestinians and all those responsible for incitement. This incident will be investigated as part of the overall investigation of these events."[8]

The statement added to the general confusion and left open the question of whether the IDF had killed Muhammad al-Dura. This was in keeping with Israel's entire response to this question, which proved disorganized and contradictory, with very different statements coming from various sources. Public relations consultant Lenny Ben-David said of the confusion, "We heard one thing from [GOC Southern Command] Yom-Tov Samia, another thing from the IDF Spokesperson's Unit, and something else from the commander in the field. There was no single version of events."[9]

For his part, Enderlin moved quickly, distributing the footage to various news agencies. It was immediately broadcast and the impact was enormous. The Arab affairs reporter for Israel's Channel 1, Shlomi Eldar, prepared the material for broadcast. "The picture was a formative experience for the entire intifada," he said.[10] The BBC reported on the major impact the story was having, noting that the picture appeared in the main headline of the *New York Times*. The IDF still offered no response to these accusations.

Deputy IDF Spokesperson Col. Elam Kott was sent to investigate the incident. After reviewing maps of the area, Kott concluded that the IDF did not shoot al-Dura. In consultation with Foreign Ministry officials Alon Pinkas, Gideon Meir, and Meir Shlomo, Kott said the IDF should immediately state that it did not shoot the boy. Meir objected: "If you come out now and say, 'It wasn't me,' you have to be ready to provide solid proof so people will say, 'Okay, it wasn't you.' "[11]

On the same day, France 2 aired another report on the incident, this time on Muhammad al-Dura's funeral. The report mentioned that the IDF had stated it was not possible to conclusively determine who had killed the boy. Meanwhile, media pressure was steadily increasing and, at a meeting of the IDF Spokesperson's Unit, Maj. Gen. Giora Eiland, chief of the Operations Directorate, proposed informing the press that the IDF planned to review its own conduct. At a press conference, he said: "Based on the information I had at the time, I explained that it appeared that he had been shot by us, and that we certainly did not intend to hurt him."[12] After he made this statement, almost all media outlets reported that Israel had accepted responsibility for the incident.[13] "I made mistakes here, I admit it," said Eiland a few years later. "I took responsibility because up to that moment it was a more logical explanation. I thought that to start to be perceived as not knowing—no one will believe you, and you come off badly twice. In retrospect, it was a mistake."[14]

That same weekend, major riots erupted in Israeli-Arab communities. Many observers have drawn a connection between the broadcast of the al-Dura video and the outbreak of the riots. Prime Minister Ehud Barak met with leaders of the Arab sector in his office and relayed Eiland's statement to them: "The boy was killed by IDF fire. . . . It appears that the soldiers, who were caught in a tight spot, shot and killed the boy unintentionally."[15]

At a meeting of the IDF general staff a week after al-Dura's death, Samia reported the results of a preliminary investigation based on conversations with the post's commanders and soldiers and aerial photos of the intersection. "Tel Aviv erred with the immediate statement to the media and the apology," he said. In the meantime, he had ordered the demolition of many structures around the Netzarim Junction, including the wall behind which the al-Duras had taken cover.[16] As a result, the original "scene of the crime" was lost. Many believe Samia acted too hastily, and he has acknowledged the error. In this instance, operational considerations outweighed the needs of public diplomacy, whose importance was not properly understood.

After publishing an investigative report of the incident in the Israeli newspaper *Haaretz*, journalist Tom Segev suggested an official investigation.[17] Samia agreed and appointed a team of investigators comprised of experts from the military, the police, and Rafael, an Israeli defense technology company.[18] The composition of the team was only disclosed seven years later.[19] Two of its members were Yosef Doriel, a mechanical engineer, and Nahum Shahaf, a physicist. Both believed that the IDF did not shoot the boy and offered their services to Samia.[20]

Samia presented his findings to IDF Chief of Staff Shaul Mofaz. Samia was absolutely convinced that the IDF did not kill al-Dura, but the investigation's findings only supported this view to a very high degree of likelihood. Discussing whether to present the findings to the public and, if so, how, Mofaz said that the IDF should close the book on the case: "The chief of staff rightly said . . . that some uncertainty remains [and therefore] the matter should be dropped."[21]

The IDF spokesperson supported the chief of staff's position.[22] The head of the Operations Directorate, Brig. Gen. Gadi Eizenkot, felt differently: "In my opinion, the proper thing to do was to insist on telling the real story, on the basis of the findings, realizing by this point that we were dealing with something that would remain a symbol for many years to come, and so it was important to give the public the real story."[23] Similarly, Samia persisted in his view that the investigation's findings should be made public. On November 27, nearly two months after the incident, a press conference was held to present the main findings: "The odds that [al-Dura and his father] were hit by IDF fire are extremely low, practically zero. The likelihood that al-Dura was struck by either stray or deliberate Palestinian fire is high."[24]

Did this press conference help Israel's public diplomacy efforts? The controversy continued. The Foreign Ministry believes that it simply kept the emotionally charged story in the news, causing Israel considerable damage. But some in the IDF and elsewhere came to feel strongly that Israel should continue to investigate the circumstances of the boy's death and use every means possible to make its doubts public. The debate continues to this day.

•

When government officials decided to withdraw from the al-Dura case, Nahum Shahaf resolved to investigate the incident on his own to disprove the France 2 report. "We have positive proof that the gunfire came from the direction of the Palestinian position, not from the direction of the Israeli position," he asserted. "We have Palestinians who murdered the boy in cold blood, and this is a terrible deed: Palestinians who kill the boy in front of the cameras and then blame innocent Israeli soldiers."[25]

To prove his claim, Shahaf collected visual material related to the events and sent it to the media and to Danny Seaman, director of the Government Press Office. According to *NRG-Maariv*, Shahaf doubted that al-Dura and his father were struck by gunfire at all. Even if so, he contended, the gunfire did not come from IDF soldiers.[26] Later, he repeatedly argued that the Palestinians staged the entire incident, and he went so far as to say that al-Dura was still alive. Seaman was the first official to embrace Shahaf's view and second it in press interviews.[27] Years later, al-Dura's father adamantly denied this, asserting: "In our religion, every person who is killed with a bullet is still alive—living in Paradise. He isn't here on the ground, but living with God."[28]

In the meantime, Esther Shapira, a reporter for Germany's ARD television network, produced a documentary about the circumstances of the boy's death, made with assistance from the pro-Israel group Palestinian Media Watch (PMW). It aired in Germany on March 18, 2002, and concluded that Muhammad al-Dura was almost certainly struck by Palestinian gunfire.

Another private player also decided to join the fray: Philippe Karsenty, a French-Jewish politician, businessman, and head of Media-Ratings, a French NGO that monitors media reports, saw Shapira's film and was impressed by her arguments. He decided to throw himself into the public battle over the al-Dura shooting "for history's sake."[29] Karsenty explained: "Israel is despised in France. It's perceived as a strong and wealthy country whose army behaves like the Nazis. My decision to fight infuriated many people, not only in the French establishment, but in the Jewish community too. A lot of Jews and non-Jews have told me that I'm right, but that they can't support me publicly because they can't fight against this establishment."[30]

The al-Dura case was now an issue for the French courts and the French media. On January 13, 2003, Gérard Huber published *Contre-expertise d'une mise en scène*,[31] which argued that the al-Dura incident was faked. His partners were Stéphane Juffa, chief editor of the Metula News agency where Huber worked, and journalist Nidra Poller, who translated the book into English.

The online publication *Whistleblower Magazine* supported Huber's claims and called the incident "a staged piece of street theater," adding that France 2 was refusing to reveal crucial evidence in the case. The publication also quoted Huber's assertion that it had yet to be proven whether Muhammad al-Dura was alive or dead and asked why Shapira's film had not been shown on French television.

On October 22, 2004, France 2 permitted three independent journalists to watch 27 minutes of raw footage of the incident. Two of them subsequently published an article in *Le Figaro* that cast doubt on the incident's authenticity. They had originally sent the article to *Le Monde*, which refused to publish it.

The case escalated when France 2 filed a slander lawsuit against some of its critics, including Philippe Karsenty, for claiming that the footage was fake. On February 21, 2005, the *Jerusalem Post* came out on the side of those who doubted whether Muhammad al-Dura had actually been killed. At the same time, Raanan Gissin, Prime Minister Ariel Sharon's media advisor, unsuccessfully attempted to obtain the raw footage.

By mid-2005, the controversy was gaining strength in both France and Israel. In France, Karsenty and his supporters were pressuring France 2 to withdraw its claim that al-Dura was killed by IDF fire and admit that its reporting was inadequate. In Israel, Nahum Shahaf waged a public campaign against Charles Enderlin. Karsenty, Shahaf, Gissin, and Seaman all called on Enderlin to hand over the raw footage. This was a reasonable demand in order to determine whether anyone had tampered with material. However, the raw footage disappeared and was never shown in public.

Karsenty lost his first legal battle and was forced to pay court costs plus one euro as symbolic compensation to Enderlin and Abu Rahma. On October 19, 2006, he appealed the verdict and asked Israeli officials to help him obtain Abu Rahma's raw footage in order to show it in court. This time, Karsenty was successful. Vatikai sent a memo to Deputy Chief of Staff Maj. Gen. Dan Harel explaining the need for the material. In response, Deputy IDF Spokesperson Col. Shlomi Am-Shalom contacted Enderlin and requested the material, acknowledging that it would be used as part of the legal proceedings underway in France.[32]

The French court's ruling, Seaman's letter, and the deputy IDF spokesperson's attempt to obtain the raw footage from France 2 stirred renewed interest in the al-Dura affair. Am-Shalom's appeal to the network was turned down, but the French court ultimately compelled the network to screen the requested material.[33] After viewing the raw footage, Karsenty claimed: "We saw that French 2 doesn't have any evidence to support what they are saying. There is nothing in the raw footage—just staged scenes. . . . The al-Dura hoax is over tonight."[34]

On February 27, 2008, a hearing was held on Karsenty's appeal. Jean-Claude Shlinger, a French ballistics expert, testified that, in his opinion, there was no way Muhammad al-Dura and his father could have been struck by IDF gunfire and the images were most likely staged. The network's Israel bureau sent a letter to the editor and publisher of *Haaretz*, which had published the report, demanding the immediate publication of a response stating that Shlinger's testimony carried no legal weight. The letter said the French court had consented to have the expert opinion submitted, but it had ruled that the expert himself would not be allowed to testify.

On May 21, 2008, the appeals court in Paris acquitted Karsenty of slander; France 2 immediately said it would appeal the decision. On June 4, many French journalists, Enderlin's colleagues, and ordinary readers signed a petition on the *Nouvel Observateur* website that described Enderlin as the victim of a hate campaign, citing his journalistic accomplishments and good reputation. At the same time, a handful of other journalists denounced the petition and called for an independent investigation. On July 2, representatives of the Jewish community asked then-president Nicolas Sarkozy to establish a commission of inquiry into the matter.

The next stage of the controversy also occurred in a French court. Israeli physician Yehuda David was convicted of slander in a suit brought against him by Jamal al-Dura. The case began with a report by Israel's Channel 10 in which David stated that the wounds Jamal al-Dura claimed to have received during the shooting in 2000 were in fact the injuries David had treated in 1994. Al-Dura insisted that he had been wounded at Netzarim Junction, and the court ruled in his favor. Dr. David subsequently asked the Israeli government to help cover the costs of the trial. In an unusual move, the government agreed.

Taken together, the various legal proceedings surrounding the al-Dura case appear frustratingly inconclusive. They have not and likely cannot provide an answer to the basic question of who killed Muhammad al-Dura. Theoretically, they could reveal whether France 2 had conducted itself in accordance with journalistic ethics and publicly disclosed all the information it possessed, thus reopening the debate once again.

For now, however, the parties have reached a stalemate. Israel cannot conclusively prove itself innocent, just as the Palestinians and France 2 are unable to prove the opposite. What remains is the cumulative effect of the plethora of media coverage, the issue's massive online presence, and the use of the images involved, all of which place responsibility for al-Dura's death squarely on Israel.

•

Despite the storm of controversy that surrounds the incident, there is no question that Muhammad al-Dura's death was the most influential press story of the second intifada. It was a unique media event that occurred precisely at the moment the intifada broke out. Millions of people are killed in wars and other acts of violence, but the moment of death is rarely captured on film. The fact that there was a child involved only added to the intensity and drama of the story. Children have been placed at the forefront of the Palestinian struggle before: They photograph well and arouse sympathy. "What happened with al-Dura is a totally secondary thing," says Brig. Gen. Yossi Kuperwasser, former head of research for Military Intelligence. "It's the overall situation that must be understood and analyzed. You can't discuss the ostensibly technical issues of the al-Dura story without grasping the depth of the conceptual impact that occurred here. The heart of the matter is that Jews are killing Palestinian children. All the surrounding *hasbara* is rendered unimportant at that moment."[35]

There is widespread agreement among those in the public diplomacy field that the al-Dura shooting changed the role of media in the conflict and set new rules that would profoundly affect subsequent events. Three former Israeli defense ministers related separately to the al-Dura case.

Moshe Yaalon, deputy chief of staff at the time: "Israeli officials accepted responsibility for the event and immediately began to apologize. I think this was a mistake. In this instance, we should have very quickly tried to ascertain the facts and then presented our version of the story."[36]

Moshe Arens, former defense minister and foreign minister: "The world today is very open, everything is reported. Our ability to add to the images on television or to newspaper articles and to reports on the Internet is marginal. In the al-Dura case, apparently the picture that was presented was not the reality, but they created a reality."[37]

Ehud Barak, prime minister at the time: "The pictures became part of the symbols the other side used in its effort to define who is right. The world is focused on interpreting one particular picture, but it interprets it in a much broader context."[38]

The al-Dura incident was, in effect, a test case for the impact of the media, the impressions it creates, and Israel's response to them. Atrocity stories and images have always existed in war, but due to the growth of the global media, a single camera brought the story to the world's attention and created a massive reaction.

The story of al-Dura was also one of the first cases of an image that went "viral," spreading across the media landscape, apparently of its own accord. France 2 shared the video with other news agencies and networks, amplifying the media effect and creating collective media responsibility and commitment to the story on the part of hundreds of channels and stations throughout the world. In the charged atmosphere between the Arab world and Israel, the images sparked an outburst of violence by Israeli Arabs, the adoption of al-Dura as a symbol by al-Qaeda, and the incident's use as a means of incitement at the infamous Durban conference in 2001.

While initially disseminated by television, this material can be found on websites in perpetuity, preserved in the world's collective memory. Over a decade and a half after the shooting, an Internet search for the name "Muhammad al-Dura" turns up hundreds of thousands of results. The Internet has no problem vividly recalling what is forgotten by the traditional media. The story lives forever online, so Israel is forced again and again to respond to it and defend itself in a media landscape it cannot control.

Clearly, the IDF was negligent in its handling of the incident. First, it did not follow a consistent media policy. Conflicting statements were issued throughout the affair and every step taken in the media realm was plagued by internal disagreements, some of which went public. The IDF did not immediately grasp the impact and significance of the event and so dealt with it very slowly, as if it were a routine matter.

Into this vacuum stepped nongovernmental parties, both individuals and organizations. They understood the long-term significance of the event and created a personal network that transcended borders to wage a public campaign. This did not only take place online, but also at events like the Herzliya Conference and in publications like the *New York Times*, the *International Herald Tribune*, and *Le Monde*. The campaign eventually moved from the media into political and legal forums, such as the French and Israeli judicial systems. In the battle for hearts and minds, these independent parties and individuals became new players in the field of public diplomacy.

•

The conflict between Israel and the Palestinians is asymmetrical in every way, including in the media realm. For example, many pictures from the first and second intifadas showed Palestinian children clashing with Israeli soldiers. The image of a Palestinian child facing an Israeli tank calls to mind the biblical story of David and Goliath, but here the roles are switched. This time it is Jewish Israelis, well armed and equipped, confronting helpless and exposed Palestinian youngsters. The images of the al-Dura shooting are perhaps the most notorious of these images. "Al-Dura became an icon, a symbol of the cruelty of Israelis, of Goliath and David, of Israelis as killers of Palestinian children, of the evil within us and of this terrible power that Israel possesses,"[39] notes Israeli diplomat Amira Oron.

But this is not the only asymmetry between Israel and the Palestinians. Israel tries to uphold democratic values and freedom of expression, while Palestinian organizations—both Fatah and Hamas—generally ignore them. "You're dealing with a society in which credibility is not a matter of principle but just the opposite. [The norm is] propaganda, distortion of facts and figures, issuing statements that have no connection to reality. They have no problem being perceived as noncredible since they're already perceived that way anyhow. They fill the headlines and shape the story."[40]

The al-Dura incident exemplifies the overlapping nature of different low-intensity battlefields:

- The military front—a violent encounter between the IDF and the Palestinians.

- The diplomatic front—the Durban conference held a year later was heavily influenced by the presence of Jamal al-Dura.

- The legal front—the various court proceedings in France and Israel.

- The economic front—this event and others influenced Christian churches and other institutions to divest from corporations trading with Israel.

- The public diplomacy front—where the battle between Israel and the Palestinians for world public opinion played out.

Israeli institutions proved decidedly inept when faced with the al-Dura incident. At the time, Israel did not have a formal public diplomacy system. Due to the lack of such a system, the al-Dura affair began as a *hasbara* failure and became a clash between different players: the traditional media versus the NGOs and individuals who took up the case. In many ways, the mobilization of hundreds of professional journalists to defend Enderlin was meant to protect him and them from the new forces that had begun gnawing away at the traditional media. The achievements of Karsenty, Shahaf, Prof. Richard Landes and the organizations that dedicated themselves to the al-Dura case demonstrate just how powerful these new forces can be.

•

What conclusions can we draw from the al-Dura case that can be applied to the overall field of new public diplomacy?

First, this case illustrates the "CNN effect"—the presence of cameras on the front lines. This was a prerequisite for the incident's wide exposure and the magnitude it acquired relative to similar events. Without Abu Rahma's footage, it's unlikely anyone would have paid much attention to the incident. In turn, the "Al Jazeera effect" helped make the al-Dura incident widely known in the Arab world. This fueled the wave of violence in the territories and in the Israeli-Arab sector that occurred in the wake of the incident. Without question, the media played a decisive role not only in searing the al-Dura incident into the world's consciousness, but also in promoting the violence that followed.

Second, the case proves that long-term planning is extremely important. Israel wavered between providing a quick response and investigating the facts in-depth. In the absence of strategic thinking, Israel zigzagged between accepting and denying responsibility for the incident, so that it was quickly found guilty in the public mind.

Third, the incident resulted in a blurring of political, legal, media, and economic arenas once considered separate. This is characteristic of a globalized world and a globalized media in which traditional boundaries have broken down.

Fourth, the narrative of asymmetry between the weak and the strong peaked in this incident. The victim seemed to be obvious, while the Israelis were depicted as faceless and unfeeling, unseen in the video except as anonymous gunfire directed at defenseless targets. The media captured this asymmetry, which photographs very well, and made much use of it in bashing Israel and blaming it for al-Dura's death.

Fifth, the incident and the enormous attention it received are further confirmation that we are now living in a post-heroic age, characterized by high sensitivity to the lives of noncombatants. This requires liberal democratic countries to wield their military power judiciously and precisely, so that terrorists and their accomplices are the only casualties—and this is sometimes a near-impossible task.

Finally, the episode attests to the success of individuals and organizations in shaping the public diplomacy arena, especially through the Internet. These new players joined forces with colleagues in other countries and together focus on common goals. The power they demonstrated here will affect the Israeli-Palestinian conflict in years to come.

Chapter 2

The Durban Conference

A Strategic Ambush

On November 19, 2008, at the General Assembly of the Jewish Federations of North America (previously, UJC) held in Jerusalem, Israeli Foreign Minister Tzipi Livni announced that Israel would not attend the second World Conference against Racism in Durban, South Africa. "We call on the international community not to take part in the conference, which seeks to give legitimacy to the hatred and extremism called 'the struggle against racism,'" she said.

Livni was referring to Israel's experience at the first Durban conference in September 2001, an event marred by vicious anti-Israel activities that took Israel and its supporters by surprise. This time, Israel chose to avoid another such ambush. Livni's announcement shed light on the mistakes Israel had made in preparing for the first Durban conference in 2001—in particular, the failure to understand the political aspect of the event.

In Israel, it was assumed that the event would be just another international conference, similar to others held by the United Nations. It soon became clear, however, that Israel had fallen into a trap. The international community had become more critical of Israel and new forces—particularly NGOs—succeeded in hijacking the conference for their own purposes, turning it into an international demonstration of hatred for the Jewish state.

More than anything else, the first Durban conference was a public diplomacy event. The use of the media, street propaganda, and incendiary symbols like the al-Dura shooting made it distinct from other UN conferences. The event included all aspects of the battle for world opinion—military, political, and public diplomacy. At Durban, Israel learned the hard way that terror attacks were not confined to the West Bank and Gaza but were global in nature. Just as terrorism is a global phenomenon, the Palestinians, supported by the Arab states and NGOs, and through them the media, succeeded in globalizing the intifada.

For Israel and for American Jewish organizations, the Durban conference was a strategic surprise, a rude awakening to the reality of the new public diplomacy. Israel gradually learned its lesson, however, and decided not to take part in the second and third Durban conferences. But the damage had already been done.

∾

The 2001 Durban conference was marked by four new factors in the Israeli-Palestinian conflict: the combination of a political struggle with the military struggle, the internationalization of the Israeli-Palestinian conflict, the role of NGOs, and the connection between anti-Israelism as the new anti-Semitism.

Israel was entirely unprepared for all of this. Mordechai Yadid, head of the Division for the United Nations and International Organizations at the Foreign Ministry, recounts that the ministry's preparations for Durban were insufficient: "No one in the leadership was very interested in this issue. In spite of reports from the different conferences and my alarm, the Durban conference was not given high priority."[1]

At a preliminary session in Tehran in February 2001, "a series of allegations took shape, initiated by Syria and the Palestinians, which alleged that Israel is an apartheid state. These claims were passed to the Durban preparation committee as draft resolutions or parts of informal declarations."[2] In March 2000, Deputy Foreign Minister Michael Melchior arrived at the Human Rights Council in Geneva and learned about the preparations for the Durban conference. "I saw that it was going to be a very serious thing and that we weren't prepared . . . I was hit in the face with it," he says.[3]

Nonetheless, Israel was concerned that the final resolutions at Durban would be extremely hostile. During July and August 2001, it tried to head this off through diplomacy. Foreign Minister Shimon Peres sent Melchior to Europe and the United States to discuss whether there was any point in participating in the conference at all. Melchior met with Jewish members of Congress, the undersecretary of state for the Middle East, the Ethiopian deputy foreign minister, and others. Israeli Cabinet

Secretary Israel Maimon was in touch with the U.S. government via the National Security Council. Peres met with his British counterpart, and the director-general of the Foreign Ministry met with the Canadian prime minister. In all these meetings, Israel warned of what was expected at the conference.

For the first time, the United States began to consider the possibility of downgrading its participation in the Durban conference to junior officials only.[4] On August 24, President George W. Bush announced that if Israel were isolated and Zionism defined as racism at the conference, the United States would not participate. Two days later, Deputy Foreign Minister Melchior announced that if the United States boycotted the conference, Israel would do the same. In the end, President George W. Bush decided that the secretary of state would not travel to the conference and a junior official would represent the United States.

Israel followed suit. "I received a call from [Prime Minister Ariel] Sharon, and he informed me that the head of the American delegation would not attend, and therefore the head of our delegation, that is, me, would not attend," says Melchior.[5] In his place, Yadid was appointed to head the delegation. Ambassador Tova Herzl believes that the decision to appoint Yadid was a mistake because it missed the public diplomacy ramifications of the event: "The most talented of our UN experts could not deal with both the political aspect and the *hasbara* aspect. A director-general of the Media and Public Relations Division or the head of the Bureau for World Jewish Affairs could have aided us greatly—someone with an overall and strategic view, not an individual one."[6]

~

The Durban conference was actually a series of four different conferences. The primary conference was between nation-states, but it was preceded by a youth conference, a conference of international parliamentarians, and an NGO forum. Observers pointed out that in fact there was a fifth "conference": It took place in the public sphere and encouraged an atmosphere of hostility toward Israel throughout the conference.

A delegation of fifteen Israelis, led by Peleg Reshef, attended the youth conference. "Already when we arrived at the hotel," says Reshef, "we saw young people at the entrance wearing shirts with a picture of Muhammad al-Dura printed on the front and 'Israel = apartheid' on the back. They were wearing caps with pictures of al-Aqsa and Israel."[7] Al-Dura appeared in other contexts at Durban; his picture was distributed and his father arrived for a round of lectures.

Along with the representatives from Israel, the World Jewish Congress sent a delegation of Jewish students to Durban. The students prepared extensively and were surprised by Israel's lack of awareness of the conference and its importance. "The mere fact that the official Israeli delegation arrived only on Friday afternoon, on the day the interstate session began, and even when the other sessions had already convened at the beginning of the week, bears witness to how Israel related to it," says Ari Rudolf from Johannesburg. "Where were the Israeli NGOs? Why didn't they join us?"[8]

The youth conference was just the preamble to the other conferences. Furious disputes between the Israeli and Jewish students and the other attendees erupted.[9] The result was inevitable. "It was enough for us," says Reshef. "We saw that this session was one-sided and it would only come to no good. We decided to leave and slammed the door on our way out."[10] The Israeli students remained in Durban in order to engage in *hasbara* activities at the major conference and elsewhere.

The interparliamentary conference turned out differently. Member of Knesset Ran Cohen was the only Israeli who attended. After analyzing the situation, he decided on a confrontational tactic: Very early at the conference, Cohen clarified to the Palestinian delegation that he would not allow the conference to become an anti-Israel event.

In retrospect, this attitude paid off. The conference was conducted with mutual respect, no violence, and no extreme rhetoric. Unfortunately, the interparliamentary meeting had little public impact and media coverage was minimal.

～

On August 31, the Durban NGO forum was convened with approximately 4,000 representatives of organizations in attendance, and their intentions were perfectly clear.

The rise of the NGOs in Durban is essential to understanding the events. In recent years, NGOs have become extremely strong and their number has risen precipitously, mainly as a result of globalization and the media revolution. Until the beginning of the 1970s, nation-states were the primary participants in the international arena. "After World War II, the first new authorities [NGOs] appeared on the international legal scene and received a singular standing. Gradually, the nation-states lost their monopoly over the international arena—as strongly demonstrated at Durban. Now we're in a stage of digesting the new situation,"[11] Israeli diplomat Daniel Taub explains. The turning point in the status of NGOs was the 1998 Rome Conference, when hundreds of them arrived to lobby for the Statute of the International Criminal Court.

"Only a few people in Israel appreciated what an NGO is and what its power is," says Shimon Samuels, the director for international relations of the Simon Wiesenthal Center, an NGO. "Some NGOs' economies and resources are greater than many states; conferences attended by celebrities, religious leaders, and people with respect and standing can do enormous damage."[12]

Dina Porat, an Israeli historian, asserts that the negative attitude toward Israel in the NGO world stems from the alliance established in the 1990s between the radical left in Europe and Islamic fundamentalism.[13] Israeli diplomat Zvi Mazel agrees: "NGOs are one of the most dangerous phenomena in the global world. They are not understood in Israel. Civil society is composed of human rights organizations, anti-globalization organizations, organizations against air pollution, etc., but they are also involved in political issues against America and against Israel. To them, Israel is anathema. They are ready to go as far as anti-Semitism, as we saw at Durban."[14] Former Canadian Justice Minister Irwin Cotler, who participated in the conference, saw this as part of the rise of the new anti-Semitism: "Classic anti-Semitism denied the Jews' right to live equally in society. The new anti-Semitism denies the Jewish people's right to equality in the family of nations."[15]

The final declaration of the NGO forum was issued on September 3, 2001, and its language was ferocious, extreme, and vitriolic. It adopted the Palestinian narrative entirely and accused Israel of colonialism, ethnic cleansing, war crimes, violation of human rights, and apartheid. "Durban was the cornerstone of the formation of the apartheid accusation against Israel. It was the intended goal of the conference and it continues to this day. Allegations of this kind were rarely raised before Durban, but have since become common."[16]

Eleven Jewish organizations tried to initiate a resolution condemning anti-Semitism, but failed. Some of the them, like the Anti-Defamation League, B'nai B'rith, Hadassah, and the Simon Wiesenthal Center, said "enough is enough" and decided to leave. Eran Lerman, director-general of the Israel office of the American Jewish Committee, described the atmosphere that led to the walkout: "Durban was a catastrophe; hatred and expressions of anti-Semitism. A Jew could not walk around with a Star of David. The threat was real and the danger was acute."[17] Indeed, in the streets outside the conference, stands were set up selling *The*

Protocols of the Elders of Zion and slogans like "What if Hitler had won?" were publicly displayed.

The radicalization of the conference was so intense that it deterred two of the most important international NGOs, Human Rights Watch and Amnesty International; they announced that the resolution's anti-Israel language was unacceptable and refused to vote on it.[18] Mary Robinson, the UN High Commissioner for Human Rights, stated she rejected the resolution.[19] "This was the first time the UN refused to accept an NGO document," Ambassador Herzl notes.[20]

In Israel, there was little awareness of the conference and its importance. Israel was preoccupied with a major escalation in terror attacks and had little attention to spare. The Israeli media, for example, proved largely indifferent. Arad Nir, editor of foreign news for Israel's Channel 2, was among the few Israeli reporters who traveled to Durban: "I knew it would be an assault, a brutal arena where Israel would be crucified and therefore I asked to go there, but I left Israel without a camera crew. . . . The other news networks in Israel paid little attention to the issue, mainly because the political echelon ignored it and chose to bury their heads in the sand."[21]

Nonetheless, the Israeli government expected the conference to be extremely hostile and tried to diversify the makeup of the Israeli delegation, for example, with activists from the struggle against apartheid and immigrants from Ethiopia. Unfortunately, the inherent problems remained. "The preparations for the trip were insufficient. We were given a thin, shallow background file, and we didn't know what we were going to do. We had half an hour of preparation," says Nigist Mengesha, former director of Fidel, the Association for Education and Social Integration of Ethiopian Jews in Israel.

In contrast, the anti-Israel organizations and their supporters were very well organized. The Israelis who arrived late to the conference found that the public arena, the streets of Durban, had been captured by hostile forces. Arad Nir recalls: "A procession passed us in the street with Palestinian flags and pictures of dismembered bodies. At the same time, [Jamal] al-Dura, Muhammad's father, made a series of appearances in South Africa. I called the director-general of the Foreign Ministry and asked: 'Do you see what's happening in Durban?' . . . I felt helpless."

"There was no direction and no coordination and no strategy," says Reshef. "Whatever we did was meaningless."

∽

Israel made two major public diplomacy initiatives during the conference: a press conference for all media representatives and a public speech in the conference plenum. In the press conference, Dina Porat used the opportunity to distribute a comprehensive document on global legislation against racism, xenophobia, and discrimination and proved Israel is one of the most progressive nations in the world on legislation against racism.

Arad Nir of Channel 2 describes the press conference as a total failure: "Porat spoke very academically and did not reach the media. The media attendance at the event was low and the impact barely registered."

The second effort was Yadid's speech to the conference itself. The speech, originally written by Melchior, dealt with the Jewish tradition's eternal opposition to slavery, the Holocaust, the Zionist rebirth, and the miraculous return of the Jewish people to the land of Israel. It also referred to the atmosphere surrounding the conference: "We came here in order to aid the victims of racism, and found ourselves victims of racism."

Benjamin Pogrund, a member of the delegation, said afterward that the speech was excellent but that Yadid's delivery was poor and harmed the content. Unfortunately, there were not enough copies of the speech to distribute to attendees and the media.

∽

Over 150 countries took part in the interstate conference that convened on September 1, 2001. Israel and the United States were represented at a junior level, while prime ministers and foreign ministers represented other states. Nonetheless, Israel attempted to influence the proceedings. Israel was concerned about the content of the final resolution, and Adi Scheinman, a legal advisor, tried to amend it: "There was an entire discussion about whether 'holocaust' should be spelled with a capital 'H' or a lowercase 'h.' They wanted to add an 's' to the end—so it would speak about 'holocausts' and not a single 'holocaust.' This was another attempt to obfuscate the uniqueness of the Holocaust in world history and equate it to the tragedies of other peoples." Israel's efforts were in vain.[22] Norway and other countries worked energetically to moderate the extreme wording of the resolution, but they were unsuccessful.[23] The draft resolution was tough and hostile. Slowly, the idea of leaving the conference arose again.[24]

The final decision was made at senior levels in Washington and Jerusalem after intensive talks between the two countries. On September

3, 2001, Secretary of State Colin Powell told Foreign Minister Peres that there was no chance to improve the draft final resolution. Following this conversation, both countries decided to leave the conference. Deputy Foreign Minister Melchior assumed that additional states would follow suit and withdraw from the conference, forcing the organizers to moderate the wording of the resolution, but no countries did so.[25] Nonetheless, attempts continued—mainly by Canada and the European Union—to restrain the problematic language.

Ultimately, South Africa assumed the role of mediator and succeeded in moderating the resolution, reflecting its desire to end the conference in a spirit of goodwill. "In the end, they cleaned up the text and adopted only general declarations that were okay from our point of view," says the Foreign Ministry's legal advisor, Alan Baker.[26] The only reference to the Palestinian issue was relatively benign, similar to previous UN resolutions. Noam Katz, a member of Israel's diplomatic delegation at Durban, says: "While the NGO resolution was emotionally anti-Israel in the most vitriolic terms, the states' resolution was relatively moderate, reflecting their desire to move the wheel back a bit."[27]

In Jerusalem, the final resolution was seen as "one of our biggest successes in an international organization," and according to Foreign Minister Peres it was "a stinging defeat for the Arab League."[28] But Benjamin Netanyahu, then serving as finance minister, had an opposite opinion: "Israel's attitude to the *hasbara* war was similar to its attitude on the terror front, exercising restraint and avoiding the use of its full power. That restraint at the Durban conference bought us no international 'goodwill.'"[29]

On September 8, 2001, the Durban conference was adjourned, not before it had formulated a plan of action for the coming years, including additional conferences. Three days later, on September 11, al-Qaeda attacked America. The world agenda changed, the Durban conference disappeared from the world's radar, and a new global war against terror was launched.

～

It would be a mistake, however, to assume that the Durban conference's resolutions—and, most importantly, the atmosphere of the event—disappeared after 9/11. Less than a year after Durban, the United Nation's World Summit on Sustainable Development convened, again in South Africa (Johannesburg). The Palestinians attempted to recreate their previous success. This was expressed mainly through street demonstrations and huge banners denouncing Israel and Prime Minister Ariel Sharon. But this time, it didn't work. "The ugly Palestinian rhetoric did rule over the demonstrations," says Noam Katz, who was again sent to organize media activities. "Nonetheless, it didn't reflect the spirit of the conference and was far from the Durban events."[30]

The Johannesburg summit was the first opportunity for the Foreign Ministry to apply the lessons of the Durban conference—mainly, to demonstrate a different attitude toward NGOs based on a new ministry policy. Senior Foreign Ministry official Avi Miluah formulated a plan to build new relationships with NGOs, recognizing their power. Since then, the ministry has maintained working relations with NGOs, relations that are totally different from the previous period.[31]

In 2003, this was manifested in the new Foreign Ministry department specializing in NGOs. Orli Gil, head of the department, said: "We must cultivate [the NGOs] and cannot just label them as pro-Israel or anti-Israel."[32]

~

In retrospect, Israel dealt with the conference through traditional diplomacy and abandoned public diplomacy. It ignored the NGO conference that happened to be the most anti-Israel. Israel arrived late to the NGO forum, did not prepare for the virulent anti-Israel atmosphere, and suffered a serious defeat. Even the Jewish organizations involved, which know the NGO world quite well, had not planned for the hostility they encountered.

Moreover, the conference demonstrated a new international reality in microcosm—the blurring of borders between various fronts and areas of action. The event appeared to be political in nature but in effect combined various fields. For example, media coverage of the Israeli-Palestinian conflict encouraged hostility toward Israel; the main symbol of this was the death of Muhammad al-Dura.

In times of crisis, managing media information is an important tool in public diplomacy. Here, as well, Israel was taken by surprise.

An additional aspect of the Durban conference is the link between anti-Semitism and anti-Israelism. Beginning in the year 2000, Israel and Jewish organizations increased their vigilance regarding anti-Semitic incidents. The link between the second intifada, the Second Lebanon War, Operation Cast Lead, and the rise in anti-Semitic incidents was obvious. Historian Rivka Shpak-Lissak claims: "the new anti-Semitism in Europe is a new stage in anti-Semitism. It hides its true nature behind the claim that it is just legitimate criticism of Israel's actions in the territories."[33] According to Yehuda Bauer, a professor emeritus of history and Holocaust studies at Hebrew University, there have been four waves of anti-Semitism since the 1950s. The first came after the Sinai War, the second following the Six Day War, the third after the First Lebanon War and the first intifada, and the final wave during the second intifada.[34] This trend has continued. For example, after the Gaza flotilla incident in 2010, there were ten attacks on Jews in France and five in Austria. "Jews and Israelis are often seen as a single community, and events in the Middle East cause anti-Jewish groups and individuals to take hostile actions against them," says a report by the Stephen Roth Institute for the Study of Contemporary Antisemitism and Racism at Tel Aviv University.

This statement proved true again in 2014–2015. According to a report from Tel Aviv University's Kantor Center, there was a steep increase of violent anti-Semitic incidents in 2014, making it one of the worst years of the past decade. A total of 766 such incidents were recorded, 38 percent more than in 2013. The explanation is simple. In the summer of 2014, a war in Gaza erupted, also known as Operation Protective Edge. As expected, the flare-up in the Israeli-Palestinian conflict sparked a rise in anti-Semitism. This connection was again evident in 2015, when the scope of violent anti-Semitic incidents throughout the world fell sharply as the situation calmed. There were "only" 410 incidents of violent anti-Semitism in 2015, a drop of 46 percent from the peak level. The report's authors note that the attacks had become more brutal, and attribute this to the Islamic State organization and the violent character of other incidents and organization in the Middle East since the so-called Arab Spring.

Figure 2.1 shows the rise in anti-Semitic incidents from 1989 to 2015. As shown, the number of incidents spiked during Operation Cast Lead in 2009, as in 2014. "During the operation, anti-Semitic incidents reached heights we haven't seen in the last two decades, both in terms of the numbers and in terms of the level of violence,"[35] says Amos Hermon, head of the Jewish Agency's Task Force Against Anti-Semitism. "The connection to the Israeli-Palestinian conflict is clear," says Patrick Klugman, president of the French Union of Jewish Students. "In 1999, we received reports of 69 anti-Semitic incidents in France, and their number has gone up . . . to 743 in 2000."[36]

In 2004, President Bush ordered the State Department to monitor global anti-Semitism and rank countries according to their relationship with Israel. "The U.S. will monitor this; we promise that the urge to

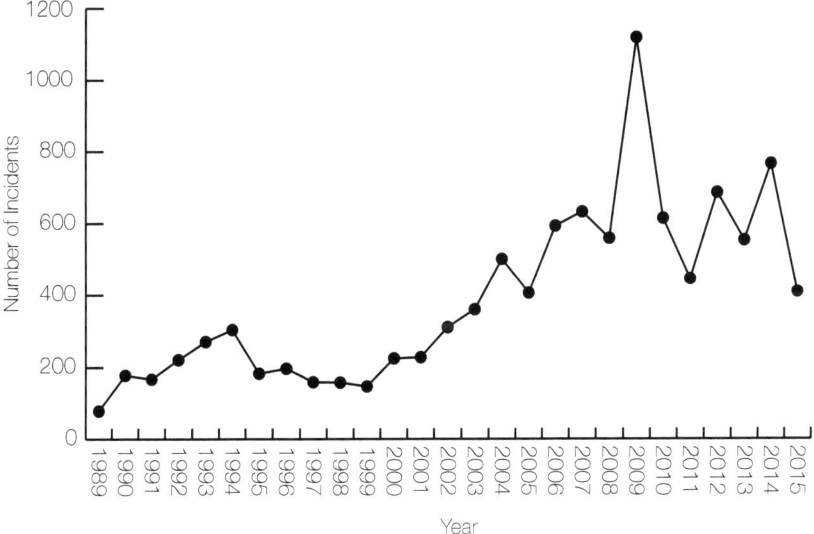

Figure 2.1. Anti-Semitism: Violent Incidents Worldwide, 1989–2015.

anti-Semitism will not gain another foothold in the modern world." Since then, the State Department has issued annual reports on the issue.[37]

The reaction of the United States and the international community to the second Durban conference in April 2009 reflected their disappointment with the Durban process, which had collapsed into an anti-Western and anti-Israel crusade. Fourteen countries boycotted the third Durban conference, which convened in New York on September 22, 2011, in tandem with the UN General Assembly. This conference was attended by then-president of Iran Mahmoud Ahmadinejad. The states that took this step openly declared that their boycott was a consequence of the first conference's anti-Semitic character.[38] The Durban process was dead.

Chapter 3

"Smart Power"

The roots of public diplomacy can be traced to ancient Greece (fourth and fifth centuries BCE). The word "diplomacy" is derived from a Greek term meaning "folded documents," and several versions of the word appeared in European languages in the late 18th century to refer to the range of factors and interests affecting the relations between states. Diplomatic representatives serve as a mechanism for the systematic study and execution of foreign policy. Some call diplomacy the art of the possible, involving efforts aimed at leading others to sympathize or identify with the interests the diplomat represents—without resorting to the use of force.

Classic diplomacy entails the exchange of messages between sovereign states. This type of diplomacy remains relevant as long there are personal interactions in the system of diplomatic relations. Public diplomacy, on the other hand, is characterized by exchanges of culture, designed to explain and defend government policy to foreign audiences. It includes a state's efforts to influence the views of the public or the elites in another state, with the goal of effecting positive changes in the target state's foreign policy. The primary objective is to present the ideals of the home state, its ideas, institutions, and culture. The new media—radio, television, and Internet—provides powerful tools for promoting the classic goals of diplomacy.

Public diplomacy is distinct from traditional diplomacy in its transparency and broad distribution; in its focus on public opinion and conduct rather than governments and their policies; and in the emphasis it places on the multiplicity of opinions and ideas, including conflicting voices. Another distinction pertains to their respective range of action: Traditional diplomacy concentrates on the short term and primarily addresses immediate events and crises. Public diplomacy has medium- and long-term goals, and it builds public systems for long-term positioning of the state's image.

In order to demarcate the bounds of public diplomacy, it should be distinguished from other efforts to exert influence, such as public relations, psychological warfare, and propaganda. This distinction pertains to the way information is used: In public diplomacy, the information is open and transparent. In public relations, the information is filtered to produce a positive image. In psychological warfare, there is negative use of information to affect the mindset of enemy soldiers. And in propaganda, the information aims to change public opinion in the enemy state and even in the home state.

∿

During the Cold War era, the West and the East used public diplomacy in competing for hegemony in the world. When the Cold War ended in the late 1980s, the United States decided there was no longer any need to invest in public diplomacy and it cut over $2 billion in overseas projects. The U.S. Information Agency, which had been responsible for disseminating information and coordinating among the branches of public diplomacy, was disbanded in 1999 and its information functions incorporated in the State Department. Public diplomacy seemed passé.

Al-Qaeda's attack against the United States on September 11, 2001, was a turning point. The American government declared a war on terror, and it renewed a public diplomacy strategy in the framework of this war, supporting it with additional funding. The format was different this time: The principle objective was to uproot and wipe out international terrorism. During the years between the end of the Cold War and the September 2001 attack, changes had occurred that engendered a new type of public diplomacy.

The new public diplomacy was built upon the familiar foundations of earlier forms of public diplomacy, with the addition of new factors, including media technologies and NGOs. There were no longer clear distinctions: between traditional external dissemination of information and parallel internal activities, between public diplomacy and traditional diplomacy, and between cultural diplomacy and the marketing and management of news.

There was a rapid increase in the number of NGOs and the clout they wield, initially in the domestic arena and later in the international arena via global networks. NGOs became a driving and provocative factor, analyzing and promoting global issues and making a worldwide impact.

As the role of NGOs grew, the nation-state lost its hegemony and exclusivity in the public diplomacy arena. NGOs now assumed an equally powerful role in the processes of shaping and disseminating messages. These organizations are not only a new target audience that states must take into consideration; they are influential entities that work to promote their own independent worldviews and a new global agenda.

Another key factor is the emergence of two-way communication between a state and the public. This dialogue, based on new technologies, helps the state to disseminate its messages in different ways in order to adapt them to other cultures and subgroups. Two-way communication also enables the state to listen to individuals, with the aim of persuading them, and it enables individuals to listen and respond.

Unlike earlier generations of traditional diplomacy and public diplomacy, the new public diplomacy combines three time frames—short, medium, and long. In the immediate and short term, it reacts to current news events in order to minimize damage and garner positive coverage. Here, the new public diplomacy uses tools of advocacy, international broadcasting, and online diplomacy. In the medium term, weeks or months, it takes preemptive action to neutralize damage and gain an advantage in the public presentation of various issues. Tools in this medium-term effort include international public relations, commercial diplomacy, and Diaspora diplomacy. Long-term action entails forging personal connections with elites and officials in another state. The focus is on individuals who have a promising political future or other influence on public opinion, and the goal is to draw them closer and build long-term relations with them. The tools of diplomacy here include cultural diplomacy, exchange programs, and branding.

The tools of the new public diplomacy are multidisciplinary, touching upon distinct worlds of theory, research, and practice. Some of them emerged from diplomacy itself, while the rest were adopted from other fields—including the world of culture and the world of business. The list is long: listening, advocacy, diplomacy of exchange, international broadcasting, foreign assistance, international public relations, information management, branding, nonstate players, international law, online-virtual diplomacy, Diaspora diplomacy, cultural diplomacy, commercial diplomacy, assessment, and evaluation. While the worlds of culture and business are driven by different values, they share a common goal: ongoing and long-term change in the home state's public image in the target state.

~

Joseph Nye, the former dean of Harvard's School of Government, formulated a key theory that combines the use of force and public diplomacy. The theory is based on three basic terms: *hard power*, *soft power*, and *smart power*.[1] Focusing on the end of the Cold War and the emergence of the new public policy, Nye identified the need for new tools to boost influence in the international arena without the use of force and noted the growing role of nongovernmental actors in the global arena and the need to be attentive to their views.

Nye's theory is helpful in formulating the general theoretical model of the new public diplomacy and adapting it to the Israeli context. He developed a complete model of new public diplomacy and presented tools for promoting this diplomacy, including a new international discourse between states and NGOs, and between public and private organizations. Nye reiterated the need to distinguish between actions designed to have a long-term impact (in essence, the new public diplomacy) and short-term action (primarily in everyday communication).

While based on previous theories in political science, the new terms added innovative meaning drawn from contemporary international processes. Hard power features elements of realism, the use of force in the international system and the fight against anarchy, while soft power is characterized by liberalism, negotiation, peace, and international order. Nye defined power as "the ability to alter the behavior of others to get what you want" and outlined three basic ways of exercising power—"coercion (sticks), payments (carrots), and attraction (soft power)."[2]

Hard power was previously regarded as essentially military power, but Nye expanded this concept to include economic measures and noted that changes in the world economy were being incorporated into the international system as hard economic power. The combination of military and economic forces creates power that can shape the behavior of others to achieve desired results.[3]

Soft power, which began to develop in the 1990s, stems from the major changes that occurred in the international system, including globalization and the information revolution. The use of soft power includes three components:

1. *Culture*—The system of values and practices that define the society—both "high" society (pertaining to the elites) and popular society (focusing on entertainment for the masses). When the state has universal values and its policy promotes interests shared by others, this elicits attraction and commitment, thus raising the likelihood of achieving desired results—that is, influence.

2. *Political values*—Values the state emphasizes in its internal policy, such as democracy, or promotes in international institutions, including collaboration with other states, will affect the policy preferences of other states vis-à-vis the home state.

3. *Foreign policy*—Policy that promotes peace and human rights is a source of emulation and influence. States tend to connect with a particular state in identification with such foreign policy; they will not fear it and will not regard it as a threat.[4]

One of the salient advantages of soft power is that nonstate entities can exercise it, as opposed to hard power and military power that are the sole province of states. This advantage is growing as NGOs proliferate and assume an increasingly important role in the international arena. Soft power is characterized by the free flow of information and of mass culture via satellites, television, and the Internet.

Soft power and hard power sometimes complement each other, and sometimes are in conflict. The simultaneous use of hard power and soft power may compromise the values that soft power promotes; it may be seen as "talking out of both sides of the mouth." Moreover, economic pressure or military action—hard power—"speak louder" than soft power. Nye gives the example of a state that seeks to win international popularity and fears that exercising its power would hurt its popularity. If it attempts to expand its influence without considering soft power, it is likely to find that other states will also resort to hard power to oppose it. States do not want others to interfere in their foreign policy, not even through soft power. But hard power has an advantage in its ability to attract other states without actually exercising this power: The myth of an invincible state boosts its popularity.

~

The international experiences of the United States at the beginning of the 21st century—the events of September 11 and the wars in Iraq and Afghanistan—exposed the gap between the different types of power and the new reality. Though the United States ostensibly preferred to exercise soft power, a humane and moral approach, it chose to employ hard power. To adapt his theory to this new reality, Nye introduced the concept of "smart power" as a bridging concept that underlines the need to exercise a correct mix of hard power and soft power. "Smart power is the ability to combine the hard power of coercion or payment with the soft power of attraction into a successful strategy."[5]

The challenge becomes how to balance the two types of power in an intelligent way. The battle against international terrorism requires a distinction between extremists and moderates in the Muslim world, and a separate focus on each. Military force and economic sanctions should be deployed against the radicals to strike a blow against terrorism and destroy its infrastructure. On the other hand, Nye suggests using tools of public diplomacy vis-à-vis moderates in the Muslim world, highlighting the positive values of the United States. He recognizes the need to adapt soft power to an era of terrorism, a time characterized by the use of force, and believes that smart power is best equipped to mobilize the private sector and NGOs to join in the diplomatic process alongside the state.

The need to combine the two types of power arose again during the Second Gulf War, after the United States realized that the war would continue for a long time and that deposing Saddam Hussein was not enough. Thus, the U.S. administration presented a vision of soft power: democratization in Iraq to complement military efforts. In this combined approach, the United States could be seen as breaching the walls using hard power, while exploiting this breach to inject new ideas, an exercise in soft power.

The United States divided its vision of democratization into three stages: short term, medium term, and long term. But its efforts, and particularly those of President Bush, were not well received. The push for democratization compromised American political and security interests, generated global hostility toward the United States, and harmed its international standing.

The American example is not necessarily definitive. But other states drew lessons from it and adopted an inclination to connect hard power and soft power to wield smart power. Smart power is characterized by a flexible and variable combination of the two types of power and their components: culture, cultural values, politics, ideology, money, intelligence, law enforcement, diplomacy, information, and the military.

Each of these 10 components could be considered either hard or soft power, or a combination of both. Military force, for example, can be used for conquest or for emergency humanitarian assistance. Culture is ostensibly a tool of soft power only, but many view American dominance in the world of film and television as an attempt to impose its culture on other states—an expression of hard power. Money can be seen as a component of economic pressure but can also be used for foreign assistance, and so on. Therefore, the way these factors are employed and combined produces different levels of power: extremes of power, soft or hard; or a balance between the two extremes—smart power.

Cultural Diplomacy

Culture plays a central role in society and profoundly affects the lives of the individual members of a society. Cultural change lays the groundwork for a change of consciousness, and this takes time; there are no immediate achievements or quick victories.

Cultural diplomacy aims to address the long-term goals of general public diplomacy, rather than the immediate needs of the state. It slowly builds bridges and connections. The first step is to closely study the target audience to become familiar with its culture. This is followed by meticulous planning of activities. Finally, there is a slow process of building relationships.

Cultural diplomacy starts with the values of the home state and the desire to connect the public in the target state to these values. Many states—including Canada, Germany, Britain, and the United States— have established state agencies responsible for cultural diplomacy. These entities operate in five channels: exchanges of individuals, exchanges of groups, exchanges of cultural exhibits, educational and cultural centers, and international broadcasting.

Economic Diplomacy

Economic diplomacy, which developed alongside cultural diplomacy, has likewise received a boost from globalization and the media revolution. Four channels of economic diplomacy can be identified:

1. *Financial*—This diplomacy is conducted between two or more states by official representatives serving in a target state, who monitor its economic policy and report to their home state. Diplomatic delegations to institutions like the World Trade Organization, the International Monetary Fund, and the Bank for International Settlements function similarly.

2. *Commercial-governmental*—This channel is conducted via diplomatic representatives who encourage commercial activity between two states at the governmental level and at the private level.

3. *Commercial-corporate*—Representatives of companies or multinational corporations coordinate between their headquarters and local branches throughout the world. In practice, they promote the economic-cultural interests of the home state.

4. *Business*—Here, too, the multinational corporations initiate the activity, but their efforts are primarily directed at regulatory agencies in the target states.

Corporate diplomacy and business diplomacy developed during the past three decades in the wake of globalization, the dismantling of economic walls between states, and the new interorganizational network that exists in parallel to the interstate system.

In the economic arena, there is another diplomatic channel: ongoing economic assistance and humanitarian assistance in times of emergency. Defense assistance also entails economic value, since it enables a state to reduce its defense spending. Israel and Egypt, for example, each receive billions of dollars annually from the United States, and this aid supports their economies and frees large sums for investment in civilian areas. OECD countries are directly involved in economic assistance and indirectly involved via the United Nations. Members of the OECD commit to allocate a fixed percentage of their annual budget for foreign aid. States that seek to boost or maintain their international standing establish a system of foreign assistance for this purpose. For example, the Norwegian Agency for Development Cooperation (Norad) oversees Norway's network of international humanitarian assistance. After waiting 15 years, Israel was officially accepted into the OECD on September 7,

2010, and the organization's principles—including foreign assistance—are now incumbent upon it.

Branding the State

Another component of the new public diplomacy is branding, which comes from the world of marketing, business, and trade, and includes methods and tools for promoting commercial products. A "brand" connotes immediate recognition with a product and its manufacturer. As the concept of branding developed beyond reference to an individual product, it became more transferable to other arenas, including the state arena. The process of business branding can be applied to the state by replacing business definitions with state terminology. If we replace "business brand" with "state brand" or "the state as a brand," then the planning, implementation, and evaluation will be similar and parallel to introducing the "state" brand into the market.

On the other hand, some researchers suggest examining a brand according to four parameters: 1) knowledge (what is the brand? how is it built? what does it include?), 2) evaluation (how is the brand viewed by consumers? by company employees? by stockholders? by other companies?), 3) relevance (how significant is the brand to the individual?), and 4) distinctness (in what ways is the brand different from other brands?).

There are similarities and differences between branding a state and branding a commercial product. Both involve unique symbols and names that elicit beliefs, views, ideas, and emotions among the public. Both assign a central role to education and creating awareness—commercial branding aims to raise awareness of the product in order to sell it, while public diplomacy seeks to inform the individual about a particular state, its policy, culture, and heritage. In both cases, there is an implicit belief that fostering a positive relationship with people is an essential means of promoting objectives—and these relationships are planned for the long term. Mass media is used in both cases of branding for building long-term relations and communicating information. Both require in-depth research prior to activity in the field, and both can be measured (unlike many other aspects of public diplomacy).

The differences between business branding and state branding stem from the disparity between consumerism and statecraft. State branding entails changing attitudes toward it, while business branding seeks to induce the consumer to make a purchase. In the first case, success is reflected in positive public opinion; in the second case, success is measured by an increase in sales. Similarly, failure is expressed in unchanged or negative public opinion vis-à-vis the state, or a decline in sales in the case of a product. Communication in business branding is one-directional, while state branding is two-directional. Businesses can control the message to the consumer in a focused way, while the state relies on messages that are not one-dimensional or centralized. Accordingly, it is possible to control the consumer product and maintain a consistent image, while the state as a brand has multiple and even contradictory meanings.

The possibility of rebranding a state and reshaping its image appealed to many states, leading them to develop branding initiatives in their foreign relations. A salient example in the past decade is the unsuccessful effort by the United States to rebrand itself in its relations with the Arab world. Other states, such as Norway and Canada, adopted similar initiatives with the aim of positioning themselves in the international arena. Norway, which lacks visibility, looked for a suitable niche and focused on peace efforts and environmental protection. Canada, which is more prominent in the international arena, chose to pursue a new image by emphasizing the country's multicultural and diverse society.

Assessment and Evaluation

Assessment is a key component of every strategic planning process, from beginning to end. It focuses on the desired objectives, provides feedback, and ultimately responds to the basic question: Did the action meet its goals? Public diplomacy, in its various channels, must rely on assessment and evaluation.

The U.S. Government Accountability Office (GAO) examined the effort to influence public opinion in the Arab-Muslim world in 2006–2007 and concluded that the new public diplomacy lacked a systematic method for assessment and evaluation. Some of the researchers asserted that one of the reasons for the U.S. government's failure in public diplomacy was the lack of feedback and clear indexes for evaluating the activity. The U.S. State Department continues to search for methods and indexes for evaluating public diplomacy, and it established a unit for evaluation and assessment in this field.

Other states have found it difficult to set clear indexes for assessment of public diplomacy, and there are three reasons for this: 1) American methods for gauging public opinion cannot be applied universally; such methods must be adapted for each state. 2) The methods are not scientific and are insufficiently precise. 3) Disparities of culture require adaptation for each specific state.

The researcher Eytan Gilboa has proposed a World Standing Index (WSI) that includes international discussions, voting patterns, decisions of international organizations, announcements and activities of NGOs, diplomatic recognition and diplomatic relations, debates and decisions in parliaments and in political forums, political declarations by world leaders endowed with moral authority (the pope, for example), diplomatic visits by heads of state and senior ministers, rejection or acceptance of terminology, Internet sites, sanctions and boycotts, legal activity in the national and international arenas, trends in public opinion, and media coverage.[6]

Traditional diplomacy is not dead. However, the additional dimension of new public diplomacy shifts the center of gravity, moving it more and more toward openness, transparency, and the public arena.

Chapter 4

Low-Intensity Warfare

Human history bears witness to a continual stream of military clashes, with war serving as one of the grand strategies of nations. In the words of military theorist Basil Liddell Hart: "for the role of grand strategy is to co-ordinate and direct all the resources of a nation towards the attainment of the political object of the war—the goal defined by national policy. Grand strategy should both calculate and develop the economic resources and man-power of nations in order to sustain the fighting services."[1] War is not an end in itself, but rather a means of implementing a grand strategy. This helps to explain the famous statement by the Prussian military theorist Carl von Clausewitz: "War is the continuation of politics by other means."

"The sign of true strategy is that it defines its intent and sticks to it, without fear, while adapting the means to the end, and also the end to the means,"[2] Liddell Hart emphasizes. The Chinese military thinker Sun Tzu stated in *The Art of War* (probably the first treatise on military doctrine, written in the fifth century BCE): "War is a matter of vital importance to the state; the province of life or death, the road to survival or ruin. It is mandatory that it be thoroughly studied."[3] Therefore, Sun Tzu continues, it is essential to "appraise" war in light of five fundamental factors: moral influence, weather, terrain, command, and doctrine. "There is no general who has not heard of these five matters," he asserts. "Those who master them win; those who do not are defeated."[4] Some 2,500 years have passed since Sun Tzu wrote these words, and the key points of his military doctrine are still cited in current military theories.

War is not a one-dimensional and fixed concept. Over the course of history, diverse forms of warfare gradually developed in keeping with the times and technology. Clausewitz compared war to a chameleon that changes its colors and saw it as a phenomenon that is based more on continuity and conservatism than on change and revolution. For Clausewitz, war was like a chain of mutations whose nature or direction could not be foreseen.

∼

World War II is considered the last major war, but warfare is still a part of our world. Wars have evolved in new and varied ways, but they still entail violent confrontations over political-military objectives. Many scholars concur that conventional wars between states have become a rare phenomenon since the end of the Cold War—that is, since the 1990s. International conflict can run the gamut from conventional war to peaceful competition. "Most of the conflicts have occurred under the level of traditional conventional warfare (sometimes defined as 'high-intensity conflict'), but over the level of peaceful competition that routinely exists between states. These conflicts [at a middle level] are sometimes defined as 'low-intensity conflicts.' "[5]

Low-intensity violence has many definitions, including some that emerged from the Israeli experience: "A conflict with a political aim, which is decided through a change of consciousness in the society, by attrition. The political calculation is the dominant calculation in the conflict, and the military-operational calculation is secondary to it; its main results are related to consciousness and the physical outcome is secondary; it is a protracted conflict, and its moves are planned accordingly; it is focused on the struggle over consciousness; conflict management relies on the ability to control the intensity of friction; and the nonsovereign entity, which is inferior in combat strength, is usually the one that chooses the path of limited conflict."[6] The U.S. Joint Chiefs of Staff adopted another definition: "Low-intensity conflict is a limited politico-military struggle to achieve political, social, economic or psychological objectives. It is often protracted and ranges from diplomatic, economic and psychosocial pressures through terrorism and insurgency. Low-intensity conflict is generally confined to a geographic area and is often characterized by constraints on the weaponry, tactics and level of violence."[7]

Based on these and other definitions, we can describe the characteristics of low-intensity warfare:

1. The use of subtle tactics and political expertise because the conflict should not be decided only by firepower.

2. There is no distinction between the battlefront and the home front, and clashes between armies on the front lines rarely occur.

3. The principal objective of both sides is to influence the views and loyalties of the civilian population. This can be achieved by dampening support for the rival through persuasion or coercion.

4. Conflict management is conducted ad hoc, not according to advanced planning.

5. Political calculations carry significant weight in these conflicts, sometimes more than military calculations.

When all-out war, or even limited war, is conducted between states, there is symmetry. Limited conflicts, on the other hand, are asymmetric—at least one of the participants is not necessarily a state. In this asymmetry, one side has advantages over its rivals in terms of its capabilities and power. In a limited conflict (or low-intensity warfare), the strong side must exploit its advantages to diminish the rival's ability to fight, while the weak side will try to eliminate its rival's advantages by reducing the friction between them. The weak and militarily inferior side will also mobilize diverse means of communication (especially via the Internet) to neutralize the asymmetry, win the advantage, and magnify its achievements.

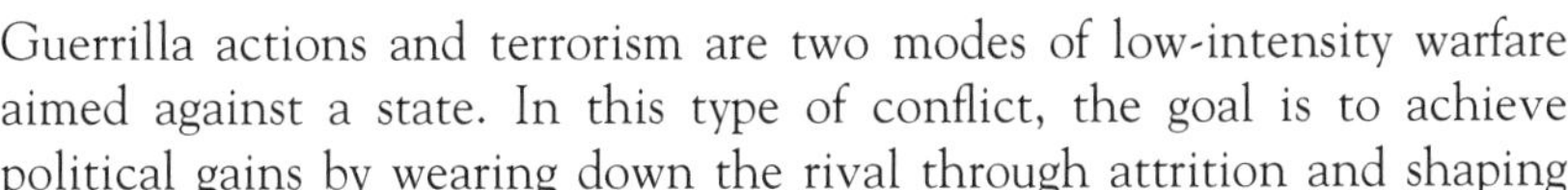

Guerrilla actions and terrorism are two modes of low-intensity warfare aimed against a state. In this type of conflict, the goal is to achieve political gains by wearing down the rival through attrition and shaping consciousness.

Yehoshafat Harkavi, a former IDF general, defined *guerilla* action as "an ancient form of warfare that preceded regular combat, because in ancient times fighting was primarily between irregular forces. Guerrilla [warfare] became a distinct method of combat only when regular combat emerged. It is characterized by small-scale fighting in a territory controlled by the enemy."[8] Guerrilla combat served as a defensive tactic in the past, but in the 20th century it became a method of attack aimed at grabbing power. Guerrilla activity combines political and military means for achieving its objectives.

Boaz Ganor defined *terrorism* as "a form of violent struggle in which violence is deliberately used against civilians in order to achieve political goals (nationalistic, socio-economic, ideological, religious, etc.)."[9]

Guerrilla warfare and terrorism have much in common, and both employ propaganda and communication in their fight to shape consciousness. However, the goals of a guerrilla struggle are material, political, and more clearly defined: Guerrilla warfare is aimed against a state and its symbols, not against its civilians; it seeks to destroy equipment and supplies; it relies on broad popular support; and it is more selective than terrorism. Its principle objective is to advance a particular ideology.

∿

In an asymmetric conflict, the inferior side chooses to balance power by influencing public opinion and building consciousness to amplify its actions and accord it legitimacy, recognition, and support. In these ways, it will seek to drive the target public in the desired political direction.[10] The information and technology revolution, the emergence of multinational corporations, and the participation of new players (such as international organizations and NGOs) in the international system created a comfortable infrastructure for the battle for consciousness.

As the centrality of this battle grew and spread across the global arena, it unintentionally helped international terrorism to proliferate. The turning point in the international arena was September 11, 2001. The United States had failed to understand the extremism and Islamization in the Arab-Muslim world and had not identified the growth of anti-Western and anti-American movements. After 9/11, it recognized the need to return to public diplomacy and to add new dimensions to it.

At the beginning of the 21st century, the United States was involved in low-intensity warfare in Iraq and in Afghanistan. On both fronts, it fought against international terrorism that had struck against it and other Western nations. Gradually, the United States succeeded in reducing the scope of Al-Qaeda's activity and especially its involvement in international terrorism. However, as often occurs in this type of warfare, a new organization inherited Al-Qaeda's position: Islamic State of Iraq and Syria (ISIS). At the beginning of the second decade of the 21st century, ISIS occupied large parts of Syria and Iraq. It developed a semi-state structure, bolstered by thousands of volunteers from around the world. Within a few years, it also succeeded in creating an infrastructure of international terrorism. An anti-ISIS coalition arose, led by the United States, with France, Britain, and other states. They were later joined by Russia, though primarily with the aim of protecting Bashar Assad's regime in Syria. While ISIS lost some of its territorial gains, it recorded impressive "achievements" in international terrorism, successfully mounting attacks in the United States, Britain, France, and Germany. Scholars expect that most of the wars in the 21st century will occur in developing states and in nations that lack a solid political structure and government and that are divided ethnically and religiously. Therefore, the wars of the United States and its allies will be against nations or terrorist movements that champion extreme ideologies and opposing cultural values, and against societies plagued by poverty and lacking stable government institutions. The principal effort will be the battle for consciousness.

There are various terms used in the world to describe the battle for consciousness. In Britain, it is called the "fight for hearts and minds." The U.S. military uses the expressions "psychological warfare," "perception management," "influence management," and "information operation." The IDF speaks about *consciousness*: "The strategy of limited conflict is to win a decision of consciousness in the society with the help of military means. The battle is for the society's consciousness and for national resilience. Decision is achieved through maneuvering to raise doubts and generate a sense of persistent uncertainty."[11]

Consciousness is not a natural and inherent concept but rather a structured process, continually shaped by interested parties and by those who wield wealth and power. According to this view, there are two states of consciousness—a situational consciousness and a basic consciousness, and there are six tools used in the battle for consciousness:[12]

1. *Physical actions* including destruction, aerial bombardment, attacks against people and property, aimed at affecting consciousness.

2. *Acts of deception* aimed at tendentiously injecting false information to influence the rival's perceptions, to mislead and surprise it, and to lead it to make erroneous assessments.

3. *Cybernetic activity* of two types: 1. actions aimed at harming the rival's computerized systems and information—command and control, communications, computers, and electronics; 2. actions aimed at protecting one's own systems and information.

4. *Humanitarian activity* aimed at strengthening the positive connection between military forces and civilian authorities in areas where military forces are deployed.

5. *Propaganda activity* via *the media*, aimed at winning support for policies and national goals—both at home and in the rival's public opinion and system.

6. *Psychological warfare*—use of nonviolent means of persuasion, such as distributing leaflets, communicating messages via the media, and spreading misleading messages and rumors. There are three types of psychological warfare: *white*—activity whose source is known, *gray*—activity whose source is unknown, and *black*—responsibility for this activity is cast upon someone else.

∾

Military experts and historians, including Clausewitz, have distinguished between a strategy of decision versus a strategy of attrition. In their view, wars are supposed to end in decision and victory, which pave the way for diplomacy and political activity. Political activity can also appear at the start of the process, and then war and the use of force signify the failure of this activity. However, Clausewitz and his generation dealt primarily with all-out conflict between regular armies, while today limited conflict is more common. This requires new definitions for the terms "decision" and "victory." The criterion that comes closest to decision in a limited conflict is victory in the battle for consciousness.

Terrorist and guerrilla organizations have adopted the strategy of attrition, concluding that it would enable them to win a decision in the battle for consciousness. Attrition is conventionally viewed as a weapon of the weak side, compensating for its technological and numerical inferiority. But the state can also seek to wear down and even defeat its rival through attrition. This requires a resilient society, capable of finding the emotional and physical strength to cope with a protracted war, despite its price.

However, the battlefield today is not clearly defined; the means of warfare have become diverse and new participants have joined the fight. The arena of limited conflict has blurred the terms "decision" and "victory," and a new perception of these terms is also required. "A situation may develop in which both sides declare themselves victors, but this enables, to some extent, manipulation of the victory."[13] We can determine the victory by changing the definition of the war's aims. This strong subjective dimension and the ability to manipulate are what differentiate between victory and decision. "There is a basic difficulty in precisely defining victory in a 'limited conflict' or in a guerrilla war waged by an organization, religious or political, from a neighboring state," Zeev Schiff writes regarding the Second Lebanon War.[14]

Low-intensity violence and the new public diplomacy come together on the battlefront of consciousness. Old and new tools have been deployed in the new battle for consciousness, including the new media and networks, the Internet, international broadcasting, and two-directional communication. Since the campaign is directed at public opinion in the enemy state, I see a fascinating similarity between the strategy of terrorism/guerrilla warfare and a state's public diplomacy. Both seek to win over public opinion in the target state and to effect change in that state. The low-intensity conflicts do not end in decision and in victory. At best, both sides declare victory and these declarations have an impact on public opinion. However, in reality, there is no "victory" in protracted low-intensity conflicts. International experience indicates that crises wane, only to erupt again in new circumstances.

Chapter 5

Globalization and the Media Revolution

Globalization can be briefly described as a process that frees social relations from geographic dependence and places them in a single global arena. This arena affects all its component parts, which in turn shapes the arena itself. Scholars note five uses of the concept of "globalization" in national contexts: internationalization, liberalization, universalization, Westernization, and deterritorialization. Globalization is characterized by *processes that equally and directly connect people from all parts of the world, beyond political, social, religious, or other systems.*[1] According to Zygmunt Bauman, "the deepest meaning conveyed by the idea of globalization is that of the indeterminate, unruly and self-propelled character of world affairs; the absence of a center, of a controlling desk, of a board of directors, of a managerial office."[2]

Technology has a decisive impact on globalization. Throughout human history, technological developments have sparked wide-scale change; thus, the past is divided into the agricultural era, followed by the industrial era. They are now joined by the *information era*, which Alvin Toffler coined "the third wave." The key feature of the information era is rapid mobility from point to point; the distances on earth have shrunk, bringing communities and people closer together.

It is customary to trace the beginning of the globalization process of communication to the 19th century, but the pace of progress was very slow and gradual then. Newspapers and magazines appeared that were intended for local audiences, and their distribution was confined to national borders due to language differences. International news agencies were the first significant form of global communication. At first, they provided local news services and information and later expanded to global news coverage. Movies and radio broadcasts at the beginning of the

20th century crossed national borders and accelerated the process. Radio became global with the development of short-wave broadcasting in the late 1920s. Its range stretched to thousands of miles, though its technical quality was low. Television emerged after World War II, especially in the United States. In the early 1980s, another significant technological change occurred—satellite broadcasting. The growing number of communication satellites made it possible to transmit broadcasts to every corner of the world. The broadcasts initially used analog and wireless technology, and later cable networks. During the 1990s, direct-broadcast satellite (DBS) technology brought programming to viewers without the need for land-based connections. There are three methods of broadcasting today—land, cable, and satellite—as well as various combinations of these methods. This range of options has boosted the role of television as the dominant medium of our time.

The Internet began to develop in the mid-1960s but only really emerged with the development of digitization, which converts all information into binary units that can be recorded as electronic signals. In this process, most of the new global information can be translated into the language of the computer, including pictures, text, and music.

The next stage was the integration of communication tools—telecommunication systems and computer systems—into a single system, with each part of the system conveying signals and content from the other parts. A shared digital language unified cinema, television, radio, newspapers, music, literature, photography, telephony, and more. These were later integrated in mobile devices, some of them telephone based. These two developments—digitization and integration—revolutionized the communications industry, opening new possibilities and creating the new media, whose consumers are partners in producing and disseminating it. The computer and the Internet began to interact with the reporter, telephone, radio, cinema, and television. New devices, led by handheld computers, streamed information from the media and conveyed relevant local data in real time. The next technological generation included smart phones that support all classic media options in a single device, as well as additional capabilities. The revolution continues and no one knows what lies ahead.

During the 1990s, there was also a revolution in media distribution. Until then, media outlets were primarily national in scope. But the new technological infrastructure enabled the formation of a worldwide communication system, spawning television and Internet networks for the global arena. The Internet revolution influenced related technological systems: advanced materials, nanotechnology, robotics, biotechnology, and more. The globalization process included technological innovations that engendered profound changes in other fields, including politics, culture, and economics.

Globalization connected the world in a single economic unit and created a new world economy. International economic institutions were created in the wake of World War II, and the new technological capabilities accelerated global monetary activity. Money could be transferred rapidly from one country to another, thus facilitating the creation of large and cross-border economic systems. Multinational corporations were drawn to the new opportunities the new economy offered. While multinational corporations focused on manufacturing, trade, and finance, their activity compelled them to also become interested and involved in political and social issues in order to create a supportive environment for their businesses.

⁓

The system of nation-states still exists today, but the sweeping tide of globalization threatens its status and ability to function. Political activity was traditionally conducted within the nation-state and among nation-states. Globalization added new activity on two levels: sub-state and supra-state. It reduces the likelihood of war between states and encourages ongoing relations and negotiation between them.

The new world order brings to the fore organizations that did not participate in the battles of the past. These organizations no longer operate on the sidelines of the international arena; they are active players in this arena, together with sovereign nation-states. On the international map today, there are about 200 governments, hundreds of thousands of organizations, including local NGOs, intergovernmental bodies (such as the United Nations and the World Bank), international organizations (for example, Amnesty International and Doctors Without Borders), and about 60,000 multinational corporations.

⁓

Two media phenomena arose from the new process of globalization: 1) the formation of global communication networks, and 2) the enhanced status of individuals and groups in the media world.

New media networks began to appear in the West in the early 1980s. CNN launched its broadcasts on July 1, 1980, paving the way for global television news stations such as the BBC and Fox News. A new configuration emerged in the global news industry, which was previously controlled by "the big four"—the AP, UPI, Reuters, and AFP news agencies. Some of them survived, while others disappeared or merged into the new international media corporations.

Ted Turner, an American entrepreneur, exploited the technological developments to create CNN, the first global news channel. The network broadcast news around the clock, with a global deployment that combined communication satellites and cable television. CNN and other global media networks gradually became central players in the international arena. The First Gulf War (1990–1991) is usually cited as the turning point, as CNN broadcast live and continuously from the battlefields. Even before the war, the network utilized its technological capabilities to broadcast directly from Iraq. Peter Arnett, a CNN correspondent, was the only reporter to broadcast directly from Baghdad during the war. President Saddam Hussein exploited Arnett's broadcasts to convey messages to the West from the Iraqi perspective. The broadcasts stirred controversy and raised questions about the network's credibility. New global networks extensively reported on international crises: the events of Tiananmen Square in China (July 1989); the revolutions in Eastern Europe (the late 1980s); the coup attempt in Russia (1991); the humanitarian intervention in northern Iraq and in Kurdistan (1991); the wars in Somalia (1992–1994), Rwanda (1995), Bosnia (1992–1995), Kosovo (1999), and Afghanistan (2002); the events of September 11 (2001); and, more recently, the stormy Arab Spring (2011) and aborted coup in Turkey (2016).

These events sparked discussion about the connection between news coverage and the shaping of foreign policy by political leaders. The generic name given to the networks' reporting was the CNN *effect:*[3] "the dynamic tension between television news in real time and policymaking, with the news enjoying the dynamic tension that exists between real-time television news and policymaking, with the news having the upper hand in terms of influence."[4] This effect has also been described as "branding" the media's technological capabilities via the new channels, which elicits significant responses among the viewers and the political elite vis-à-vis domestic and world events.

The CNN effect includes *direct* (or nearly direct) *broadcasts* of *central news events*, with an emphasis on *humanitarian crises* (and confrontations in general) that influence *public opinion* and drive *decision makers* to take action related to the crisis or the event.

Direct broadcasts have a very strong effect because they are not edited or subjected to other intervention. The picture is beamed straight from the field to the viewer's home. States can limit direct broadcasts by blocking access to the location or through administrative means, such as preventing the transmission of materials to the home station, but they are reluctant to adopt such sanctions due to their fear of the networks. As the technologies for transmitting direct broadcasts become increasingly sophisticated, the CNN effect is amplified via smartphones and other devices.

Some claim that *decision makers* are indifferent to events until the media brings them to their doorstep. Due to the emotional impact it creates, the CNN effect can accelerate political developments that might have also occurred without television reporting. The debate over the role of CNN in international crises remains open. Some note that the media has always had an impact on decision makers and political events, while others claim that the CNN effect is only a myth. One may argue about the magnitude of the CNN effect, but it undeniably exists. The media's onsite presence at events—acts of terror, military attacks, popular revolutions, or natural disasters—is required in order to bring these news stories into the public domain and generate international impact. Decision makers—in particular, military commanders who encounter reporters on the battlefield—must always be mindful of the CNN effect.

The appearance of Al Jazeera in Arabic on November 1, 1996, is considered the second wave in the development of global media networks. The network was established after the BBC's failed attempt to broadcast news in Arabic. From the outset, Al Jazeera was considered an unconventional network and continually stirred controversy. It gradually became an integral part of the political landscape in the Middle East. Its influence on policy issues and public opinion grew, and it amassed tens of millions of viewers throughout the world. The network's motto—"the opinion and the other opinion"—aims to illustrate that a single view does not suffice, as is customary in the Arab world. It has confronted Arab governments and regimes, including Egypt, Jordan, and Iraq. In response, these governments have shut down their offices and stopped their broadcasts. This has only boosted Al Jazeera's popularity.

Externally, the network has been coined "Jihad TV" due to its sensational, inflaming, irresponsible, and propagandistic broadcasts, especially after al-Qaeda chose it as a means of disseminating exclusive tapes of

Bin Laden and other terrorist leaders. This isolated the network in the global media but also led to the establishment of similar networks, thus undermining its exclusive status.

Just as CNN reshaped the global media system and influenced international policy, Al Jazeera also became an important international phenomenon. The "Al Jazeera effect" is significant in five ways: 1) The network broke the monopoly of Arab governments and regimes on information about what occurs in their territory. 2) It eroded the exclusivity of the Western networks and introduced an Arab alternative; thus, many viewers in non-Western countries distrust the Western networks and give greater credence to Al Jazeera. 3) The network granted broad coverage and international legitimacy to terrorism and violence, including false and misleading information.[5] 4) The network created a virtual Arab entity shared by 300 million Arabs in 22 states and helped to foment the revolutionary events in 2011 in Tunisia, Egypt, Libya, and Yemen. 5) Al Jazeera boosted the power of the individual to change the relationship between the government and its citizenry and to influence the management of affairs of state.

In parallel to the establishment of huge corporations that wield enormous influence, a sociopolitical process occurred, empowering groups and individuals who exploited the new media, and in turn helped to shape it. This powerful process is based on the rapid expansion of the Internet, virtual communities, social networks, and sophisticated applications on mobile phones. Social media such as Facebook, Twitter, Myspace, LinkedIn, YouTube, Flickr, and Wikipedia were made possible by the new technologies and their range of uses.

The new technologies engendered a series of processes that changed the face of the media arena, which now included the traditional media, the new media (in both of its stages), and the public (individuals and groups). The technologies enhanced the public's ability to contribute to the new media world, which is built upon networks that create new public spaces. The general public is broken down into individuals who gradually form networks in a range of fields: social, geographic, political, ideological, or value related. This is how new groups or new publics are created beneath or above the state level.

In late 2010 and early 2011, the Arab "Spring of Nations" erupted. Like other social revolutions, it expressed a series of processes that occurred over time. But, as always, there was a formative event that brought these processes to fruition. The journalist Thomas Friedman described the events as "the mother of all wake-up calls."[6] According to Friedman, the forces that had preserved the status quo in the Middle East were oil, autocracy, hatred of Israel, and fear of disorder. New forces were now in play, Friedman asserted, citing China, the generation of 20-somethings, and Twitter.[7]

The first signs of unrest appeared in Tunisia following the first wave of leaks on the WikiLeaks site. One of the documents, published in December 2010, referred to Tunisia as a "police state" and claimed that its president of 23 years, Zine El Abidine Ben Ali, had lost touch with the public. The founder of WikiLeaks, Julian Assange, predicted that the leaked documents would trigger revolutions in the Arab world.[8]

The revolution that began in Tunisia was named the Jasmine Revolution, after the country's popular flower, which local men tuck behind their ears. The distress of the population in Tunisia—in particular, the country's young generation—was fertile ground for a political upheaval. One dramatic, highly publicized event was needed to ignite the opposition. The social networks and other technologies then stepped in to connect the focal points of unrest and create a large camp.

Three seminal events were documented that symbolized and gave identity to the revolution: Mohamed Bouazizi, 26, who operated a fruit and vegetable cart that was confiscated by the police, lit himself on fire in the town of Sidi Bouzid, about 125 miles from Tunis, the capital. His death brought many young people to the streets. On December 22, an unemployed youth named Lahseen Naji committed suicide; two days later, a demonstrator, Mohamed Ammari, was shot to death by the local police.

The events in Tunisia reflected the unifying power of social networks, and the effectiveness of cell phones and their cameras. Pictures taken by the demonstrators themselves were posted on the Internet or sent to the media—in particular to Al Jazeera, which had no obligations toward the local government. This set a snowballing effect of events in motion.

The number of participants in the world's social networks is continually growing. Facebook is the leading network, with about 1.65 billion users as of mid-2016, followed by Twitter, YouTube, Instagram, Vine, Google+, Pinterest, and LinkedIn. Use of social networks is also growing in Arab society. During the first quarter of 2011, the number of Facebook users in Arab states soared by 30 percent. In the Middle East and North Africa, the number of Facebook users doubled in a single year. Facebook flourished in every country in the region; Iran, which waged a war against the network, recorded the lowest usage, and Turkey had the highest percentage of users. The Arabic interface, launched in 2009, was the preferred interface.[9]

The rapid victory of the demonstrators in Tunisia influenced other states in the region. The network formula operated within states and among them. Soon, demonstrations began in Egypt, Yemen, Syria, Jordan, Bahrain, and elsewhere.

Hosni Mubarak ruled in Egypt for 30 years and his regime collapsed 20 days after the unrest began. The demonstrations in Egypt were initiated by a group of young people in the April 6 Movement, established in 2008. In January 2009, the group, which operated as a social-economic opposition, numbered about 70,000 members.[10] They organized via Facebook, Twitter, Flickr, blogs, and other new media tools. In June 2010, security forces arrested a young businessman, Khaled Sa'id, at an Internet café in Cairo and beat him to death. His crime was that he used a blog to attack government corruption. Five days after his death, a Facebook page was launched, entitled "We Are All Khaled Sa'id."[11] The owner of the page, Wael Ghonim, soon became one of the leaders of the revolution.

Following the murder of Sa'id, and in solidarity with the revolution in Tunisia, the April 6 Movement called for demonstrations on National Police Day, January 21, 2011.[12] The largest square in Cairo, Tahrir Square, was chosen as the site for the main demonstration. The choice of this central locale in the heart of the capital facilitated coverage by the foreign media (the CNN effect) and effective dissemination of the message to neighboring states (the Al Jazeera effect). Mubarak's regime tried to avoid exercising force, fearing that physical clashes with the demonstrators would be documented by the media and thus harm the president's personal standing and Egypt's international standing. Mubarak was also concerned about possible dissension among the soldiers and was reluctant to test their loyalty. The demonstrators recognized this point of weakness and escalated their presence and activity. Mubarak and his officials tried to act in two ways: 1) blocking the Internet and Al Jazeera broadcasts and 2) identifying and neutralizing leaders of the revolution.

On January 28, after a week of unrest, the government cut off the five Internet providers and disconnected Egypt from the global network, as China had previously done.[13] Mubarak also decided, like other Arab leaders, to strike against Al Jazeera and stopped its broadcasts to the Middle East via the NileSat satellite.[14] Both efforts failed: The Internet sites resumed operation and Al Jazeera continued broadcasting nonstop, using other satellites or networks instead of NileSat.

Amid the cybernetic revolution in Egypt, Secretary of State Hillary Clinton delivered a seminal speech defining U.S. policy regarding the online revolutions. She cited fears about abuse of the Internet by terrorists, extremist groups, human traffickers, pedophiles, and economic hackers. But she also emphasized that the cybernetic space should remain open, enabling the free flow of information: "The Internet has become the public space of the 21st century—the world's town square, classroom, marketplace, coffeehouse and night club. We all shape and are shaped by what happens there."[15]

The American administration promised to help the protest movements overcome technological impediments and to make it harder for autocratic governments to hinder communications.[16] The United States is leading a global initiative to develop and install encrypted Internet and cellular systems for opponents of tyrannical regimes that seek to silence critics through censorship or by blocking communication networks. The initiative includes an "Internet suitcase" that can be smuggled into a closed state, development of "stealth" wireless networks, a fleet of aircraft that can reactivate severed networks, and setting up systems in military bases that cannot be violated.[17] Clinton attacked states that censor the Internet and isolate themselves. "Virtual walls are cropping up in place of visible walls," she noted.[18]

As often occurs in the interlinked world, events developed simultaneously. In Syria, Yemen, Jordan, and other states in the region, demonstrations took place, propelled by the social networks and new media. This trend of new public involvement also spurred demonstrations of unprecedented scope throughout Israel in the summer of 2011. The protests were aimed against the government's economic policy and the concentration of economic power in the hands of tycoons. An exception in this wave of demonstrations in 2011 was Iran, which had already stamped out protests following elections in 2009 by shutting down the networks and wielding a heavy hand against demonstrators. Fearing a resumption of internal unrest, the Iranian regime suddenly restricted Internet access in February 2011. However, there was an organized infrastructure for continued Internet activity, and its users had developed ways of circumventing government monitoring.[19]

Syria, heavily influenced by Iran, chose the same route as its patron. Starting in early February, large numbers of Syrians marched in provincial towns, and they continued to do so during the following months. The demonstrators communicated with each other via Twitter and Facebook. In response, the government cut off Internet access for long periods of time, along with telephone networks, both mobile and landline. Skype was also no longer available.[20]

Tyrannical regimes have also exploited the new media for their own benefit. In *The Net Delusion: The Dark Side of Internet Freedom*, American researcher Evgeny Morozov describes many cases in which governments have used the Internet to uncover subversive activity—for example, publishing pictures of demonstrators and requesting the public's help in identifying them.[21] Thus, the Internet can incriminate its users if they fail to take precautions. Michael Dahan concurs that technology can serve freedom but may also be used to suppress and monitor opponents and political activists: "The social networks provide precise information to security and intelligence agencies. This is what happened in China, in Iran, in Egypt, in the Palestinian Authority and in Moldova."[22]

Social networks try to remain apolitical and present themselves as an objective technical entity. At a conference in Paris, Facebook's founder Mark Zuckerberg argued that "it would be extremely arrogant for any specific technology company to claim credit"[23] for triggering the protests in the Arab world. "People are now having the opportunity to communicate. That's not a Facebook thing. That's an Internet thing," he explained. The Internet gives each person a voice, and people can use the Internet to share their opinions with many others. "For the first time, the general public has an opportunity to communicate with the government, to express views, to conduct a discussion."[24]

Facebook is seemingly overwhelmed by its success and fears restrictions like those imposed on Google in China, for example. Therefore, it reiterates its policy that users must operate under their real names, a demand that sometimes puts their lives in jeopardy.[25]

In July 2016, there was an attempted military coup in Turkey. Social networks also played a role. In distress, President Recep Tayyip Erdoğan turned to the Turkish people via cell phone and implored them to go to the streets and block rebel units. Erdoğan, who had fought against the Internet and social networks, was now dependent on them. In fact, he utilized both new media and old media: Erdoğan spoke to the Turkish people on a cell phone but via the national television network. The immediate lesson was that social networks are an important player, but the old players apparently still carry influence. The rebellion, incidentally, failed.

Maximum freedom, unfettered democracy, and the new town square have peaked, in my view. Social networks realize there are limits to power. In the United States, a precedent was set when the FBI hacked an iPhone and extracted terrorism-related information after Apple refused to unlock it. The networks concluded that they should monitor posts concerning pedophiles, drugs, and violence. They understood, belatedly, that ISIS is using their platforms to disseminate horrific videos of executions that amplify the organization's influence and boost its efforts to recruit volunteers. The question of terrorism on the Internet remains open. More and more states, including Israel, Germany, and France, have questioned the networks' role in incitement and the spread of terrorism. The networks reject the demand to remove messages of terrorism, but they may not remain indifferent if pressure by states and legal proceedings force them to take responsibility for the content on their networks and impose monetary penalties. Money fuels the networks. The fear of losing revenue could induce them to take action they have sought to avoid.

Chapter 6

"Drink More Water"

Public diplomacy has been on the national agenda throughout the history of Zionism. Those who dreamed of establishing a home for the Jewish people in the Land of Israel recognized that broad global consent was a prerequisite for fulfilling this dream. This required extensive *hasbara*, which began at the end of World War I and intensified after the Holocaust. The tragedy that befell the Jewish people, together with public diplomacy efforts, led to the approval of UN General Assembly Resolution 181 on November 29, 1947. However, international legitimacy was not sufficient. An ongoing series of military confrontations and diplomatic negotiations required international support, and winning this support became the primary diplomatic objective of the State of Israel.

The story of Israel's public diplomacy is not only a matter of content and messages, but also of ongoing organizational efforts—most of them unsuccessful—to integrate *hasbara* in the prestate and state systems. In the following pages, I will try to unfold Israel's diplomatic and security history through the lens of public policy.

In 1922, Col. Frederick Kisch came to Palestine to organize the Political Department of the World Zionist Organization (WZO). "He believes in publishing not only in order to disseminate news, but also as a means of stimulating effective criticism and suggestions for changes," his assistant Gershon Agron (Agronsky) recalled. "Journalism has a very important role. It is incumbent upon Zionist officials to help journalism fulfill its purpose."[1] Two years later, Agron became the press officer of the *Zionist Executive* and established the WZO's Press Office.

When the riots of 1929 erupted, the Press Office directed the *hasbara* against the Mandate government, accusing it of failing to protect the lives and property of the Jews of Palestine. Headed by Agron, the

Press Office was responsible for the Zionist movement's relations with the media throughout the world. It was the beginning of the vital connection between national institutions and foreign correspondents, whose reports shaped world opinion.

In 1934, the WZO formed a *hasbara* department to address Jewish and non-Jewish audiences in Palestine and abroad. There was also an effort to foster cooperation between the WZO and the press in Palestine. The press already viewed the WZO as a tool of the state in the making, while the WZO backed the media in its battle against the restrictions imposed by the Mandate authorities.

Agron proposed institutionalizing the connections between the Jewish Agency and the local and foreign press. In 1945, he submitted a memorandum for establishing an Information Ministry in the future state, based on the model of the British Ministry of Information during World War II.

Days after the declaration of the state, Foreign Minister Moshe Sharett asked Agron to implement his proposal to head a government "information service." Sharett explained that his plan was to establish a state *hasbara* bureau with two units, one for the local press and one for the foreign media. Prime Minister David Ben-Gurion was opposed to creating a separate ministry for public diplomacy and believed that *hasbara* services should be subordinate to the Prime Minister's Office (PMO). Sharett made another offer to Agron, which the latter rejected, and during the War of Independence, Moshe Perlman headed the joint *hasbara* bureau of the IDF and Foreign Ministry, with Abraham Herman serving as his deputy.

The documentary material from that period indicates that foreign correspondents were already complaining about rigid censorship, claiming that local reporters were receiving preferential treatment. Most importantly, they felt they were not receiving crucial information and were being denied physical access to the battlefront. There was also criticism from the local press: "How do we expect to win in the propaganda arena in Israel and abroad if we assign commanders who have no affiliation with the press, no training and no understanding. Why haven't journalists been mobilized for the journalism front?"[2]

In April 1949, an effort was made to renew the activity of the *hasbara* services in the PMO, subordinate to the prime minister himself, via the director-general of the PMO. Ben-Gurion's dominant personality dictated the *hasbara* policy and its execution, including placing it under the PMO's purview.

Philanthropic organizations—including Keren Hayesod, Keren Hakayemet (JNF), the United Jewish Appeal, and Israel Bonds—mobilized in support of the diplomatic efforts of prestate Israel. They continued this activity after the creation of the state, thus establishing two paths of public diplomacy—the state system and Jewish NGOs (in Israel and overseas).

In the Suez Crisis of 1956, weaknesses in *hasbara* became apparent. Israel's ambassador in Paris, Yaakov Tsur, wrote in his diary: "Officials in the French Foreign Ministry are concerned about our weak *hasbara*. All of the acts of provocation by the Egyptians have been forgotten. . . . Only the fact of the attack remains [Israel's attack on Egypt] and Nasser is quickly succeeding in spreading his version throughout the world. Due to the secrecy of the operation and its speed, it is impossible to prepare public opinion and we will need to be accountable for this."[3]

To improve the coordination between *hasbara* organizations, an interministerial committee was formed (the "Teddy Forum"), chaired by Teddy Kollek, the future mayor of Jerusalem and then director-general of the PMO. The committee included representatives of Israel Radio ("Voice of Israel"), Army Radio, the Government Press Office, the Hasbara Ministry, the Foreign Ministry, the IDF Spokesperson's Unit, and the WZO. After Kollek left in 1965, Minister of Hasbara Yisrael Galili coordinated the forum. A year later, the Israel Broadcasting Authority (IBA) was established, still subordinate to the PMO. An initial effort was also made to coordinate Israel's public diplomacy arrays: The government decided to assign Galili responsibility for the *hasbara* services in the PMO, including the IBA. Galili oversaw the activities of the *Hasbara* Center, Government Press Office, Government Advertising Agency, and Israel Film Service. Due to the coalition makeup, the appointment of Galili did not resolve the fundamental problems, including the multiplicity of organizations engaged in *hasbara*, and the failure to formulate a state *hasbara* policy or designate an official government spokesperson.

These deficiencies remained on the eve of the Six Day War. In May 1967, during the waiting period, Israel embarked on a public diplomacy campaign in Western countries to mobilize international support and stave off the threat to its existence. On the other hand, the Arab states relied on diplomatic, military, and propaganda support from the Soviet Union. There was public confusion and diplomatic stuttering in Israel during this period, but the atmosphere changed with the formation of a national unity government and the appointment of a national explainer: Chaim Herzog, a retired general and former head of military intelligence. Herzog, an eloquent and credible spokesperson, was asked to lead the internal *hasbara* via Israel Radio, the media outlet with the strongest impact. This was before the dawn of the television era in Israel. There was only educational TV at the time.[4]

Prior to the outbreak of war on June 5, hundreds of foreign correspondents flocked to Israel, as would occur in future wars. The logistics effort of the PMO, the Foreign Ministry, the IDF Spokesperson's Unit, and the Government Press Office was successful. Foreign correspondents covered Israel in a positive way, despite the lack of a central *hasbara* focus. Galili's *hasbara* mandate did not extend outside of Israel, and the IDF spokesperson, Col. Aryeh Shalev, received his orders from the head of military intelligence and the IDF chief of staff, not from the government.

Israel's swift victory in the war boosted its image as a state with impressive military capabilities. However, the occupation of the territories quickly eroded its positive image and made world opinion forget the dangers Israel had faced only weeks earlier.

A new *hasbara* effort was required in light of Security Council Resolution 242, international criticism of Israel's control in the territories, and the lack of internal consensus in Israel about the new situation. The government sought to contend with the problems of public diplomacy through two decisions: First, it decided to form a permanent ministerial committee, chaired by Galili, to coordinate the state's *hasbara* organizations.[5] Second, it decided to appoint a public committee to examine Israel's *hasbara* array, in Israel and abroad.[6] In particular, the committee was charged with examining the coordination and demarcation of authorities between the ministries in the field of public diplomacy in Israel and abroad. The committee was chaired by Maj. Gen. (ret.) Elad Peled, and its members included Binyamin Eliav, Yitzhak Taub, Avigdor Levontin, and David Shaham.

Over the course of nine months, 52 people appeared before the committee and its subcommittees, including ministers, senior government officials, journalists, IDF officers, and representatives of Jewish organizations in Israel and overseas. The committee concluded that Israel's *has-*

bara efforts should be expanded in light of the objective and diplomatic difficulties. Its principal organizational conclusion was that a *"hasbara* authority" should be created, subordinate to a minister in the PMO.[7] As expected, Foreign Minister Abba Eban opposed this recommendation. "The Foreign Ministry's opposition to the erosion of its authorities was the only obstacle preventing the new authority," says Elad Peled. "To the best of my knowledge, the Foreign Ministry has always objected to a *hasbara* authority external to it."[8]

The committee's recommendations were brought before the government immediately after the 1969 elections. The assumption was that if Prime Minister Golda Meir offered Galili the Hasbara Ministry, he would agree to take on this job. He indeed agreed, but when he realized that a clash between the Information Ministry and Foreign Ministry was inevitable, he asked to be completely relieved of these responsibilities. On March 31, 1970, in light of broad ministerial opposition to the committee's recommendations, the prime minister announced that a *hasbara* ministry would not be formed. Thus, the first attempt to establish a *hasbara* ministry ended in failure.

~

The Yom Kippur War (1973) was substantially different from the Six Day War. It was a complete strategic surprise for Israel and a real threat to its security. Foreign correspondents again came to Israel in droves. Their work exposed basic flaws in Israel's spokesmanship, organization, and censorship activities. Israel ultimately achieved a military victory but failed—as usual—in its public diplomacy. In public opinion, a clear picture remained of an Arab achievement and an Israeli failure. During the war, the IDF assumed responsibility for national *hasbara*. Generals Aharon Yariv and Shlomo Gazit, working together with the IDF spokesperson, Brig. Gen. Pinhas Lahav, led a national *hasbara* forum including officials from key government ministries. "I was a sort of unappointed '*hasbara* minister,' Gazit says. The forum was established because [Defense Minister Moshe] Dayan did not have confidence in the IDF spokesperson, who was the chief of staff's man, so he created a national forum and placed me at the head of it. Such a step was only possible in times of emergency, and not during a period of calm. During an emergency, a consensus emerged among the majority in the political system and the majority in the public, so it was possible to create and run a national *hasbara* system."[9]

A ceasefire was reached after three weeks of fighting, but long exchanges of fire continued in the north and in the south, in the form of a low-intensity war. The *hasbara* system was not designed for a situation of protracted warfare, and the interministerial coordination collapsed.

In early 1974, Maj. Gen. (ret.) Gazit was again assigned a role in this arena. He was asked to head an internal IDF committee that would study IDF spokesmanship and the media during the Yom Kippur War. Its main recommendations were to unite *hasbara* operations into a single system and to create a central address in the IDF to guide *hasbara* in order to ensure coordinated reporting by the authorized entities.[10]

On March 31, 1974, the government again decided to create a "Ministry of Public Diplomacy to be led by a *hasbara* minister" and to transfer areas of activity to the new ministry from other government ministries (the PMO, Finance, Defense, Foreign Affairs, Education, and Culture). On April 1, 1974, Justice Minister Haim Zadok announced in the Knesset that a new ministry would be established to coordinate public diplomacy activity in Israel and abroad: "The Ministry of Public Diplomacy will work closely with the Foreign Ministry in formulating *hasbara* programs abroad; clearly, employees of overseas missions will continue to report to the foreign minister and his ministry."[11] Shimon Peres was appointed minister of public diplomacy, but Golda Meir resigned as prime minister ten days later. When the new government headed by Yitzhak Rabin was formed on June 3, 1974, Peres was appointed defense minister and Aharon Yariv was selected to replace him as *hasbara* minister. This was the second attempt to form a public diplomacy ministry.

In January 1975, Yariv asked to resign. "He had a lot of good intentions, but was unable to position the ministry as a focal point for joint consultation of *hasbara* bodies and certainly not with the prime minister,"[12] says Alouph Hareven. "The chance of establishing an effective ministry to coordinate all of the *hasbara* authorities in the state turned out to be impossible in the context of the Israeli reality of internal rivalries, bureaucracy, personal and partisan struggles, and interministerial competition," adds Israeli diplomat Moshe Yegar.[13] The ministry was canceled.

~

In 1977, the Likud won the elections and formed a government for the first time. The party's leader and new prime minister, Menachem Begin, decided to mount a third attempt to establish a ministry to coordinate overseas *hasbara*. Begin wanted to appoint his friend Shmuel Katz, who was considered an expert in this field, to head the new ministry. But Moshe Dayan, the new foreign minister, rejected this appointment, and

Begin proposed sufficing with a *hasbara* authority instead of a ministry. Dayan also opposed this idea and Katz ultimately left public service.[14]

Under Prime Minister Begin, there were no substantial organizational changes in the *hasbara* system. After his initial effort to create a national *hasbara* array failed, Begin left the Foreign Ministry to deal with this matter in its own way. "In general, the subject of *hasbara* received almost no attention during that period," says his military secretary, Brig. Gen. Azriel Nevo. "The field was marginal and completely dependent on the people responsible for the subject of *hasbara* or spokesmanship. . . . There was no *hasbara* team and there was no guideline on this topic."[15]

Nonetheless, key events—such as the attack on the Iraqi nuclear facility in 1981 and the "Peace for the Galilee" Operation in 1982— required a *hasbara* policy. Regarding the Iraqi bombing, there was total silence. However, this collapsed after the news broke in the foreign media: "The slow Israeli response was something I'll remember my entire life," says Yegar. "We only issued an authorized version several weeks after the bombing because there was no preparation in advance—the topic was so secret that no one at the Foreign Ministry knew about it."[16]

In June 1982, Shlomo Argov, Israel's ambassador in London was shot and critically wounded in an assassination attempt by a Palestinian splinter group. In response, the government instructed the IDF to attack Lebanon. The "Peace for the Galilee" Operation was the first time the IDF unleashed its full military force against terrorism. The war was conducted amid profound public discord at home and harsh criticism abroad. "The IDF activity exposed the *hasbara* system and its agents to an enormous wave of criticism. The fighting in Lebanon, the prolonged siege of West Beirut and the massacre in Sabra and Shatila—perpetrated by the Christian Phalangists—sparked unprecedented attacks against Israel in the world media,"[17] Yegar asserts. In this war, which continued for 18 years, Israel learned for the first time about the power of psychological warfare and the enemy's use of public diplomacy tools, such as operational documentation and the media. Perhaps the war for consciousness began here. "Ultimately, the war in Lebanon was not decided in the *wadis* [valleys] of that country, but rather by television reports in Israel and in Lebanon," says Brig. Gen. (ret.) Moshe Tamir. "We withdrew from Lebanon because of the pressure of consciousness exerted by the enemy and the response of public opinion in Israel."[18]

One of the main issues Israel debated at the time pertained to media coverage of the siege of Beirut. The siege was aimed at isolating Yasser Arafat and severing him from his fighters and from the outside world. Many television crews reported from Beirut and conducted frequent interviews with Arafat. However, there was no equipment in Beirut for direct satellite broadcasting, so reporters had to deliver the material for broadcast to foreign correspondents stationed on the Israeli side, who would then take it to a satellite broadcasting facility in central Israel. Representatives of the IDF Censor's unit waited at the broadcasting facility in order to review the material before it was broadcast, as required by Israeli law. They did not allow the interviews with Arafat to be broadcast. The censor's decision to reject this material was not based on security considerations. Rather, it aimed to serve *hasbara* objectives—to isolate Arafat. The global television networks pressured Israel, arguing that it was not entitled to prevent the broadcast of material filmed in Beirut, territory that was not under its control and not of a military nature. In the end, Israel capitulated and permitted the material to air.

$\backsim$

On December 8, 1987, four Palestinian laborers were injured by an Israeli truck. The next day, riots broke out in refugee camps. That was the first day of the "intifada"—which became the accepted name for those violent events. The Arabic term's literal meaning "is the shivering that grips a person suffering from fever, or the persistent shaking of a dog infested with fleas; but in political terms, it has always been associated with relatively brief upheavals."[19] Arafat himself decided to apply this term to the uprising.

The violence erupted unexpectedly and found the government in Israel unprepared. Defense Minister Yitzhak Rabin, who was in the United States at the time, decided to continue his visit. Eitan Haber, his media advisor, recalls: "The first intifada caught us not only with our pants down but without pants at all, and even without underwear. People had spoken for years about the possibility of such an occurrence, and still, in 1987, everyone—despite the Yom Kippur War and even the Lebanon War—felt like it was the seventh day of the Six Day War."[20]

Israel did not digest what was happening. There was no response, no action, no *hasbara*. At first, it seemed to be another round of violence that would quickly peter out. But it was a new phenomenon, prolonged and broad in scope.[21] In similar security-related circumstances—the Six Day War and the Yom Kippur War—Israel immediately formed a media center to coordinate among *hasbara* and media entities. Arik Gordin, who headed the *hasbara* branch in the IDF Spokesperson's Unit, admits that the center was formed too late but says it was successful and received the cooperation of all of the state entities.[22]

The Palestinian violence presented new *hasbara* challenges for Israel. IDF Spokesperson Ephraim Lapid notes that the Palestinians were able to challenge Israel's exclusive control of the media—via direct contact with the foreign press and the use of Palestinian stringers.[23] The American Colony Hotel in East Jerusalem became a meeting place for Palestinians and foreign correspondents. The Palestinians dispatched talented and eloquent spokespersons—Hanan Ashrawi and Saeb Erekat. Thus, they created an effective *hasbara* array for the first time, which successfully competed against its Israeli counterpart.

In 1989, the third year of the intifada, Lapid asked Maj. Gen. Gazit to lead an internal committee to analyze the activity and deployment of the IDF Spokesperson's Unit. The committee reiterated four recommendations that had already appeared in the previous report, submitted in the wake of the Yom Kippur War. The most important of these recommendations was to create a central state *hasbara* agency and an IDF center for guiding and coordinating policy.

In late 1989, I was appointed to serve as IDF spokesperson, the first civilian to fill this military position. As my first mission, I set out to prepare the IDF Spokesperson's Unit for a future war. The First Gulf War broke out on January 15, 1991. Two days later, Scud ground-to-ground missiles were fired at Tel Aviv from Iraq. By the official end of the war, on February 27, 1991, the Iraqis had fired 39 missiles in 17 separate salvos. It was not the first time that an enemy had penetrated Israeli air space—during the Yom Kippur War, short-range Syrian missiles landed in Israeli territory. However, this war was different due to the magnitude of fire and the fear of missiles carrying nonconventional warheads.

Israel had anticipated attacks by the Iraqis. Following Iraq's invasion of Kuwait on August 1, 1990, revenge for the Israeli air force's destruction of Iraq's nuclear facility in 1981 became a salient motif in Saddam Hussein's declarations. Indeed, the Iraqi operation was named the "Road to Jerusalem." Israel prepared to defend the home front by deploying batteries of ground-to-air missiles, including Hawk and Patriot missile interceptors, and by reinforcing air force activity to prevent the penetration of enemy aircraft. The population was offered a personal defense system that included sealed rooms at home and personal gas mask kits. It was the first time the government of Israel had ever decided to provide such kits to the civilian population. The initial plan was to provide the kits to part of the population, but following a public debate, the distribution was extended to include the entire population. The distribution was conducted as part of a national *hasbara* campaign orchestrated by the IDF Spokesperson's Unit.

On the eve of the war, the ministers of defense, education, and communications decided to unify all of the state radio and television channels in Israel; Army Radio and Israel Radio operated together via a joint broadcasting center. This unified deployment was aimed at maintaining maximum control over the information reaching the public. This was possible because there were only state channels at that time and almost no reception of foreign television broadcasts. The United States announced that it would attack Iraq on January 15, 1991, if Iraq did not withdraw its troops from Kuwait. During the interim period, the United States formed a broad coalition to wage the "mother of all battles," as Saddam Hussein defined it. This "grand coalition" included Western nations and a substantial representation of Middle Eastern states. The United States sought to assemble a united international front against Iraq, though it was clear that the Americans would bear the primary burden of battle. Indeed, on January 15, the Americans launched an attack. It was primarily an aerial assault, but it also included sea-launched cruise missiles.

On Thursday afternoon, January 17, rumors circulated about missiles landing on the beach in Tel Aviv. These reports were found to be untrue. Discussions continued at IDF headquarters and in the Defense Ministry until 10:00 p.m.; the participants then went home. At 12:45 a.m., the phone rang in my home. On the line was Anat Schori, a producer at the unified broadcasting center. "Nachman," she said. "What happened? Can you update us? There were sirens. Did missiles fall?" I promised to check and then called the IDF Spokesperson's Unit on a secure telephone line. From the unclear mumbling on the other end of the line (the soldiers were wearing gas masks), it was impossible to understand anything. The chief of staff's bureau informed me that missiles had indeed fallen and told me I should come immediately. On the way to IDF headquarters in central Tel Aviv, I listened to the radio and could discern that there was great confusion. I called the broadcast studio and asked if they could put me on the air. "Certainly," they said. I actually had little information, just whatever could be gleaned from a few telephone conversations. There was a feeling that things were out of control, due to the lack of available and reliable information. I directly addressed the public from the car, via the studio, primarily trying to explain to the public how to defend itself: "When we have information that is more confirmed, we will announce it," I said. "At this stage, the most important thing for each of us is to have the personal equipment we received and to know how to act. We've seen this in recent days and everyone should wait quietly in order to protect himself and the members of his family. We'll continue to update you in the coming hours and minutes, the moment we can. We'll keep you in the picture. Everything we can—we'll say. At this moment, we ask everyone to do the same drill we've gone over so many times."[24]

At IDF headquarters, I found the defense minister and IDF chief of staff busy reviewing the operational plans, which were primarily offensive. I apologized for interrupting them and said: "Six million Israelis are sitting in their homes this very moment, frightened and waiting for instructions. What do you think we should do?"

"Take care of them," the chief of staff, Dan Shomron, laconically replied.

I set up an improvised broadcasting station in the chief of staff's cubicle, adjacent to the command center. All information on the missile attacks arrived there. The basic idea was to quickly collect the information and to pass it along by telephone to the radio and then to the television, which began special broadcasts. During the night, I left the command center bunker twice to appear on television and update the public. But I soon realized that I should not leave the strategic broadcasting spot alongside the chief of staff, who was the chief source of information. From that night onward, we established a special and unprecedented broadcast procedure. Under orders from the chief of staff, it was my exclusive role, as IDF spokesperson, to brief and instruct the public. No one else was allowed to make any public statements. The defense minister agreed. This was a heavy responsibility, and I consulted several times a day with a team of officers from the fields of psychological warfare, special measures, military censorship, field security, and education. The broadcasters in the studio chatted with me about this and that while the public waited tensely in sealed rooms. It was a difficult atmosphere and I tried to inject a bit of humor. "What do you suggest we do?" they asked me. "Drink water," I said. "Drink more water."

Next to the IDF's underground command center, referred to in Hebrew slang as the "pit," a special caravan was set up where American liaison officers received satellite warnings of missiles launched toward Israel. They briefed the officers in the "pit," who then activated the system of warning sirens. At the same time, I received notice of how many missiles were fired and where they were headed. I would immediately go to the improvised broadcasting post and update the public. I usually had three minutes before the missiles hit, and when necessary

I started broadcasting on the go. After the first night of missiles, the head of the Operations Directorate, Brig. Gen. Meir Dagan (who later served as director of the Mossad), prepared a map of six regions in Israel, each designated with a different letter of the alphabet. We used this map to provide specific instructions for each region when the sirens sounded. The challenge was to release the citizens as quickly as possible because the use of gas masks was very stressful and there were cases of heart attacks and suffocation. Quick communication enabled an effective response—only a few moments elapsed between receiving the report of missile fire and instructing the public. We followed this special procedure in all 17 missile attacks, and in several cases of false alarms.

The prime minister during the First Gulf War was Yitzhak Shamir. His military secretary, Brig. Gen. Azriel Nevo, says that Shamir was not interested in "what we say and how we say it." From Shamir's perspective, "there was a vacuum and Nachman Shai filled it."[25] After the first salvo of missiles and in accordance with the IDF chief of staff's directive, I initiated the formation of a *hasbara* coordination forum, which included the prime minister's media advisor, the Foreign Ministry's deputy director of *hasbara*, the defense minister's media advisor, and the director of the Government Press Office. This forum met often and coordinated the *hasbara* messages and their dissemination. We were briefed on the strategic objective defined by Israel's political echelon, which the IDF was ordered to implement. The forum shaped a national policy of public diplomacy based on the government's directives, the latest military intelligence, and the level of national resilience. The forum was presented with recommendations from the IDF Spokesperson's Unit think tank, comprehensive feedback from media monitoring, and the results of public opinion surveys.

The IDF's Behavioral Science Department conducted public opinion surveys daily. Compared to the multiyear norm of the IDF spokesperson's credibility (69 percent), the survey results showed a level of nearly 100 percent, and this level of public trust continued throughout the war. Dr. Mina Tzemach of the Dahaf Institute conducted similar surveys, which provided further feedback and helped to improve the instructions for the population on the home front.

The *hasbara* forum initiated the creation of two media centers that addressed both diplomatic and security issues. One was set up at the Hilton Hotel in Tel Aviv and the other at the International Convention Center in Jerusalem. Benjamin Netanyahu, who served as deputy foreign minister at the time, would appear for briefings with foreign correspondents and discuss the war's diplomatic aspect. According to Eyal

Arad, Netanyahu's media advisor: "[It marked] the first time that the Foreign Ministry, the IDF, and the Prime Minister's Office worked in a coordinated way with the media. There was collaboration in providing operational data to a unified center with a clear manager. They all filled their roles with great success. Even today, when the system cooperates, this is the model for their work."[26]

The new characteristic in the media coverage of the Gulf War was live broadcasting from the various battlefronts by television news networks, led by CNN. They set up mobile broadcasting systems in the states of the region, including Israel, and operated them continuously. This forced Israel to ease its censorship of the media, including foreign news networks, and to allow broadcasts based on agreements and understandings between the broadcasting companies and the military censor.[27] On January 19, the head of military intelligence, Maj. Gen. Amnon Shahak, convened a discussion at the Tel Aviv Hilton to define policy on the question of live broadcasts. Participants in the discussion included the IDF spokesperson, the chief military censor, and the head of the Field Security Department. It was clear that Israel had no way of preventing direct broadcasts of the war. But the problem was that these broadcasts could help the Iraqis zero in on their targets in Israel. Shahak approved the continuation of live broadcasts during the war, but only under certain conditions: Foreign correspondents would be briefed in advance about restrictions on reporting, and representatives of the military censor would be deployed at the broadcasting posts. The networks did not comply with these new restrictions, and this created a real security problem. Thus, on another occasion, I appealed to the foreign correspondents to act responsibly: "If you want to commit suicide, so be it. But don't kill us too."

Live broadcasts connected the domestic and foreign audiences in real time. The Israeli public was given full access to the foreign media, just as foreign audiences received pictures straight from Israel. The world media operated nonstop during this crisis period, in an unprecedented way that reflected globalization and media transformation. Direct broadcasts, and especially pictures of the bombardment of Baghdad, reached international audiences, particularly in the United States, and had an immediate impact on decision makers.

The IDF spokesperson filled the function of "national explainer" during the war and briefed the public, providing vital and practical instructions on how it should protect itself. The war took place exclusively on the home front; it was the first war in Israel's history in which IDF troops remained uninvolved. This passive stance was contrary to the classic Israeli concept of defense—bringing the battle to enemy territory. IDF troops were prepared and ready to act outside Israel's borders, but the government decided that defense of the home front would suffice. Thus, the war demanded a twofold *hasbara* effort. On the strategic level, it was necessary to explain why the IDF was not fighting back as dictated by Israel's national security doctrine; and on the tactical level, an effort was needed to convince the public of the reliability of protective measures. "We did not mislead the public," says Col. Ralph Shein, head of the IDF's "Special Means" Department. "We didn't lie to the public. We tried to put things in proper perspective. . . . The messages were credible and so the public became accustomed to the new situation."[28]

The Gulf War did not engender the required change of establishing a permanent *hasbara* array, a need that would again be demonstrated very soon. In October 1991, a peace conference convened in Madrid, launching a new diplomatic process. Deputy Foreign Minister Netanyahu led the *hasbara* effort and recruited a team of 40 experts with security and diplomatic backgrounds to join Israel's delegation in order to mount a "media blitz." Here, too, Israel's system of public diplomacy was based on improvisation.

∾

Shimon Peres became foreign minister on July 13, 1992. During his term, secret talks were held between Israel and the Palestinians, leading to the Oslo Accords. The agreements were officially signed on the White House lawn on September 20, 1993. Since the talks were secret, they were not accompanied by the *hasbara* aspects and considerations typically associated with publicized diplomatic meetings. After the signing of the accords, and in the atmosphere of conciliation that prevailed between Israel and the Palestinians, Peres decided that the Foreign Ministry's *hasbara* array should be revamped for the first time in Israel's history.[29] "Peres folded the flags of *hasbara* and said there would be a policy of peace that would explain itself, and that there would no longer be a need for *hasbara*," says Israeli diplomat and researcher Alon Liel. "When there's good policy, there's no need for *hasbara*. The State of Israel did not even write new *hasbara* materials from 1994 to 1999. Even Bibi [Netanyahu], who's an adamant supporter of *hasbara*, told us to stop using the Palestinian Covenant for *hasbara* purposes."[30]

Nonetheless, due to internal political considerations, the government decided on December 25, 1994, for the fourth time, to create a ministry to coordinate public diplomacy and information. The purview of the new ministry, headed by Minister Moshe Shahal, would not include foreign affairs.

A low-intensity conflict is never-ending, and the spotlight shifted from the West Bank to Lebanon. Operation Grapes of Wrath, which Israel launched in Lebanon on April 11, 1996, was also a media failure. In the general elections held the next month, Netanyahu was elected prime minister for the first time. He came with rich experience in public diplomacy, dating back to his student days at MIT and including roles at Israel's embassy in Washington, the Israeli UN delegation, and the Foreign Ministry in Jerusalem. Netanyahu fully understood the importance of the battle for world public opinion, but his first action, soon after his election, was completely contrary to this and caused substantial damage to Israel. He decided to open the Western Wall Tunnel in Jerusalem, with the aim of strengthening the Jewish people's connection to Jerusalem, which he referred to as the "rock of our existence." Netanyahu ignored security assessments that this move would spark riots; he was determined to demonstrate national leadership in contrast to what he regarded as the appeasement in the Oslo Accords. Indeed, riots ensued, killing 17 IDF soldiers and about 70 Palestinian police officers and civilians. Hundreds of Jews and Arabs were injured. President Clinton urgently summoned Netanyahu, King Hussein, and Arafat to Washington and pressed them to sign the Hebron Accord, which transferred most of the city of Hebron to the Palestinians. Thus, Netanyahu's initiative actually ended up promoting the Palestinian cause. The dynamics of the tunnel events were similar to those of the first intifada in 1987 and the events of October 2000. The difference was that the rapid intervention of President Clinton succeeded in halting the deterioration this time.

When Ehud Barak became prime minister in July 1999, he immediately set out to fulfill his campaign promise to withdraw IDF troops from southern Lebanon. This significant move was accompanied by *hasbara* activities at the national level, aimed at winning benefits in the arena of consciousness vis-à-vis the population in Lebanon. The withdrawal was planned secretly, in parallel to failed attempts to coordinate with the Lebanese government. The IDF spokesperson, Brig. Gen. Oded Ben-Ami, prepared a detailed media plan for the withdrawal. However, in the end, the IDF left Lebanon hastily in late May 2000 without media coverage and without exploiting the *hasbara* advantages. Representatives of the media waited for the soldiers on the Israeli side of the security fence: "Three weeks earlier, I spoke with the GOC Northern Command," says Ben-Ami. "Gabi [Ashkenazi], I said to him, we need to start organizing for letting journalists into Lebanon. Gabi agreed at first to embed media representatives, but later changed his mind and said he was unwilling to take responsibility for 62 civilian journalists. I told him I disagreed and that it was part of the withdrawal directive. We both decided to turn to the chief of staff [Lt. Gen. Shaul Mofaz] to receive his opinion. I stated my position and he stated his, and the chief of staff said: 'I have to side with the GOC Northern Command.'"[31] Ben-Ami adds: "There was strong criticism in the media about the hasty withdrawal—in part, because reporters were not allowed to accompany it from the inside."

Years later, Netanyahu told the Winograd Commission that the withdrawal from southern Lebanon left a deep impact in terms of consciousness, with implications for future security moves: "I see a connection between the hasty withdrawal and the start of the [second] intifada. It became implanted in consciousness and was perceived, whether correctly or not, as Israel fleeing from terror, and that [Israel] could thus be forced to flee from other sectors."[32]

~

This detailed description of security and diplomatic events in Israeli history indicates that the State of Israel lacks a strategic approach to public diplomacy and has failed to build an agreed-upon and sustainable organizational array. Over the years, frequent changes were made in the public diplomacy system: *Hasbara* responsibilities were transferred from one ministry to another, a ministry for *hasbara* was created and closed four times, and public committees (such as the Peled Committee) submitted reports that were immediately shelved. *Hasbara* entities continued to function without a unified structure. The government's decisions were generally guided by political and personal considerations, and the real interest—the essential need for a national array of public diplomacy—was neglected. This type of array was needed in emergencies, especially in times of war, as well as in Israel's diplomatic negotiations; in fact, it should serve as an integral part of all government activity. Occasionally, public diplomacy efforts were indeed coordinated under a single authority, as occurred during the First Gulf War, for example. However, when the emergency was over and the urgency diminished, the system returned to its previous patterns of operation. If Israel retained an organizational memory and maintained continuity from one event to the next, its organizational behavior would not be purely reactive. Personal disputes, political differences, and bureaucracy were and remain the primary impediments to establishing an essential, centralized array of public diplomacy and coordinating all governmental and nongovernmental entities involved in *hasbara*.

Chapter 7

"Even When We Do Something, Nothing Comes of It"

In July 2000, President Bill Clinton convened a summit with Israeli Prime Minister Ehud Barak and Palestinian Authority Chairman Yasser Arafat at Camp David, where the historic peace accords between Israel and Egypt were brokered in 1978. This time, however, the summit was a failure, paving the way to violent confrontation.[1]

Israel was convinced it had made every effort to reach an accord at Camp David, and that it could lay the blame on the Palestinians for the summit's failure: "The Camp David summit greatly improved Israel's political standing in relation to the Palestinians in the international media and the diplomatic community," says Gilead Sher, who was a member of the negotiating team, "but the seeds for the disturbances were also planted there."[2] Sher believes that the world understood that Israel wanted an agreement and the Palestinians thwarted it.[3] Ahead of the summit, Barak prepared a *hasbara* team, with security and diplomatic experts in Jerusalem, Camp David, Washington, and New York.[4] Despite the failure of the summit, to this day he is convinced that Israel was able to gain significant *hasbara* advantages: "We were prepared to go very far in return for an accord that would help to resolve the conflict. The Palestinians turned to violence and we defended ourselves. In the world, there was clear recognition that the Palestinian side bore responsibility."[5] However, the assessment of two of Barak's media advisors, Gadi Baltiansky and Merav Parsi-Zadok, is that Israel was not properly prepared for a disappointing outcome at Camp David.[6]

The violence erupted after opposition leader Ariel Sharon's visit to the Temple Mount.[7] "It was Sharon's visit to the Temple Mount that got

the wheels of the intifada moving," says Maj. Gen. Danny Yatom, who
was Barak's diplomatic-security chief at the time. "The bloody clashes
began the next day and seven Palestinians were killed, and things evolved
from there without anyone being able to control them."[8] Others hold the
view that the Palestinians prepared and planned the violence ahead of
time, and that Sharon's ascent to the Temple Mount was just used as a
pretext. Journalists Amos Harel and Avi Issacharoff say, for example: "The
second intifada did not break out because of Sharon's [Temple Mount]
visit. Whether you accept the Israeli establishment's version of events
(that Arafat plotted the outburst of violence) or that of the Palestinians
(that it was a spontaneous outburst of popular anger), one can state with
a large degree of confidence: The bloody conflict would have begun at
some time or another around the last quarter of that year."[9]

During the long Rosh Hashanah weekend, the violence spread to
Netzarim Junction. Hundreds of Palestinian youths hurled rocks and
Molotov cocktails at an IDF post there and advanced upon it.[10] On
October 1, Israeli Arabs declared a general strike, which led to protests
and solidarity demonstrations. Thirteen protesters were killed in clashes
with police. In Nablus, Palestinians attacked the site of Joseph's Tomb,
causing the death of Border Police officer Madhat Yusuf. On October
6, the IDF retreated from the site.[11] Describing the events of that day,
IDF Chief of Staff Shaul Mofaz says: "These events are the result of a
loss of control in the field or of some directive to create friction in the
wake of the Temple Mount incidents."[12]

There had been other outbursts of violence in the years before the
second intifada, but they subsided within a short time. This time the
deterioration was immediate; events quickly spread and escalated and
Israel was taken by surprise yet again.[13] "The intifada was anticipated in
Barak's instructions throughout the year that preceded Camp David, but
it's no secret that somehow it still took everyone by surprise," says Isaac
Herzog, who was cabinet secretary at the time. "As Barak has said—it
was the match that ignited the twigs and the entire bonfire. From a
hasbara standpoint, Israel was not prepared. There was no orderly system
of *hasbara*, and things were organized on the go."[14] Israel attempted to
rein in the violence militarily, while simultaneously conducting political
negotiations. "We negotiated as if there were no terror and we fought
the terror as if there were no negotiations,"[15] says Shlomo Ben-Ami,
who was foreign minister then. This created a severe *hasbara* problem.
Gilead Sher believes that the government had trouble explaining this
duality to the citizenry.[16] And so the second intifada began.

The combat over the course of the second intifada may be divided into four main periods:

1. *Prior to Operation Defensive Shield, September 2000–March 2002*: An attempt was made to contain the conflict, with an emphasis on defensive efforts and avoiding a total breakdown of relations with the Palestinian Authority.

2. *Operation Defensive Shield, March 2002*: Transition to a major offensive, retaking control over all of the West Bank, while undermining relations with the Palestinian Authority.

3. *Following Operation Defensive Shield, April 2002–November 11, 2004*: Ongoing and extensive strikes at the terror infrastructure, with full and broad freedom of action; combat within the sector while asserting control over the territory and the population.

4. *Following the death of Arafat on November 11, 2004*: A reshaping of the military efforts, putting the emphasis back on defensive actions, while maintaining components of offensive action.[17]

•

The second intifada entailed a cycle of threats and responses. Palestinian terrorism confronted Israel with new security challenges: suicide bombings, mortar and rocket fire, and turning the home front into the battlefront. With suicide bombing, the Palestinians essentially developed a human bomb, which they considered a strategic weapon, enabling them to infiltrate Israeli population centers and strike at the country's "soft underbelly." From 1993 to September 2000, there were 34 suicide bombings that killed a total of 155 Israeli civilians.[18] But then suicide bombing greatly intensified: From 2000 to 2007, there were 155 suicide bombings, killing 425 Israelis out of a total of 1,065 killed during that period.

The initiative generally came from the Palestinian side, which sought to undermine the status quo and cause Israel to withdraw. When the conflict erupted with the Palestinians, Israel did its utmost to contain and quell it. Operation Defensive Shield was the offensive move that came in wake of the bombing of the Park Hotel in Netanya on Passover Eve, 2002. In fact, there had been a series of suicide bombings during the month prior to the Park Hotel bombing. The major military operation was a one-time action and halted the rise in terror attacks, especially the suicide bombings, but the attacks continued. Israel also continued to counter with offensive initiatives—primarily targeted killings.

Targeted killings were designed to strike at terrorist leaders and militants, as Israel had done in the past—for example, in the Mossad's liquidation of the Black September terrorists responsible for the massacre of Israeli athletes at the 1972 Munich Olympics,[19] and in the establishment of special IDF units in the Gaza Strip in the early 1970s (Sayeret Rimon) and in the 1980s (Duvdevan and Shimshon), which waged an active war against Palestinian terror. During the second intifada, a new term was coined to describe this type of action: "Targeted killing" (*sikul memukad*) was meant to impart the idea that Israel was upholding the rules of war and not allowing its security forces and young troops to descend into carrying out unethical assassinations.[20] Attorney General Elyakim Rubinstein proposed the term to replace "liquidation" (*hisul*), which had become very problematic for Israel.[21]

The first targeted killings were ground actions with direct gunfire; later, Israel moved to using a combination of ground intelligence with shooting from the air. The killings evoked negative public reactions in Israel and abroad. Ron Prosor, the director-general of the Foreign Ministry at the time, found it hard to convince the United States to supply Israel with telescopic sights for rifles, as the Americans feared they would be used for targeted killings.[22] On July 22, 2002, the air force dropped a one-ton bomb on a building in the Gaza Strip, killing Hamas leader Salah Shehadeh, his wife, and 17 civilians. In this action, the basic principle of a targeted killing—hitting just the terrorist and sparing civilian noncombatants—was violated. The large number of civilian casualties sparked widespread public protest. Twenty-seven pilots sent a letter to the air force commander expressing their opposition to carrying out "illegal and unethical orders," and many of these pilots were subsequently released from reserve duty in the IDF.

Over the course of the conflict, Israel has improved its capacity to operate from a distance against terror targets through a combination of intelligence information provided by the Shin Bet and intercept capabilities from the air: "In 200 to 250 instances of targeted killing, there wasn't a single instance of misidentification,"[23] says Maj. Gen. (ret.) Giora Eiland. Targeting killing has been adopted by other countries, including the United States and Britain, which have used this tactic extensively to strike at terrorist leaders in Afghanistan and Iraq-Syria. In recent years, most of these attacks have been conducted with drones, a new dimension in warfare.

Defensively, the main effort went into erecting the separation fence, a land obstacle designed to protect Israel's citizens and prevent terrorists from crossing into Israel. In April 2002, after lengthy public debate and political controversy, the government approved the construction of a 709-kilometer section of fence in the West Bank. By 2011, 525 kilometers of the barrier were in place, including dozens of kilometers of a protective wall. Construction of the barrier entailed land seizures and interrupting urban and rural contiguity in places, and its completion has been delayed due to legal problems. "We failed in our *hasbara* regarding the fence. It's most often described as a wall, which indicates an appetite for territory. We didn't explain it well," says Shimon Peres.[24] Some 150 petitions have been filed against construction of the fence, and the UN General Assembly and International Court of Justice were both asked to address the issue. Israel tried to explain to the international community why the fence was being built, but Maj. Sharon Feingold, head of the International Department in the IDF Spokesperson's Unit, calls these efforts "a prime example of Israeli bumbling."[25]

The fence issue illustrates three major aspects of the Israeli-Palestinian conflict: First, it signifies a shift from the local arena to the *international arena* of public opinion; second, it underlines *Israel's isolation* in its fight against terror (despite the September 11 attacks and broad international recognition of the need to fight terror); and third, the *legal arena*—as seen in rulings by the International Court of Justice and Israel's High Court of Justice.

Whenever Israel found an answer to the Palestinian threat, the terror organizations searched for new ways to sustain the asymmetry between them and the IDF. Faced with the IDF's offensive capabilities and the defensive effectiveness of the separation fence, they had to find a cheap, readily available, mobile and lethal weapon. Ultimately, they adopted the method used by Hezbollah on Israel's northern border from 1982 to 2000 and during the Second Lebanon War in 2006—firing rockets into Israel.[26] Hamas also adopted other tactics used by Hezbollah, such as abducting soldiers.

In 2001, Hamas and other terror organizations began developing short-range rockets and firing them at southern Israel. This strategy gradually became more advanced; the warhead, accuracy, and range of the rockets improved; and the pattern of action became more varied and unpredictable.[27] Surprisingly, a certain similarity may be seen in the modes of action used by Israel and the Palestinian terrorists, mainly in the use of weapons fired from a distance (though their respective weapons remain asymmetrical in terms of firepower and sophistication). The IDF uses helicopters and other aircraft that fire guided weaponry at ground targets, and the Palestinians fire Qassams and other rockets from their territory into Israel. Thus, a certain symmetry is created amid the asymmetry of low-intensity combat. However, there is an essential difference when it comes to targets: The IDF attacks hostile terror targets and makes an effort to avoid harming civilians, while the Palestinians fire indiscriminately at civilian population areas.

The IDF responded to Palestinian rocket fire again both offensively and defensively. Defensively, it fortified public and residential buildings in the areas adjacent to the Gaza Strip, including the city of Sderot. Another defensive measure is to intercept incoming missiles in flight. In February 2007, Israel decided to develop its own system for intercepting short-range missiles—the Iron Dome—and the United States agreed to help fund its development and future production.[28] The system was successfully tested and put into operational use in February 2011. It has a very high success rate of 75 percent. And there is nothing else like it anywhere in the world.

Offensively, the IDF uses helicopters and other aircraft to thwart rocket fire from the ground. Such action is based on cooperation among the air force, intelligence, and Shin Bet, and it has foiled a large number of attempted rocket launches.

During this period, the home front became inseparable from the battlefront. The blurring of this dividing line constituted a new reality that continued from 2000 on and intensified during the Second Lebanon War: "The home front was involved in the war involuntarily. The northern Galilee had experienced Katyusha fire before, but this was the first war in which the northern home front (from the Hadera line northward) was under assault."[29]

As the home front becomes increasingly involved in low-intensity warfare, it is vital that information be relayed to it in an emergency as part of a comprehensive *hasbara* policy. Immediately after the Yom Kippur War, the IDF examined the importance of the information communicated to the public in a time of emergency and concluded that the public should receive as much accurate information as possible. Concrete information and instructions can reduce the level of anxiety in the public and help people cope with the threat.[30] This requires systematic organization to control the information and make a clear assessment of the situation; the information should be conveyed to the public by skilled professionals. This is vital on the individual level and fosters trust between the public, the IDF, and the national leadership.

On the eve of the Gulf War, Israel decided to distribute gas masks to the population. The defense minister and IDF chief of staff instructed the IDF spokesperson to prepare a *hasbara* campaign for the gas mask distribution, which aside from the particulars of the distribution itself was also meant to mentally prepare the population for war. When the first barrage of missiles came, the public turned to the institutional information channels to obtain information and instructions; these were perceived as accessible and as purveyors of reliable information. Experts in the field advocate that such information be consistently conveyed by a single authoritative figure, through a number of different channels. This analysis fit the model of the "national explainer" that was used during the war and focused on relaying instructions to the different groups that constitute the home front.[31]

In the aftermath of the Gulf War, Defense Minister Moshe Arens felt that the civilian front should be prepared for a new reality, and he issued a directive to establish the Home Front Command for this purpose. The Home Front Command began operating in February 1992 and gradually received professional and command responsibility for the five districts of the State of Israel in a time of emergency. During the second intifada, the Home Front Command proved to be just as crucial during low-intensity conflict as in all-out war, particularly since the new terror strategy concentrated on the home front and its weak links. The importance of the Home Front Command was recognized, and yet it was left out of the Israeli system of *hasbara*.

During the first intifada (1987–1993), Palestinians made use of the media to increase international sympathy for their cause. They developed a mechanism for collecting and disseminating information, distributed cameras to document and report, and forged a closer relationship with the foreign media, recognizing that it held the key to international coverage.[32] Palestinian journalist Inam al-Obaidi argues that despite the Palestinian efforts, the story was still being told by European or American news crews for Western viewers and was also presented to the Palestinian public in this way—that is, until the second intifada, when a big change occurred: "The second intifada was covered by the Arab satellite channels, whose crews were made up of locals aware of the history of the conflict and attuned to the feelings and culture of the people. Their viewers were also familiar with the history of the struggle; they spoke the same language and shared their feelings and beliefs. For the first time, Palestinians felt that their story was being told by them."[33]

Shlomo Ganor, director of Arabic television, says the change was not just the scope of the satellite broadcasts but also their content: "The intra-Arab competition in the coverage of events led to greater extremism, increased violence, and the continuation of the terror attacks. . . . The Arab and intra-Arab media, which wished to justify its existence, artificially resuscitated the intifada. Even when the Israelis and Palestinians agreed to halt the violence, the intra-Arab media, for its own reasons, revived the issue."[34]

Al Jazeera and the Arab broadcast satellites provided a broad stage for the events of the second intifada, greatly enhancing their exposure and reaching a very large audience. "The broadcasts are raising the level of hatred of 1.2 billion Muslims in 57 countries," says Zvi Mazel, former Israeli ambassador to Egypt. "The power of the media, via print journalism and every other means . . . affects public opinion in Europe and the entire world and so affects us."[35]

On November 23, 2000, Maj. Gen. Yaakov Orr, coordinator of government activity in the territories, sent a letter for wide distribution among the government offices, pointing out the need for Arabic radio and television broadcasts from Israel: "In the Palestinian territories, listening to the media—television and radio—is one of the most influential factors affecting the Palestinian public agenda and the behavior of the population. The entire field has been left open to Palestinian radio and television that is under Palestinian Authority control, to local stations that are filled with extremism and incitement, and to other Arab stations."[36]

After the network had been around for a decade, a new era of Al Jazeera broadcasts began: English-language broadcasts aimed at Europe and America were introduced. The station thus realized its plan to compete with the international networks.

Another aspect on the public diplomacy front was the inclusion of the Internet in the Palestinian arsenal. Israel's enemies swiftly put the new technology to use in the battle for public opinion: "Both sides fire bullets at each other. These bullets are the written word, the speech, the television movie and so on. . . . Clever use of them gives the highest added value to the real weapons used in combat."[37] This type of combat became one of the key arenas in the battle waged by Iran and the terror organizations it supports against Israel.

Palestinian and international terror organizations use the Internet to disseminate messages that promote terror, without oversight or censorship restrictions, and as a means of communication between the organizations and command centers and their activists and other target audiences.

Hezbollah emulates Al-Qaeda's mode of activity: "It operates satellite and Internet television; it operates a radio station (A-Nur) on a wireless network and on the Internet, as well as a publishing house and dozens of websites. It hosts foreign journalists for guided propaganda tours; it produces and stages media events; it supplies processed dramatic material and not just the fiery speeches of Sheikh Nasrallah. The charred body of a boy in Kafr Kana will be waved in front of the cameras again and again, usually at the direction of a Hezbollah producer," says communications researcher Gabriel Weimann of the University of Haifa.[38]

This challenge calls for a two-part response—intercepting Hezbollah broadcasts and blocking their dissemination, and creating broadcasting systems to counter them. While it is impossible to prevent the international Arab networks from broadcasting throughout the world via satellite, it is possible to hinder their access to the Internet. An international effort was launched against terrorist organizations like Islamic Jihad, Hamas, and Hezbollah to cut them off from local communications providers. At a May 23, 2005, meeting of EU culture ministers, the French culture minister called for Al-Manar's broadcasts to be blocked throughout Europe. In August of that year, the broadcasts to Asian countries were blocked.[39] In the face of hundreds of Arabic-language television channels, Israel finds itself weak and even helpless.

•

Israel's state television began Arabic broadcasts in 1968, ostensibly aimed at the Arab population in the territories it had recently captured. But only a few hours per day were allotted to these broadcasts, far from prime time. This neglect continued for years. All attempts to broadcast in Arabic to the Arab population in the territories and to Arabic-speaking citizens of Israel failed. The new public broadcasting corporation launched in 2017 operates an Arabic channel, but commercial television in Israel does not offer Arabic programming. The i24 channel broadcasts from Israel in English, French, and Arabic, but it only won regulatory approval for cable broadcasts in Israel after an amendment I sponsored was enacted by the Knesset in October 2018. This was an important step forward. The channel is continuing its satellite broadcasts in the Middle East.

Since the establishment of the state, Voice of Israel radio broadcasts in Arabic have been a highly credible and influential media channel for the Arabic-speaking public in Israel and abroad. However, due to technical failures and budget constraints, the scope of these broadcasts decreased. Moreover, the impact of radio diminished as television strengthened, and it could no longer compete with the power of Arabic-language television.

In the absence of Israeli television broadcasts in Arabic, another way to deal with the challenge of the Arabic networks was to participate in their broadcasts, especially Al Jazeera, and to present Israel's perspective. For several years, efforts were made to get Israeli spokespeople on these broadcasts, such as Maj. Eitan Arussi and Maj. Avichai Adraee from the IDF Spokesperson's Unit, Amira Oron from the Foreign Ministry, and even heads of state. Brig. Gen. Yoav (Poli) Mordechai, a fluent Arabic speaker, was particularly prominent in this arena, frequently giving interviews in Arabic during his term as IDF spokesperson.

In March 2008, the Foreign Ministry decided to limit its cooperation with Al Jazeera and possibly to end it completely. "Zero is being invested in *hasbara* directed at the Palestinians, even less than zero," said Yaakov Orr, four years after he called for Israel to provide a response to the hostile broadcasts in Arabic. "The field has been left wide open and it's no wonder that Palestinian society is devolving to a state of very strong resistance."[40] Experts and observers following the media revolution in the Arab world and Israel's lack of a response to it concur: "The Arab world is an audience that we don't deal with, even though it is very important to them. We don't know it well and we don't know how to deal with it. This is certainly a terrible mistake. We don't have good tools with which to speak to this audience. Even when we do something, nothing comes of it. We've made cardinal errors."[41]

•

The low-intensity conflict obliged Israel to alter the IDF's strategy versus terrorist threats. Maj. Gen. Israel Ziv, chief of the IDF Operations Directorate, was tasked with this challenge. "We understood that we were captive to a conception. . . . We didn't fully understand the asymmetrical cultural-conceptual challenge we faced. . . . We realized that we had to upgrade our own conceptual tools, our way of approaching the problem."[42]

The IDF recognized that it had to shift to an approach of managing the conflict, minimizing the terror, and enabling normal life in Israel to continue. The IDF was accustomed to managing combat on the strategic and tactical levels. Now a third aspect was added, the systematic level, which was promoted by three reservist officers—Shimon Naveh, Dov Tamari, and Zvi Lanir. "We shifted to talking in terms of effects, of effects as objectives. For instance, if we wanted to achieve separation between a civilian population and a terror-supporting population, we took the challenge of separation and translated it into a different kind of action toward them. We gauged this activity over a longer period of time and by new criteria that we invented and improved on the go, through learning and doing."[43]

The IDF's new doctrine comprised three military levels and a fourth, higher, level that acted as a liaison between those three and the political echelon. The *political echelon* formulates the aims in terms of international diplomacy, the policy for military conflict with the enemy and for strengthening society from within. The *general staff* operates in accordance with instructions of the political echelon and applies the policy on military conflict in four operational sectors: abroad, internally, Lebanon, and the West Bank/Gaza. The *command level* manages psychological warfare, economic warfare, intelligence, and physical warfare. The *operations sector* oversees physical warfare and the intelligence effort, including counterterrorism and offensive efforts.

Combat doctrine stipulates that battles are fought in seven areas: political, military, economic, legal, civilian, settlements, and consciousness. "The aim [of the consciousness campaign] is to preserve and expand the internal Israeli basis of consensus and the external international legitimacy for IDF actions, and thus to achieve effects vis-à-vis the enemy, particularly for the purpose of bolstering the deterrence factor for our forces and isolating the civilian population from the guerillas and terrorists."[44]

•

The IDF's new operating concept, along with the measures and language derived from it, required the establishment of new organizational mechanisms for combating terror, which had previously been one of the secondary roles of the IDF's intelligence branch.[45] The aim was to create the desired media effect: "We took the space and turned it into a proactive campaign of generating achievements in the realm of consciousness by using tools aimed at making an impact that could change mindsets."[46] To do this, Maj. Gen. Ziv realized that he had to establish a new organizational entity, and at his recommendation, Chief of Staff Yaalon approved the creation of the Center for Consciousness Operations (known by the Hebrew acronym MALAT). The new center, which replaced the information warfare unit, was founded in mid-2004 and its staff included civilian psychologists and Middle East experts.[47] To integrate the operational and intelligence aspects, it was made subordinate to the Operations Directorate, but it was guided professionally by the head of military intelligence. The center's mission was to "exploit the rifts in Palestinian society and the way it understands IDF activity in order to accelerate the processes desirable to Israel."[48] Its job was to support efforts to achieve a victory of consciousness.

Ziv coordinated the two units under his command that dealt with public diplomacy and psychological warfare. The IDF Spokesperson's Unit established a Strategic Department under the command of Col. Amit Livni, which worked in tandem with the Center for Consciousness Operations.[49] Livni created a "consciousness forum" that determined ways to implement covert consciousness operations in the IDF's overt spheres of activity.[50] IDF Spokesperson Brig. Gen. Ruth Yaron had reservations about the close relations between the Center for Consciousness Operations' activity and her own work. She was concerned that activity based on the manipulation of information ("black" or "gray" measures) might impugn the credibility of the IDF Spokesperson's Unit, which uses open ("white") measures. Therefore, she advocated separating the two.[51] Yaron's commander, Maj. Gen. Gadi Eizenkot, then head of the Operations Directorate, agreed: "I wanted to see a total separation between the Center of Consciousness Operations, which aims to manipulate the enemy, and the IDF Spokesperson's Unit, which is responsible for credible *hasbara*; credibility is the very heart of the matter."[52]

The Center for Consciousness Operations was also in charge of executing the consciousness operations it devised.[53] This occurred, for example, during Operation Defensive Shield, the largest military action of that period. "If you really look at what affected Palestinian consciousness, it wasn't so much the radio and television [reporting] and how we broadcast it, but what we did. It was the major assault that really affected the enemy. If you start with the premise that every guerilla organization is going to fight for its connection with the population, then our goal is to break that connection and the power the group draws from the population."[54]

Other actions focused solely on consciousness, such as dropping leaflets during the Second Lebanon War and in clashes with the Palestinians.[55] In the absence of Arabic-language mass media (radio and television), leaflets served as a poor substitute. Other measures included drone photography[56] and the use of false documents (primarily during Operation Defensive Shield).[57] The IDF also managed to infiltrate Hezbollah television broadcasts and Hamas radio stations and use them to broadcast its messages, with the aim of undermining the confidence of those organizations and hurting their credibility. Another method was to create deterrence and intimidation by means of low-altitude flights and supersonic booms. This was done in Syria, Lebanon, and Gaza.[58]

•

The Center for Consciousness Operations and the IDF Spokesperson's Unit represented different dimensions of the battle for consciousness. The center's covert actions included some with a "low signature," subject to a sweeping gag order and documented solely by the IDF and not the media. In the overt sphere, for which the IDF Spokesperson's Unit was responsible, there were varying levels of openness, including filming operations for the media's use and embedding reporters.

In IDF terminology, "blackout" is defined as "maintaining the secrecy of information or concealing it from people or organizations (aside from a few who are in on the secret), because spreading this information could cause security damage or diplomatic damage." Most of the operations of the Israeli security community—the IDF, Shin Bet, and the Mossad—are secret. Sometimes, a secret operation is exposed and then a media response is required, as occurred in several botched Mossad operations (incidents that occurred in Amman, Cyprus, Switzerland, New Zealand, Abu Dhabi). In Israel's military history, there are many examples of operations that began under a total blackout and were gradually exposed: the bombing of the Iraqi nuclear reactor, the assassination of Abu Jihad, the liquidation of the murderers of the Israeli Olympic athletes, and, more recently, an air force operation against a nuclear site in Syria. The same holds true regarding the quiet war between Israel and Iran. A number of hits on senior Iranian nuclear scientists have been ascribed to Israel, as well as some mysterious explosions at strategic facilities in 2011.

The policy on publicizing a given operation may change according to the results of the operation, information that has leaked from other sources, or a change in political circumstances. In such cases, preparations should be made in advance for dealing with the media, and these should be known to all relevant parties.

The *Dictionary of IDF Terminology* defines a "signature" as "typical features of a target as seen by various detection and identification devices."[59] A low-signature operation thus involves either limited or total nonidentification of the forces, activity, and outcome. In an action of this kind, there is no self-initiated media coverage and very minimal public reporting on it. According to Harel and Issacharoff, the IDF made an effort to carry out low-signature actions starting in September 2001: "At the start of the intifada, there were armored nighttime raids on Palestinian Authority command posts in the centers of West Bank cities. The attacks were moderate in scope and mainly conducted in response to terror attacks. Operations were deliberately carried out at night, for a set amount of time, with all the forces exiting the Palestinian Authority by dawn, in an attempt to avoid media coverage that would include images of Israeli tanks on Palestinian streets."[60]

At a discussion in Prime Minister Barak's office on October 31, 2000, the participants were asked to propose a military response to a terror attack. I participated in the meeting in my role of coordinator of national *hasbara* and presented the media aspects, describing the situation as a low-intensity and high-exposure conflict. The Palestinians commit terror attacks, I said, to trigger an Israeli response that would be viewed as an escalation and excessive use of force and come to overshadow the terror incident. There was also the fear that an Israeli response would encourage the Palestinian population to perpetuate the terror and would intensify external pressure on Israel and calls for international intervention. My recommendation, in terms of the media aspects of the conflict, was that low-signature military measures would be best, combined with linking the Palestinians to terror in Israel. At the end of the discussion, the prime minister approved military moves consistent with the proposed low-signature approach.

Soon afterward, in November 2000, a roadside bomb was detonated under a bus carrying Israeli schoolchildren in the Gaza Strip settlement of Kfar Darom. Two teachers were killed and three children lost limbs. Prime Minister Barak wanted a rapid military response using helicopters, while Giora Eiland, the chief of the Operations Directorate, preferred to use tanks, arguing that deploying helicopters would be seen as an excessive use of force.[61]

This reflects an ongoing dilemma in the IDF about how to respond to terror attacks, using appropriate and proportionate measures. When Benjamin Ben-Eliezer took over as defense minister in 2001, he opposed the use of heavy weaponry but later changed his mind and approved the use of helicopters.[62] Col. (ret.) Orly Gal, a former deputy IDF spokesperson, explains: "We talked about what tools to use, about the danger involved with each one. Bear in mind that in the past it was an F-15, then we moved to helicopters and later to UAVs; each time there was a change, it was due to public opinion. It had a lot to do with public consciousness and reactions to the destruction and to innocents being harmed."[63]

The presence of cameras on the battlefield and the instant television reporting were key considerations in shaping the IDF's media policy. The dilemma was whether to respond immediately and broadly to a terrorist attack or to wait a while. An immediate response is more effective but also generates negative media coverage; a delayed response may reduce the media damage, though it is less effective. These are the two aspects of the war for public opinion: "If we understand that a tank doesn't look good on TV, then the decision of whether or not to use a tank has to take into account the picture of the tank on CNN," says former Chief of Staff Yaalon. "The military action should be completed within fifteen minutes, because in this time the media will prepare to film the combat helicopters."[64] Yaalon's comments reflect the IDF's dilemma in combating terror—the desire for a low signature to avoid international accusations of excessive force versus the need to act proactively.

The IDF chose to adopt operational documentation, recognizing that media openness is not possible or desirable. The *Dictionary of IDF Terminology* from 1998 does not contain an entry for "operational documentation." It does include "documentation" and "oral documentation," which refer to the gathering of material for historical purposes or information management, but not for *hasbara*. In the distant past, the IDF used to film its secret military activity and keep the footage "classified" until an unspecified date.

The different nature of the new wars, the advanced technologies, and the accessibility of the media obliged the IDF to operate in a media-saturated arena. Media scholar Guy Bechor says: "Since the real war is in the field of worldwide *hasbara*, on the level of propaganda and imagery, the IDF should equip a few hundred selected soldiers with video cameras so they can document daily, systematically, the ongoing occurrences in the territories and on the northern border. In the current reality, the camera is a more effective weapon than the rifle."[65]

At the start of the second intifada, it became apparent that foreign media crews, partly composed of local Palestinians, were regularly filming operations by IDF troops. The Palestinian side often organized mass events and invited the media to cover them. Col. Raanan Gissin, former deputy IDF spokesperson and an advisor to the prime minister on foreign media, described Israel's response to such events: "We started to bring in cameras because we realized that the media and the Palestinians agreed that it was a crime scene. So we said, let's cover ourselves first of all. Instead of taking a lawyer along, we should always have a camera there to document things. If it's being considered a crime scene, then the burden of proof is on us; when something bad happens, the one who committed the crime—[as we are being accused]—doesn't want to be accused, and he doesn't leave evidence in the field."[66]

Aware of the importance of video footage in the media arena, the

Defense Ministry instructed the IDF to record its activity.[67] Col. Elam Kott, deputy IDF spokesperson, was tasked with instituting operational documentation in the IDF. It was a lengthy and slow process.[68] In light of the experience gained during the intifada, operational documentation became an integral part of the IDF's doctrine on limited conflicts: "In certain operations, the fighters will be accompanied by operational documentation crews. These teams of soldiers or individual soldiers will film or record the fighting. The recorded material will be used by military officials for research, *hasbara*, propaganda, evidence in lawsuits, and more. This documentation is of great importance since it will sometimes be used as legal material in a lawsuit or in defending against lawsuits brought by the enemy."[69] However, "the IDF's operational documentation was a major failure," according to the Gellert Committee appointed by the general staff to evaluate the performance of the IDF Spokesperson's Unit during the Second Lebanon War. "This is particularly striking in light of Hezbollah's achievements,"[70] the committee noted.

Embedding reporters among fighting forces enables the media to document their actions. This is done in coordination with and under the supervision of the army. The IDF only rarely permitted journalists to accompany its operations during the second intifada. The need arose when the IDF was operating in large-scale operations like Operation Defensive Shield. But the IDF blocked the media from entering the field of action. In the summer of 2005, the IDF carried out the disengagement from Gaza. The war in Lebanon erupted a year later. In both instances, the prospect of embedding journalists with the forces was considered as a component of media policy. Reporters were embedded under agreed-upon terms, including the IDF's right to vet the materials. In this context, the method of pooling resources is normally used—one media representative enters the field of action and then relays the raw material to colleagues from other media outlets.

The IDF intended to embed reporters in IDF units during the disengagement, but the controlled coverage turned into full media openness: "Everything happened faster than expected and we didn't see any logic in restoring the original rules, but things were done with coordination and control,"[71] says Brig. Gen. (ret.) Eival Gilady, who helped oversee the disengagement. In the Second Lebanon War, the IDF adopted a similar approach. About 50 reporters and cameramen entered Lebanon, and military installations were open to the media. In some cases, commanders objected, despite directives from the chief of staff and the IDF Spokesperson's Unit. From the IDF's perspective, the outcome was disappointing, as the media's freedom of action led to a series of embarrassing incidents and information leaks.

Media openness is a basic principle in a democratic state, but the IDF places legitimate restrictions on its scope, content, timing, and location. However, given the media's presence in combat zones, the IDF should realize that it can no longer control what the media publishes and broadcasts.

•

Since Operation Cast Lead, there were two additional operations in Gaza: Pillar of Defense (October 2012) and Protective Edge (July 2014). This recurrent pattern is typical of low-intensity warfare between Israel and the Palestinians. There were also numerous terror incidents, especially since September 2015, which is viewed as the start of the third intifada. The large operations and terror attacks inevitably draw extensive media coverage, despite the IDF's reluctance to embed reporters in IDF fighting units. As the battles spill into civilian areas, creating an overlap between the home front and the battlefront, the media can cover the war without the army's assistance or involvement. A new phenomenon that arose in the recent rounds of fighting is the use of personal cell phones to cover the war. Despite orders forbidding soldiers from carrying phones with them, they have leaked pictures from operational activity. Furthermore, civilians have documented events with their cell phones and posted photos and videos on social media, and this documentation is soon picked up by the news media.

The bottom line is that the IDF's ability to manage information from the battlefield is diminishing due to the activity of the Palestinian rival and the availability of new technologies.

Chapter 8

Voice of Israel

The next three chapters map the players involved in Israeli public diplomacy (*hasbara*) in 2000–2006, the most significant years in the transition from a decentralized system to a concentrated array of public diplomacy. Some of them engaged directly in *hasbara*, while others played only a supportive role. The official entities include the Prime Minister's Office (PMO), the Foreign Ministry, the Defense Ministry—including the IDF Spokesperson's Office and the Home Front Command—and the Public Security Ministry and Israel Police. We discuss these entities in this chapter.

•

Israeli public diplomacy was characterized by three processes during this period. The first was the transition from a decentralized system to a centralized one; the second was the integration of new tools of *hasbara*; and the third process, which occurred primarily in the IDF, was a conceptual change in the field of consciousness.

Three prime ministers served during the years 2000–2006: Ehud Barak, Ariel Sharon, and Ehud Olmert. Each attributed great importance to *hasbara* and tried to reorganize it.

Ehud Barak entered office on July 6, 1999. He planned to rebuild the *hasbara* array to serve the Prime Minister's Bureau, the PMO, and external national needs. He decided there should be a director of public diplomacy and media in his office but never appointed anyone to fill this position. "Ehud works in a thousand and one channels that you never know about," says Gadi Baltiansky, who served as his media advisor. "He calls journalists directly, issues messages via people you don't even know. Each channel operates separately. . . . When Ehud would do an interview, he'd receive pages of messages, what he should say in the interview, four different pages with contradictory messages."[1]

Barak's bureau chief, Gilead Sher, and the prime minister's political-security chief of staff, Danny Yatom, also worked on *hasbara*. On October 5, 2000, early in the second intifada, I was asked to join the bureau's team in a temporary appointment as coordinator of *hasbara*. During that period, I was serving as director-general of the Ministry of Science, Culture, and Sport. The letter of appointment stated: "In this role, Nachman Shai will guide and coordinate the public diplomacy and media activity of all relevant entities." In practice, this job description only further complicated the complex relations at the bureau. "It was a situation in which all of the players both inside and outside of the bureau were in complete chaos, doing whatever they pleased," says media advisor Merav Parsi-Zadok.[2]

There was no hierarchy in the Prime Minister's Bureau on the various issues of spokesmanship and the staff competed among themselves, each acting in their own way.[3] Throughout Barak's term, no one filled the position of director of *hasbara* in the PMO.

Ariel Sharon won the 2001 elections and brought a new team: bureau chief Uri Shani, bureau director Dov Weissglass, cabinet secretary Israel Maimon, foreign press advisor Raanan Gissin, and personal spokesperson Arnon Perlman. "The State of Israel's *hasbara* is not managed from the Prime Minister's Bureau," Perlman learned.[4] Sharon consulted often with the "Ranch Forum," which included Reuven Adler of the Adler-Chomsky advertising agency. "Arik was protected from overexposure, in complete contrast to Ehud Barak, who was burned by overexposure," says Adler, a personal confidante of Sharon.[5] Under Sharon's directive, the bureau staff gave top priority to the prime minister's image in the print media and in the weekend editions.[6] "Arik was active in weekend interviews, in commentaries, in background conversations with publicists, and they presented the remarks indirectly, attributing them to a 'senior source.'"[7]

Sharon's bureau radiated order and organization. There were no more leaks. The bureau chief, Shani, renewed the efforts to reorganize the national array of *hasbara*. One of the first steps was to consolidate the external team that already began to operate during Barak's term. Asaf Shariv, a media advisor who replaced Perlman, called them "bulldogs,"[8] and Gissin presented them as "gladiators."[9] "I formed a small group that would react swiftly," says David Baker, Gissin's deputy at the time. "I also brought in people from the Foreign Ministry. I marketed everyone to the media. I was forced to do this because other components of the *hasbara* system did not function successfully."[10] This initiative came in response to the media's strong demand for spokespersons who were approved by the prime minister. Baker was the liaison between the foreign press and the "gladiators." Thus, he helped the PMO create an independent system of spokesmanship on foreign affairs, in parallel to the Foreign Ministry and even in competition with it.

When Ehud Olmert took office on January 4, 2006, he retained the existing organizational structure, though most of the personnel from the Sharon period gradually left. In 2007, after the government adopted the Maimon Report—a comprehensive review of Israel's *hasbara* system— Olmert formed a national *hasbara* staff and, for the first time, appointed a special coordinator for public diplomacy in the PMO, though the role was not clearly defined.

•

The *Government Press Office* (GPO) is a unit in the PMO that is responsible for coordinating communication between the government of Israel and the foreign press community in Israel. It issues press credentials and facilitates sound media coverage of Israeli affairs and of state visits. The GPO included four departments at the time: Foreign Press, Arab Press, News in English, and Photography. Until 1970, it was solely responsible for dealing with foreign journalists visiting Israel; later, this role was divided between the GPO and the Foreign Ministry. In competition between the two, the Foreign Ministry gained the upper hand, and the GPO today has a diminished role in public diplomacy and the media.

During his term as prime minister, Barak wanted to form a national array of *hasbara* in the PMO. Lacking resources, he was forced to downsize the staff at the GPO and instead built the new Media Monitoring Center. Early in the second intifada, the Foreign Ministry decided to establish a national media center instead of relying on the GPO. The GPO's situation did not improve during the Sharon period, even though one of his political advisors, Eyal Arad, proposed upgrading its status and assigning it responsibility for *hasbara*.

•

The *Government Advertising Agency* (known by the Hebrew acronym LAPAM) is a sort of advertising and production arm for government ministries, government corporations, and public institutions. LAPAM, which is subordinate to the PMO and the Finance Ministry, provides a range of professional services, including developing advertising-marketing strategy and preparing, producing, and communicating messages to the media. It is not involved in the PMO's political-security activity or other *hasbara* efforts. Instead, it focuses on domestic issues, and its creative-marketing potential is not expressed at the national level.

•

On March 7, 1999, the government unanimously decided to establish the *National Security Council* (NSC). The effort to create the NSC entailed deliberations, calculations, and difficulties that were very similar to those encountered in the effort to form a national *hasbara* array. The government stipulated that the council would operate within the organizational framework of the PMO, with the head of the council reporting directly to the prime minister. The council was assigned a number of national security roles—providing consultation and guidance, conducting integrative assessment and long-term planning, preparing for discussions and offering recommendations to the government, as well as coordinating and collaborating with parallel entities in other countries.

From the outset, the NSC was designed to strengthen the government in the decision-making process on matters of state. This need intensifies during periods of low-intensity violence, when security decisions are frequently required. According to Deputy State Attorney Shai Nitzan, the government sought to address two principal factors: "complexity and diversity in issues pertaining to national security, and the need to overcome human limitations [involving relations between senior officials] related to the decision-making process."[11] Despite the government's decision in 1999, the NSC only began operating in 2002. As Benjamin Netanyahu would later note: "The entire system opposed it and continued to oppose it. . . . In the State of Israel, the defense establishment has the monopoly . . . , which is not a desirable situation."[12]

Barak's bureau chief, Gilead Sher, included the NSC in a plan he proposed for organizing a national *hasbara* array based in the PMO. Sher believed that the NSC could play a supportive role in the public diplomacy effort in light of its information, integrative capability, and involvement with the prime minister's staff. Uri Shani, who succeeded Sher, asked the NSC's director, Uzi Dayan, to prepare a report on a national *hasbara* array: "They [the PMO] did not like the Foreign Ministry's hegemony and thought we would present something they would like to hear," Dayan says. "The PMO should coordinate this subject, and that's what we said in the end."[13] The report was prepared by Brig. Gen. (res.) Israela Oron, Dayan's deputy and a former deputy IDF spokesperson. This was the first time the NSC dealt with the issue of *hasbara* at the national level.

Throughout the years, the NSC has been plagued by instability and frequent turnover in personnel, a phenomenon that indicates its inability to fulfill its primary purpose—integration of the government's work in the field of national security. Former heads of the NSC—including David Ivry, Uzi Dayan, Efraim Halevy, Giora Eiland, and Ilan Mizrahi—quit in rapid succession, claiming that the NSC was not empowered to perform its work.[14] Mizrahi finds a parallel between the reasons for the NSC's failure and the difficulty in establishing a public diplomacy array: "First, the government structure in Israel lacks a powerful focal point; there is no force capable of transferring national issues to the prime minister from the hands of other ministers. Second, there is the extraordinary power of the military-defense establishment, which refuses to collaborate with other entities. And finally, the Israeli trait of 'trust me.' 'Why the need for long-term thinking? Integration? Things are working and everything will be okay, tactics defeat strategy.' These central factors prevent a body like the NSC, and *hasbara* too, from finding their place."[15] The state comptroller also noted the impact of the rapid turnover of NSC directors on long-term planning in the field of national security.[16]

The main factors that hampered the NSC are not attributable to one person or another. They stem from fundamental problems of decision making at the highest levels of state. According to Chuck Freilich, a former deputy director of the NSC, these problems include a lack of long-term thinking, a focus on the short term, the extreme politicization of the decision-making process, the ongoing deterioration of the government's standing, and the dominance of the defense establishment over other entities.[17]

The hearings of the state commission of inquiry (the Winograd Commission) formed in the wake of the Second Lebanon War in 2006 highlighted the acuteness of this problem. Haim Ramon, Tzachi Hanegbi, Ephraim Sneh, Amos Malka, and Isaac Herzog all expressed dissatisfaction about the NSC's weakness. The prime minister at the time, Ehud Olmert, summarized: "All those who established the NSC did not want it."[18] In an interim report, the Winograd Commission recommended reconstructing the NSC to engender a change in its status. In general, it repeated previous recommendations but also proposed defining the job of NSC director as a "position of trust" appointed by the prime minister.

In its final report, the Winograd Commission reiterated its recommendation: "The NSC will have a central role in formulating and integrating intelligence assessments."[19]

Despite legislative and other initiatives aimed at bolstering the NSC's status, including a new government decision on October 14, 2007, nothing changed in practice. For example, in preparing for the Annapolis Conference in late 2007 and at the conference itself, the Prime Minister's Bureau bypassed and ignored the NSC.[20]

•

The *Foreign Ministry* is responsible for Israel's foreign policy and represents the state vis-à-vis foreign governments and international organizations through its diplomatic missions. Its duties include explaining Israel's positions and unique problems. The Jewish Agency Executive, led by David Ben-Gurion, decided to form the ministry in the summer of 1946 in preparation for statehood. Walter Eytan, spokesperson for the Jewish Agency and future director-general of the ministry, was responsible for planning the ministry in the framework of the "Situation Committee" chaired by Zeev Sherf. In January 1948, a plan was formulated that included a *hasbara* division with "a department that will engage in propaganda for our Foreign Ministry in foreign countries. Through its employees, who will be experts in the field of propaganda, it will disseminate the ideas and news we want them to receive in those countries and those government circles. It will employ all of the modern means of propaganda. This department will produce government publications, propaganda materials and information for our representatives."[21]

This propaganda department would later become the *Media and Public Affairs Division* in the Foreign Ministry, led by one of the ministry's fourteen deputy directors and responsible for Israel's public diplomacy. The division is responsible for one of the most complex sectors of activity in the field of Israeli foreign policy and the practice of Israeli diplomacy.

In addition to the Media and Public Affairs Division, the Foreign Ministry includes three tools of public diplomacy: the Agency for International Development Cooperation (MASHAV), the Cultural and Scientific Affairs Division, and the UN and International Organizations Division. MASHAV was established in 1958 and has since trained 250,000 interns from over 100 countries.[22]

MASHAV is a prominent tool of public diplomacy, offering foreign assistance as a long-term investment. Most of the ministry's media and *hasbara* activity is short- and medium-term; MASHAV is the long-term arm of public diplomacy. Israel directly invests 40 million shekels in international aid, but some activity is conducted in conjunction with other countries and international organizations, effectively multiplying this sum several times. Israel was accepted into the OECD, the prestigious organization of the world's developed countries. Member countries are committed to investing at least 0.7 percent of their gross national income in international aid, but Israel invests only about a 10th of this percentage.

Cultural diplomacy, another type of long-term investment, is the purview of the *Cultural and Scientific Affairs Division.* In an international reality in which Israel is portrayed in a context of violent confrontation with its neighbors, these investments also contribute to its soft power: "Israel is regarded in the world as a cultural power. People who are involved in culture, creative artists, producers, festival directors, museum curators, and professionals position Israel as a cultural powerhouse . . . in terms of quantity and quality."[23]

Nonetheless, the Foreign Ministry was forced to reduce the number of its cultural attachés in 2007 from 14 to four due to budget cuts and new bureaucratic rules. Precisely in this arena, where Israel could win points and present its finer qualities, there is a lack of resources.

The third Foreign Ministry branch that engages in public diplomacy is the *UN and International Organizations Division,* which is responsible for Israel's range of activities with international organizations. Following the Durban conference, a department for NGOs was formed in the division, in recognition of their importance in the international arena.

•

During the second intifada, the Foreign Ministry tried to adapt its activity to the new circumstances and demands. The confrontation with an Arabic-speaking population and the success of satellite broadcasts in Arabic required a new approach and deployment in a ministry whose primary focus was the West—Europe and the U.S., in particular. At the beginning of the second intifada, *hasbara* in Arabic was conducted within the framework of the Press and Spokesmanship Department. During Silvan Shalom's term as foreign minister, a special department for *hasbara* in Arabic was created in the Media and Public Affairs Division.

Another adaptation was to create an Internet site in Arabic. The site was launched in 2006, a very tardy response to the second intifada. The new needs underlined the lack of ministry employees fluent in Arabic, contrary to the situation in the past. Many among the ministry's founding generation came from Arabic-speaking countries and were fluent in Arabic.

•

Israel has technological capabilities that place it in the front ranks of the world's developed nations. The Foreign Ministry realized that Israel could not lag behind in the new media environment. When the second intifada erupted, the visual dimension of the *hasbara* war was accorded low priority. However, the ministry discovered that television stations and Internet sites outside of Israel were flooded with visual reports of clashes. Ilan Sztulman, a ministry official, decided on his own initiative to serve as a photographer/documenter and would go to the scenes of terror attacks and send the documentation to the broadcast networks.[24]

Israel had blocked TV crews from approaching the scenes of terror attacks to prevent the display of horrific pictures—out of respect for the casualties and fearing that it would hurt morale. The foreign minister at the time, Silvan Shalom, decided to change this longtime policy. "We did a lot of active *hasbara*, we presented shocking presentations of acts of terror, and reporters who saw them shed tears and wept."[25] Israel Police also changed its traditional approach and opened the sites of terror attacks to press coverage. A similar argument arose following the attack at the Itamar settlement in 2011, where five members of a family were murdered. Yuli Edelstein, who served as minister of public diplomacy and diaspora affairs at the time, decided to disseminate the ghastly images for purposes of *hasbara*, despite concerns of respect for the dead.

•

The Foreign Ministry gradually adopted public diplomacy tools, including *branding*. This process began unofficially in 2003 at the initiative of seven American businesspeople and media experts who had concluded that Israel needed to rebrand itself. David Sable, global CEO of Young & Rubicam Advertising, was one of the seven. He argued that the main problem regarding Israel's image in the U.S. stems from a lack of knowledge about Israel and proposed that his company conduct research on branding Israel in the United States. Meanwhile, the Foreign Ministry decided to create a new *hasbara* department for promoting Israel's achievements and positive activities.

At the same time, the government decided that the Foreign Ministry would coordinate the Brand Israel Project. Ido Aharoni, head of the ministry's branding team, formulated a new proposal for branding Israel based on three values: passion, inventiveness, and an ability to integrate human, behavioral, and technological contrasts. Partners in the branding process included the government, the business sector, the third sector, Diaspora Jewry, and the general public. The British firm Acanchi was assigned the strategic stage in the rebranding process. The state budget for 2010 included 20 million shekels for the branding project. In 2013, the ministry announced that the project was complete, branding Israel as "a state of creative energy."[26]

Meanwhile, again because of an independent initiative unrelated to the Foreign Ministry, Israel was rebranded as the "start-up nation"— thanks to a book by that name that achieved unprecedented success. The bestseller, written by Dan Senor and Saul Singer, is Israel's most effective "sales promoter" in the international arena.

•

The branding project illustrates the importance of collaboration in the field of *hasbara* between the Foreign Ministry and professionals in the private sector. The ministry had refrained from privatizing public diplomacy through outsourcing; however, in 2011, it decided to hire a number of public relations firms in selected states in Europe. However, the ministry canceled these contracts soon afterward, in July 2012, due to budget constraints—despite the ongoing deterioration of Israel's public image in Europe. Meanwhile, dozens of *hasbara* NGOs sprouted in Israel and abroad; the ministry did little to encourage this phenomenon and sometimes even opposed it.

The *Department for NGOs* was created in the wake of the Durban conference and was already active during the second intifada. NGOs were previously handled by the UN and International Organizations Division. However, the Durban conference was a wakeup call that illustrated the new power of NGOs, and the ministry realized that a conceptual and organizational change was required. Among its roles, the department focuses on Israeli NGOs and tries to integrate them in the international civil society and with the international organizations active in Israel.

•

The *Defense Ministry* is not obligated to engage in *hasbara*, but it is obvi-ous that the Israeli reality and the ministry's powerful status in security matters require its cooperation in public diplomacy pertaining to the IDF, domestic Israeli affairs, the Palestinian-Arab society, and international issues. The defense minister's personal advisor is usually the dominant figure in the Defense Ministry on media-related matters, and the advisor also orchestrates the ministry's *hasbara* policy. Historically, there has been inherent tension between the defense minister's media advisor and the IDF spokesperson.

Due to the reluctance of defense officials to include the media advisor in discussions, most of which are secret, the advisor is absent from decision-making processes and unable to make a professional contribution to them. "Those who need to represent the *hasbara* considerations of the State of Israel are not participants in the key discussions and decision making at the political level in general."[27]

Circumstances sometimes compelled the Defense Ministry to make an exception to its entrenched patterns of action vis-à-vis the media. For example, Yehiel Horev, who as the head of the security department (MALMAB) was one of the ministry's most powerful officials and had always avoided the spotlight, had to face the media in the case of Mordechai Vanunu. (MALMAB is responsible for information security at the ministry, the defense industries, and defense research institutes, including nuclear research. Vanunu served 18 years in prison for leaking information about Israel's nuclear program.) Horev asked the court to impose restrictions on Vanunu upon the latter's release from prison, and Horev's readiness to explain this policy in personal briefings and conversations with reporters was a rare occurrence, though it was consistent with the general atmosphere of growing cooperation with the media by organizations like the Shin Bet. "We had to explain—because lies were published and we wanted to counter them," Horev says. "We have no doubt that the media damaged our image, but it also empowered us and created deterrence."[28]

In May 2011, it was announced that the ministry would establish a *hasbara* division, to be led by Col. (ret.) Shlomi Am-Shalom, a former deputy IDF spokesperson. The division's roles were not described in the announcement. Not surprisingly, the division was never created.

•

The *IDF Spokesperson's Unit* is organizationally part of the general staff's Operations Directorate, but it reports directly to the IDF chief of staff. The unit's roles and line of reporting vary from time to time. Today, it is the largest spokesmanship entity in Israel. The spokesperson has the rank of brigadier general; a deputy spokesperson (colonel) and a media department director (lieutenant colonel) serve under the spokesperson. The unit is divided into seven branches of professional activity.

Near the end of his term as IDF spokesperson, Brig. Gen. Oded Ben-Ami completed a comprehensive report entitled "Spokesmanship 2000," composed by a team of experts from both within and outside of the unit. Ben-Ami sought to adapt the unit's activity to the new media environment—including, for example, the Freedom of Information Law and technological changes. "Due to its unique characteristics, Israel is expected to be more open and transparent. When the development of modern technology is added, which helps to broaden exposure, the need arises for a suitable spokesmanship response,"[29] Ben-Ami says. But at the beginning of 2000, Brig. Gen. Ron Kitrey replaced Ben-Ami and the report was shelved.

In times of emergency, the IDF spokesperson convenes a team of the unit's officers and reservists, headed by the director of the *hasbara* branch. This team also participates in the large annual military exercises and is responsible for its media plan. During the second intifada, three such teams operated, clashed with each other, and ultimately fizzled out.[30] "Higher-ups in the military command got cold feet, each one with their own political calculations," says Col. (ret.) Irit Atzmon, head of the *hasbara* center for emergency periods.[31] This type of team is essential for broadening the conceptual approach to the media and taking it "outside the box."

In 2002, Moshe Yaalon replaced Shaul Mofaz as IDF chief of staff. Both would later serve as defense ministers. Yaalon entered the role of chief of staff with firm views on media policy: "One of the things that horrified me was the lack of readiness of the IDF Spokesman's Division for this sort of war. Already at the Central Command and even before at the Judea and Samaria Division, I understood the importance of the media arena—the need to issue reliable information as quickly as possible in order to take control of the vacuum. Because if you don't fill it, someone else will and in effect will set the tone and tell the story."[32]

Yaalon instructed the head of the Operations Directorate, Maj. Gen. Israel Ziv, to develop a new operative conception, including the formation of a consciousness arena in the Operations Directorate: "This was a revolution in consciousness in the IDF that integrated the new function within the military system, within the processes of situation assessment, within the processes of decision making in the IDF,"[33] says Brig. Gen. Meir Klifi, who implemented the IDF's new approach to public diplomacy as head of the IDF Doctrine and Training Division. This view of the media and its impact on consciousness in warfare boosted the

status of the IDF Spokesperson's Unit in the general staff and required
the restructuring of the unit. One of the repercussions was the inclusion
of the IDF Spokesperson's Unit in the "operations and sorties" forum
that discusses each IDF operative activity, including activity over the
border. Thus, the IDF spokesperson became privy to secret operations,
which again raised reservations among some intelligence and operations
personnel.

•

Already in 1998, the IDF issued a new directive entitled "*hasbara* and
media as a component in the work of the commander and staff," designed
to integrate media considerations in IDF activity. The directive was written at the initiative of Brig. Gen. Doron Almog, then the head of the
Doctrine and Training Department. However, the IDF Spokesperson's Unit
found it difficult to execute this directive. The heads of the northern,
central, and southern commands, as well as other senior commanders,
sought to define their own media policies that were not necessarily consistent with IDF policy: "The IDF spokesperson, Brig. Gen. Ruth Yaron,
encountered what she called 'military juntas'—military commanders who
didn't honor her professional directives. The military commander runs it
as he sees fit, he activates the forces as he sees fit, and he also manages
hasbara as he sees fit,"[34] says Lt. Col. (ret.) Yoni Dahuh-Halevi.

In the midst of the second intifada, the Ground Forces Command
was asked to prepare new instructions for integrating the media in the
battlefield. *Combat Directives—Media Techniques: IDF and the Media—Integrating Spokesmanship* explained: "The IDF's combat doctrine states that
victory will be achieved in the field of consciousness. The media has a
significant impact on the consciousness of the general public in Israel and
in the world, so it is important to be familiar with it, to understand it
and its motives, and to choose the ways to use it for our benefit."[35] The
new directives reiterate that operational orders should include a media
appendix composed by the IDF Spokesperson's Unit and specifying how
the media will be integrated in the operation.

The new military operative doctrine includes the strategic principles
required for achieving the desired effects in the field of consciousness.
"The concepts of *hasbara* and spokesmanship belong to the past. To
shape public opinion, the IDF Spokesperson's Unit does not necessarily
explain or act as a spokesperson. In its current professional orientation,
it aspires, first of all, to understand the target audiences and the most
effective channels for addressing them, to analyze the threats and the

opportunities, to identify the connections and interactions among the target audiences, to formulate a precise message, to choose the effective platform and spokesperson, to wrap it in a specific sensitive tone and to prepare other ways of media action. This is not *hasbara* and spokesmanship; it is a design process intended to influence perceptions of reality, views and consciousness."[36] A new department was created in the IDF Spokesman's Unit—the *Department of Strategy and Initiatives*—to direct the subject of consciousness in the unit and to represent the IDF spokesperson in the consciousness arena in the Operations Directorate.

The IDF Spokesperson's Unit was not involved in the Palestinian-Arab arena. The circumstances that compelled the Foreign Ministry to form a department for Arabic media in August 2003 similarly led the IDF Spokesperson's Unit to create an *Arabic Media Desk* in May 2004. The Arabic desk proved its critical importance in the Second Lebanon War and in the violent events that followed it.

Another organizational change Yaron initiated was to establish operational documentation in the IDF via a new profession—*operational documenter*. Infantry soldiers, after a one-month training course in video and still photography, documented military activity in real time, despite the operative difficulties. This activity included incidents that were also documented by foreign media crews or by the Palestinian Authority.

•

The IDF Spokesperson's Unit has always struggled with the issue of maintaining credibility in the face of challenges posed by the media. All spokespersons want their words to be accepted: "Public trust in the IDF is the key provision in the backpack of each soldier at every rank and en route to every mission. Without the public's trust, it is difficult to function over time,"[37] says Brig. Gen. Avi Benayahu, former commander of Army Radio. Clearly, if the spokespersons' announcements are rejected, their work is in vain. Their efforts are aimed at ensuring that every piece of information they release is true, even if the information does not include the entire truth due to the circumstances.

The unit's main difficulty stems from the fact that it depends on external sources of information and cannot verify information on its own. "A very problematic situation develops, where you don't know whether to rely on information you receive from your sources. This really stands out in the army. I received investigation reports that I didn't believe and the IDF Spokesperson's Unit also didn't believe," says Maj. Gen. (ret.) Uzi Dayan.[38] One example of a crisis in credibility was an IDF attack against terrorists in the Nuseirat refugee camp in October 2003, when the chief of staff admitted that the IDF had deliberately misled military reporters in order to conceal the use of classified means of warfare (a missile fired from a considerable distance).[39] Another example occurred in October 2004, when Israel accused UNRWA of transporting weaponry in a civilian ambulance but could not prove this.[40] It is even more difficult to maintain credibility in the new media environment and amid the competition between military and other sources of information. The IDF cannot keep pace with the competition posed by real-time reporting and live broadcasts.[41] The foreign media and the Palestinians can publish military information quicker because the IDF is required to repeatedly check information and is committed to credibility rather than speed. Former deputy IDF spokesperson Elam Kott notes: "We would receive lots of information that was not correct, or was not complete or that included an attempt to cover up."[42]

The tension between credibility and speed has characterized the work of IDF spokespersons over the years, but the second intifada intensified the pressure: "The media wants the information about an incident 'already yesterday,' so there is no way to provide this, certainly not under the conditions in which the IDF operates, with its hierarchical structure."[43] The IDF Spokesperson's Unit deliberates whether to conduct a long and thorough investigation of the information or to release it quickly, at the expense of accuracy and credibility. There is no solution for this in IDF doctrine, and this deliberation reoccurs in every military incident.

The problem intensified not only because of technological changes but also due to the circumstances of low-intensity conflict. In an asymmetrical situation, the weaker side allows itself to compromise credibility and to lie, if only to preempt the stronger side. "The Palestinians are 'schooling' the IDF," says the journalist Rafik Halabi, formerly the news editor at Channel 1 television. "The IDF Spokesperson's Unit must place its full weight on credibility and not on public relations. It doesn't know how to contend with low-intensity violence, with terrorism."[44]

The IDF Spokesperson's Unit looked for ways to address the problem of speed versus credibility. It sent representatives to the division level in the field in order to receive firsthand information on events and pass it along to the unit's headquarters. The unit repeatedly asked IDF commanders to check information before sending it and appeared in a range of military frameworks to emphasize the importance of accurate reporting. It also fought to punish soldiers and commanders who did not report the truth. The unit preferred to sometimes issue announcements to the media attributed to "official military sources" or "senior IDF personnel" instead of officially quoting the IDF spokesperson, in order to protect the latter's credibility. Nonetheless, the credibility versus speed dilemma persists.

In the years following the second intifada, this dilemma took on additional weight. The advanced communication technologies completely neutralized the IDF's ability to control information on "the battlefield." NGOs and private individuals became purveyors of information, usually preempting the army and placing it in a permanent mode of defending itself. A particularly salient event occurred in Hebron on March 24, 2016. Two Palestinian terrorists stabbed an IDF soldier. One of the two was shot to death, while the second, Abd al-Fatah a-Sharif, was shot but still alive, lying on the ground, until IDF Sgt. Elor Azaria approached and shot him in the head. The entire incident was documented by a Palestinian photographer, Imad Abu Shamsiya, who sent the footage to the B'Tselem organization, which monitors IDF activity in the territories. The video was disseminated in social media, eliciting strong local and international responses. The soldier's commanders denounced his action and Azaria was brought to trial in military court following an IDF investigation. The media pressure generated by the early publication of the video undoubtedly forced the IDF to take swift action. Under different circumstances, it would have proceeded at a slower pace. In any case, the incident became a seminal event in regard to the IDF's rules of engagement and its code of ethics, and vis-à-vis the media's role in exposing incidents in the urban "battlefield."

•

The new IDF player in public diplomacy is the *Home Front Command*, established in 1992 in the wake of the first Gulf War. In Israel's previous wars, waged on average at least once every decade, the IDF was able to keep the enemy at a distance from the home front and conducted its battles in enemy territory. In the past, the home front was not completely immune to enemy attacks, but the first Gulf War in 1991 marked a turning point: Iraq was able to systematically strike against the home front of the State of Israel over a period of five weeks.

Enemy states and terrorist organizations are today equipped with ground-to-ground missiles whose range covers most of the State of Israel. In recent years, terrorist organizations have acquired the ability to launch missiles and rockets into Israel—Hezbollah from the north and Hamas from the south—and have deployed missile installations that significantly threaten the Israeli home front. The current assessment, in 2016, is that about 150,000 long-range missiles and rockets are aimed at Israel—from Iran, from terrorist organizations in Lebanon, and from the Gaza Strip and the Sinai Peninsula. Defending the home front, especially since the Second Lebanon War, has become a cornerstone of Israel's defense strategy. In the past, the national security doctrine called for taking the war into enemy territory and conducting it there. The approach changed; the missile attacks, particularly in 2006 and in 2009, brought considerations about home front defense to the center of strategic thinking. Thus, the resilience of Israelis in cities and towns near the Gaza Strip (for example, Kiryat Malachi, Ashdod, and Ofakim) determines the duration of fighting against Hamas. The home front serves in a sort of combat support role.[45] In the new war, the borders between battlefront and home front are blurred. Consequently, the home front has become a factor in Israel's public diplomacy.

•

During the period discussed here, the *Public Security Ministry* and Israel Police stood on the forefront of combatting terrorism, together with the IDF and Shin Bet. The Shin Bet and police focus on thwarting terrorism, and the police also deals with the sites of attacks and is responsible for public order. At the beginning of the second intifada, the police kept journalists at a distance until the sites of attacks were "cleaned." As noted, it later decided to open these sites to the media, encouraged coverage, and deployed English-speaking spokespersons. Israel Police, recognizing that in times of emergencies a centralized system is preferable to a decentralized one, formed a central spokesperson's department, led by a senior officer.

As the new dimensions of low-intensity fighting develop, including the decline in suicide terrorism and the increase of steep-trajectory weapon fire, the interface between Israel Police and the IDF Home Front expands. Terrorism inside the state is the purview of the police (with the Shin Bet), while cross-border shooting is addressed by both the Home Front Command and the police. This situation also boosts the status of the Home Front Command within the system of public diplomacy.

Chapter 9

The Unseen Shield?

The intelligence community in Israel includes the Foreign Ministry's Center for Political Research, the IDF's intelligence branch, the Mossad, the Shin Bet, Israel Police's Intelligence Division, and the Defense Ministry Security Authority (MALMAB). All of them can contribute to Israel's public diplomacy by providing information, analysis, and assessment.

The transition of the *decentralized system* to a *centralized* one entails many changes, including the participation of new players. Most notably, the Shin Bet gradually became involved in public diplomacy, adopting its approach and tools.

The Shin Bet (also known as the General Security Service—GSS) is directly subordinate to the prime minister. Its mission is defined in the Shin Bet Law (2002): "The 'Service' is responsible for protecting the state's security, [and] the arrangements and institutions of democratic rule, against the threats of terrorism, sabotage, subversion, espionage and exposure of state secrets; the 'Service' will endeavor to protect and promote other vital state interests for the national security of the state, and all as determined by the state and subject to law."

The Shin Bet's motto—the Unseen Shield—was adopted at its inception. Over the years, and particularly during the years of intensive fighting against terrorism, the Shin Bet developed a strategy of public diplomacy. The "unseen" organization began to reveal itself in part.

The Shin Bet was established on February 8, 1949, but its existence became widely known only after the murder of Dr. Israel Kastner in March 1957. (Kastner had been accused of collaborating with the Nazis.) Until then, its activities had been wrapped in complete secrecy, surfacing only occasionally in a political-party context. For example, it was discovered in 1953 that the Shin Bet had planted a covert listening device in the desk of Meir Ya'ari, the leader of the socialist Mapam party. *Haolam Hazeh*, a popular news weekly at the time, called the Shin Bet "the apparatus of darkness."

After the Six Day War, the Shin Bet's responsibility expanded and it grew to be a complex and large organization with thousands of employees. It became the principal counterterror agency in the territories and in Israel. As one former Shin Bet official explains: "The 'Service' had always been a compartmentalized and secret organization. No one knew where it was located. It received public exposure following its entry into the territories of Judea, Samaria, and Gaza; its contact with the police and State Attorney's Office; and its court appearances. All of these exposed the Shin Bet. Still not as the people wanted, but it was the first stage."[1] To give public expression to the counterterror operations, the head of military intelligence, Maj. Gen. Shlomo Gazit, and the head of the Shin Bet's Arab Affairs Division, Avraham Ahitov, decided to attribute the Shin Bet's activities in the territories to "the security forces" in statements issued by the IDF Spokesperson's Unit.[2]

⁓

On April 12, 1984, four terrorists hijacked a bus (No. 300) heading from Tel Aviv to Ashkelon. Security forces stopped the bus in the Gaza Strip and surrounded it. Defense Minister Moshe Arens, GOC Southern Command Maj. Gen. Moshe Bar-Kochba, Chief Infantry Officer Brig. Gen. Yitzhak Mordechai, and the Shin Bet's director Avraham Shalom and operations chief Ehud Yatom all arrived at the scene. Negotiations were conducted with the terrorists, who demanded the release of 500 Palestinians imprisoned in Israel on security-related charges. The defense minister then gave the green light for Sayeret Matkal anti-terrorist commandos to raid the bus. Two terrorists were killed in the assault and two others were captured. One passenger, a soldier named Irit Portugues, was also killed. The two captured terrorists were taken from the scene by Shin Bet investigators, including the operations chief, Ehud Yatom.

At a press conference with the defense minister and IDF chief of staff, nothing was said about the fate of the two terrorists who were apprehended alive. Hours later, the IDF spokesperson announced in response to questions that two terrorists had died during the assault and the other two died on the way to the hospital. It was later revealed that the latter were executed by their interrogators and that this information had been concealed from the media. "Bus 300 was not a special operation," says Avraham Shalom, the Shin Bet director at the time. "Four terrorists came. Two were killed. I gave an order, after receiving the prime minister's approval, to kill the remaining two. All in all, they were half dead when we received them. My people did this [the killing] very poorly. Very sloppy work. I heard all the details a week later, and it was chilling. But I wanted to protect the system because the Shin Bet is a secret organization, and this was a mistake. I shouldn't have protected the security system in that situation. I had to protect a national consensus. All that fabrication . . . I didn't realize it could be such a mess. Nothing went right. About 200 to 300, 400 people were there, and each one had something to say. Each one ran around with a photographer and with a journalist."[3]

The episode—which came to be known as the "Bus 300 Affair"—lasted three years. The media was involved from the first moment: Reporters and photographers gathered at the scene and reported as the events unfolded. The photographers documented the two surviving terrorists being led out of the bus. The *New York Times* was the first to question their fate. Three days later, the now-defunct Israeli daily *Hadashot* quoted the *New York Times* article. *Haolam Hazeh* and *Hadashot* had a photograph of one of the terrorists being led by Shin Bet agents. The photograph was published only a month later, when *Hadashot* decided to report on the appointment of a committee that would examine the circumstances of the terrorists' death. The newspaper's decision was contrary to the stance of the Editors' Committee, which had acceded to the defense minister's request and refrained from publishing this news. (The Editors' Committee included all the chief editors of the Hebrew media in Israel.) The chief military censor submitted a complaint against *Hadashot* to Israel Police, claiming that the newspaper had violated Regulation 87 of the Defense (Emergency) Ordinances. The complaint charged that the report was published without first submitting it to the military censor and receiving approval. The next day, the military censor, after consulting with the prime minister and defense minister, issued an order to shut down the newspaper for four days. (After a court hearing, the closure order was reduced to three days.)

On May 24, 1986, about two years after the incident, an internal dispute at the Shin Bet became public—a rare occurrence. Three top Shin

Bet officials—Reuven Hazak, Peleg Radai, and Rafi Malka—demanded the dismissal of Shin Bet director Shalom, accusing him of issuing the order to kill the two terrorists and then trying to cover it up. The day after this dispute was reported on television, the Israeli media devoted extensive coverage to the affair, whose details were still largely unknown to the press. The military censor continued to do its utmost to keep newspaper editors in the dark.

In light of the security establishment's fears that excessive exposure would damage the Shin Bet's ability to function, President Chaim Herzog pardoned the Shin Bet personnel and senior IDF officers involved, before any legal proceedings were initiated. After the sweeping clemency, the government continued to back the Shin Bet. Legal commentator Moshe Negbi asserts: "The government's effort to place the top Shin Bet officials above the law, and, even more, its readiness and determination to pursue this goal at any price, while recklessly trampling basic principles of law, raised questions about the future of Israel as a democratic law-abiding state."[4]

The Bus 300 Affair is considered one of the seminal events affecting the Shin Bet's public standing and its relationship with the media. "The security service after the Bus 300 Affair, and particularly in the public-media perspective, is not the same security service it was before," according to attorney Yechiel Gutman. "Though the professional-operational strength of the 'Service' was not impaired, the media, through its intensive coverage of this affair, penetrated its sensitive corners; and the subsequent media coverage of the 'Service,' its personnel and its activity has not always been balanced and fair, to put it lightly."[5]

Shin Bet personnel felt they had been excessively exposed.[6] "It was an incident that revealed the Shin Bet's work methods and really opened them to the media," says Ehud Yatom, one of the Shin Bet officials involved in the affair. "Until then, the Shin Bet was a completely closed organization. Everything there was done quietly and in silence. It was a terrible rupture that created a situation in which the Shin Bet lost the trust of politicians and the public. They had to make substantial changes in the structure of the 'Service' and in its public image."[7]

After Shalom resigned in 1986, one of his predecessors, Yosef Harmelin, was asked to return to the director's post on an interim basis. A year and a half later, Yaakov Peri was appointed to head the Shin Bet. "The Bus 300 Affair shattered two theses," Peri says. "First, there is no such thing as total political backing—when you fall into the mud and are drowning, they won't lend you a hand. Second, there is a much more open media reality out there, censorship has weakened and the defense establishment is no longer treated as such a sacred cow."[8]

Peri changed the relations between the Shin Bet and the media dramatically, starting with a decision to call the Shin Bet by name instead of referring to unnamed "security forces." He sought to improve the Shin Bet's public image through fostering working relations with the political echelon and the media.[9] However, representatives of the media were still prohibited from accompanying Shin Bet personnel in the field.

A series of security-related affairs—the Bus 300 incident, Jonathan Pollard, Mordechai Vanunu—forced the Shin Bet to change its media deployment. "After all of the committees, the 'Service' said that it would start to operate in the open world and received a lot of credit for this in the media," says Yehiel Horev, MALMAB director. "At its initiative, certain things were suddenly highlighted. . . . The Shin Bet benefited from this change. It was under attack, and now it's in its glory days."[10]

~

Another incident that shocked the Shin Bet and exposed it to the public and the media was the murder of Yitzhak Rabin. This occurred during the term of Peri's successor, Carmi Gillon.

Gillon continued Peri's policy vis-à-vis the media: On the one hand, the Shin Bet's formal spokesmanship activity was conducted, as in the past, by the IDF Spokesperson's Unit; inquiries were submitted to the Shin Bet via the PMO, and the director of the Prime Minister's Bureau served as the press liaison. On the other hand, the Shin Bet initiated actions on its own. In August 1995, for example, Gillon met with Israeli military correspondents in order to warn of the possibility of the murder of a prime minister in Israel. His remarks were published and Gillon viewed this as a turning point in the relations with the media. "Previous directors of the 'Service' had also maintained contact with the media, albeit in a very low dosage, and the information they provided had always been masked. You couldn't figure out who was behind it unless you were really in the know. This time the action was direct and everyone knew who the source was."[11]

Tragically, Gillon's worst fears came to pass: Prime Minister Rabin was murdered on November 4. This marked the next seminal stage in the Shin Bet's relations with the media. The murder again sent shockwaves through the Shin Bet and led to the resignation of Gillon and the appointment of Ami Ayalon as the new director. Ayalon, a former

IDF general, understood that a new era had begun in media-government relations and decided to prepare the Shin Bet for this era. He commissioned two reports; the first was by Hezi Kalo, a senior Shin Bet official. Kalo: "Our main conclusion was that some entity should be created in the Shin Bet to serve as a media advisor or something of the sort, but not a spokesmanship operation. A spokesmanship operation would create a constant connection with the media, something the 'Service' doesn't need. The less they write about the 'Service,' the better. The 'Service' should minimize the contact with the media, and perhaps a media advisor of this sort is the solution."[12]

The second report Ayalon commissioned was written by his bureau chief, Lior Akerman. The report outlines the potential harm stemming from the lack of a media strategy: a belated response or failure to respond to the publication of misleading information that is liable to tarnish the Shin Bet's image and hurt its interests; erosion of the public standing of the "Service" and the danger of it falling outside of the consensus; a diminished ability to recruit and retain employees and agents/collaborators as a result of its eroded image; harm to the motivation of personnel and of morale at the "Service"; abandoning the media arena to manipulative entities who promote their own interests at the expense of the "Service."[13]

Akerman concluded, after consulting with experts, that the Shin Bet should develop a professional media strategy centered on a media department that would be subordinate to the director's bureau chief.

The Akerman document sparked a revolution in the Shin Bet, which began to adopt the tools of public diplomacy. Ayalon approved the working paper and ordered the implementation of the new media strategy.

From one director to the next, the Shin Bet became more widely exposed—both on its own initiative and as a result of external events. Avi Dichter, who was appointed to head the Shin Bet on May 15, 2000, shaped the organization's involvement during the fateful period of the second intifada.

Dichter presented four basic principles of media activity: employees of the "Service" do not give interviews; the "Service" does not grant exclusivity; the connection between *hasbara* and personal interests should be severed; the media is not allowed to accompany the Shin Bet in operational activity.[14] Dichter's deputy, Ofer Dekel, was also an advocate of this approach, viewing the media as a weapon in the battle against the Palestinians and other rivals: "This is definitely war, and it should be treated as an operation with strategic thinking, tactical objectives, formulation of messages in advance, and tactical deployment for response time."[15]

During his five-year term, Dichter was able to make public diplomacy activity an integral part of the organization's work. He was also the first Shin Bet director to speak in a public conference about its mission, activities, and achievements. This occurred in the midst of the second intifada, on December 16, 2003, at the Herzliya Conference, where he reviewed the Shin Bet's counterterror efforts. Seeking to boost national morale, he assured the Israeli public that "there is life after terrorism."[16]

Dichter built a media section in his bureau, which operated in parallel to the IDF Spokesperson's Unit, the defense minister's media advisor, and the Foreign Ministry's *hasbara* division, and it quickly became a generous source of information for the Israeli and foreign media.

Competition subsequently developed between the Shin Bet and the IDF Spokesperson's Unit. In many cases, they conducted joint operational activity, but each sought to claim credit: "The Shin Bet became a player in this war," says Ron Kitri, who served as IDF spokesperson during this period. "In my opinion, an intelligence organization must remain outside of the media world. It should express its view, but through state channels, for example, in coordination with the IDF Spokesperson's Unit."[17]

During the five years of confrontation, the Shin Bet and IDF closely collaborated and developed targeted killings, which struck against terrorist leaders, especially in the Gaza Strip, and undoubtedly had a deterrent effect. The Shin Bet also, for the first time, permitted interviews with captured terrorists. The idea was to show the Israeli and Arab public the true face of the terrorists, especially their wretchedness.[18] This decision stemmed from a media policy aimed at reducing the Israeli public's fear of terrorists and at deterring potential Palestinian terrorists. Thus, the Shin Bet became involved in the war for consciousness.

A salient event was the lynching of two IDF soldiers in Ramallah. The Shin Bet quickly understood the incident's impact on the morale of the Israeli public and on the Palestinian population. "The lynching was the only incident I remember as head of the 'Service' in which I issued a directive to bring to justice all those involved, no matter what," Dichter says. He categorized this event as a "terror attack on the Israeli soul" and was determined to respond in kind. In particular, he was thinking of the photograph of Abd al-Aziz Salha, one of the terrorists, showing his bloodstained hands at the window of the Ramallah police station where the lynching occurred: "In regard to the guy who was photographed with his two hands, I decided that the day we arrest him and are sure he's the man, he'd be photographed with his two hands in handcuffs. This picture fulfills a debt to the people of Israel."[19]

Ofer Dekel, Dichter's deputy, notes that the prevailing sentiment in the "Service" was to respond to the murder: "What does this mean, that they murder two people and we do nothing? That's considered weakness, the state's weakness, and the result is frustration."[20] According to Dekel, the Shin Bet's media activity focused on two arenas: the global arena—broadcasting pictures that displayed the brutality of the Palestinians; and the Israeli arena—foiled attacks, arrests, and trials. The Shin Bet internalized the vocabulary of public diplomacy and understood that it was engaged in shaping consciousness. Of course, Israelis and Palestinians saw things differently: The picture of the bloodstained hands was perceived as a victory by the Palestinians, and as a sign of Israeli weakness and frustration. The Shin Bet achieved the opposite result when it displayed a picture of the murderer in handcuffs: For the Arabs, this portrayed defeat and frustration, while it provided a sense of satisfaction to the Israeli public, which regarded this as an operational and intelligence achievement.

~

Six years after the assassination of Yitzhak Rabin, the Shin Bet faced a similar test. On October 17, 2001, Minister Rehavam Ze'evi was murdered at the Hyatt Hotel in Jerusalem. He disregarded the security instructions of his bodyguards and went alone to his room on the fifth floor of the hotel. His murderers were waiting in ambush and shot him. The Shin Bet, which had failed to prevent a Jewish assassin from murdering Rabin, experienced a new trauma. For the first time, a government minister in Israel was murdered by Palestinian terrorists. This time, supported by the public and by its relations with the media, the Shin Bet was able to take quick and efficient action, applying the lessons from past incidents.

It actively briefed top media figures, mobilized former senior Shin Bet personnel in this effort, enlisted the political system to help, and, in particular, made sure that information would not leak from the Shin Bet.

Several weeks after the murder, the Shin Bet was able to expose Ze'evi's murderers and thus mitigate the criticism directed against it. However, even without this, as Akerman notes, the Shin Bet's initiative, quickness, and creativity made a difference in the media outcome. Despite a second murder of a political figure in Israel within six years, the damage to the Shin Bet was negligible.

During the second intifada, the Shin Bet gained prestige and public stature: "The Shin Bet was the ears and eyes of the people of Israel, and if it hadn't been able to provide significant achievements, there would have been a disaster," says Gideon Ezra, a former deputy director of the organization. "The Shin Bet was glorified, and since it delivered the goods, it was glorified more than the IDF."[21] Other senior Shin Bet officials, including Ami Ayalon, concur with this assessment, citing the Shin Bet's dominance during the second intifada in decision-making processes in general and in counterterrorism in particular. As Ehud Yatom explains: "In light of all of its failures—and each terror attack is a failure—when the Shin Bet director or others appeared before the government and defense establishment and before the public, it was able to set the tone and acknowledge that it's true that 1,100 Israeli civilians were murdered, Jews and Arabs, but it's also true that another 1,000 or 2,000 were saved. The 'Service' was able to survive all of these enormous failures. . . . If the media had attacked the Shin Bet concerning the 1,100 killed, it would have killed it."[22]

The Shin Bet's success in developing close relations with the media amplified tensions between the Shin Bet and the IDF Spokesperson's Unit.[23] Prior to the formation of the Shin Bet's media section, the IDF Spokesperson's Unit and the prime minister's media advisor often filled a spokesmanship role for the Shin Bet. Today, journalists usually turn to both the Shin Bet and IDF in parallel. Alon Ben-David, Channel 10's military commentator, explains: "The Shin Bet's spokesperson's operation is more influential than the IDF Spokesperson's Unit. On every question, they give a precise, efficient, and reliable answer. It's a small organization with lateral communication. The spokesperson's operation is located in the director's bureau and enjoys the backing of the director of the 'Service.' They contact the relevant employee in the field, receive an immediate answer, and have the discretion to answer me, which the IDF Spokesperson's Unit lacks."[24] In events such as the abduction of Gilad Shalit (2006), the Second Lebanon War (2006) or the terror attack at the Sinai border (2011), the Shin Bet was able to establish itself as an independent source of information and received credit in public disputes with the IDF. In the case of the border attack in 2011, the military commentator Alex Fishman wrote: "The IDF's intelligence branch brought specific warnings. But the mistake was in the command echelon's assessment of the information. There, they apparently believed that the terrorists would carry out the attack during the hours of darkness, and didn't imagine they would pass through the Egyptian military post."[25]

One of the reasons journalists seek information from the Shin Bet pertains to the question of credibility, which both organizations struggle to maintain.[26] The Shin Bet's high level of credibility stems from the organizational culture of reporting and from the short and rapid pipelines of reporting.[27] The IDF Spokesperson's Unit complains that the Shin Bet controls and directs the information, leaving the IDF totally dependent on it.[28] Thus, the Shin Bet is able to reveal its achievements to the media, bit by bit, while the IDF watches in frustration.

The Shin Bet's advantages are open and known. Its personnel are subject to strict discipline, including periodic polygraph testing. Consequently, it is the media that is unable to reach independent sources of information within the Shin Bet and there are no leaks. This is also due to its centralized and hierarchical structure, organizational culture, and the complete control of field officers. Roni Shaked, a commentator on Arab affairs and a former Shin Bet employee, explains: "Tension arose between the IDF and the Shin Bet. For example, I received and reported information that a Qassam rocket was fired in the Jenin area. The IDF spokesperson immediately responded and accused the Shin Bet of leaking this. That's just one example; the Shin Bet is simply more attractive."[29]

~

During the years 1967–1973, the IDF reaped the fruits of the victory in the Six Day War, basked in the glory of success, and was immune to external criticism. These seven good years ended abruptly in the Yom Kippur War, and the IDF has never regained the same standing. The Shin Bet today enjoys similar glory and prestige, but there are also negative sides to the prominent exposure of the "Service," which stirs envy and invites criticism: "I want the Shin Bet to receive credit for the results of its activity, but the activity itself must remain secret," explains Benjamin Ben-Eliezer, a former general and defense minister. "I don't want the Shin Bet to buy favorable media coverage. It has powerful tools that protect it, and it has no need for the media. I feel that we've gone beyond this step."[30]

The Shin Bet directors who succeeded Dichter—Yuval Diskin, Yoram Cohen, and Nadav Argaman—have followed the path charted by their predecessors, each according to his own personality and management style. But the Shin Bet's relative openness and its contribution to the battle for consciousness against Palestinian terrorism have become established facts that no Shin Bet director can change.

∼

The new entity in Israeli public diplomacy is therefore a secret intelligence organization, mobilized to counter terrorism, in which media exposure has become a vital component. The Shin Bet has participated in shaping Israel's national public diplomacy policy at the decision-making level and has pursued a strategic approach with defined missions and proactive work plans. It realized that in order to solidify its public and media standing, it must adopt the tools of public diplomacy.

Chapter 10

Thinking Outside the Box

Or, We're Always Ready

The combination of globalization and technological innovation brought *nongovernmental organizations* (NGOs) into the center of global public diplomacy, including Israel-related NGOs. The Jewish people has a long history of engaging in nongovernmental action to promote its interests, and such activity was instrumental in creating the State of Israel. The institutionalization of this activity and the focus on public diplomacy peaked in the early 2000s with the outbreak of Palestinian violence. With the scope of governmental action contracting in many areas of life, these organizations filled the vacuum left by government authorities.

The need for public diplomacy grew, and NGOs became the long arm of Israeli public diplomacy. Studies of Israeli *hasbara* since 2000 concluded that NGOs were an important and relevant component and recommended that the state take them into account when planning its activity.[1]

Aryeh Green founded the Media Central organization to work with the foreign press. According to Green, "The government should do more, but it can't do everything. There's a need for more resources, more strategic planning. There are services the government is not supposed to provide, that no government provides."[2]

•

Israel conducts *Diaspora diplomacy* based on and in interaction with Jewish communities throughout the world. The largest of these communities lives in the United States—about 5.4 million Jews. There are reciprocal relations between Israel and the Jewish Diaspora: Israel accords communities of the Diaspora status and prestige, while the Diaspora reciprocates with political and financial support for Israel. Communications technologies reinforce the connection between the component parts of the Jewish people. Two-directional Internet communication boosts Israel's involvement in the communities, and vice versa. Small and remote Jewish communities can utilize the virtual space to maintain relations with other communities and with Israel. During times of crisis, Jewish communities rush to the aid of Israel with financial and political assistance. In the Jewish world, global and regional organizations have emerged that place the Jewish people and the State of Israel at the center of their activity. Some organizations completed their historic role and others arose in their place.

The Jewish world is full of organizations—some say it's excessively organized. This propensity to create organizations stems from a sense of Jewish identification, which brings individuals and communities closer together. Nonetheless, it should be noted that Jews throughout history have integrated into non-Jewish society and reached top positions in an impressive range of areas.

Alliance Israélite Universelle, the first modern international organization for Jewish advocacy and education, was founded in France in 1860 in the wake of the Mortara case in Italy. (The Vatican seized six-year-old Edgardo Mortara from his Jewish parents after a servant testified that she had baptized the boy when he was ill.) In the early 1900s, Jewish organizations were established in the United States to protect the interests of the Jewish public, particularly to fight anti-Semitism. These organizations expanded the scope of their activity over the years.

For example, the Anti-Defamation League (ADL) of B'nai B'rith was founded in 1913 to combat and document the various manifestations of anti-Semitism. Abraham Foxman, who began working at the ADL in 1965 and served as its national director from 1987 to 2015, adapted the organization's activities to keep pace with the evolving political and media arenas. The ADL monitors and exposes the connection between the new anti-Semitism and anti-Israelism. Over the years, the organization came to realize that it should fight all expressions of xenophobia and expand its activity to additional target audiences.

The American Jewish Committee was established in 1906 to advocate for Jewish immigrants. It also expanded its activities over the years, adding universal American values (such as the protection of all minorities) to its original mandate, and won international renown. The AJC's objectives today include fighting anti-Semitism and prejudice, promoting pluralism and democratic values, supporting Israel and its quest for peace, fostering Israel's independence, and strengthening American Jewish life. Over the years, the organization worked persistently and openly on behalf of the State of Israel in the American arena.

The Jewish Federations of North America (JFNA), an umbrella group of 400 communities and 155 federations, is a philanthropic organization that collects over $2 billion annually for the benefit of the Jewish people and State of Israel. In addition, it formed two subsidiary entities that specialize in public diplomacy on behalf of Israel: The Jewish Community Relations Council (JCRC), comprised of 125 regional councils, and the Jewish Council for Public Affairs (JCPA).

Other organizations include Keren Hayesod, the World Jewish Congress, Keren Hakayemet-Jewish National Fund, the Jewish Agency, the Joint Distribution Committee (JDC), and the Conference of Presidents of Major American Jewish Organizations.

•

The second intifada in the early 2000s engendered new NGOs that engage in pro-Israel *advocacy*. These were formative years in the field of advocacy. For example, the Israel Advocacy initiative is a special *hasbara* campaign the JFNA (formerly known as the United Jewish Communities) launched in the wake of Operation Defensive Shield in 2002. The campaign included five areas of activity: mobilizing the community, activity on college campuses, media action, response to anti-Israeli activity, and forging relations with non-Jewish opinion makers. The organization was the first to identify the collapse of pro-Israel sentiment on American campuses and began to build an infrastructure for protecting Israel's standing. It was also the first organization to take on the Lutheran and Presbyterian churches after they decided to divest from Israel—the first steps in the battle against the Boycott, Divestment, Sanctions (BDS) movement. At that time, the advocacy efforts were successful.

U.S. organizations focusing on advocacy expanded their activity to Canada, Britain, and South America, while new organizations with similar patterns of activity emerged in parallel in Britain, Germany, Australia, and elsewhere.

The Israel Project organization was also established following Operation Defensive Shield. Jennifer Laszlo Mizrahi was the driving force in creating the organization. She initially sought to operate within the framework of the American Israel Public Affairs Committee (AIPAC), but the Jewish lobbying group declined, saying that its target audiences are the U.S. administration and Congress. The Israel Project set out to strengthen Israel in four areas: foreign media, ongoing surveys in the United States and in Europe, training programs and seminars for spokespersons in the United States and in Israel, and strategic projects such as exposing Iranian threats against Israel.

The Israel Project opened an office for liaison with foreign correspondents in Jerusalem and offered the GPO to organize media events and even to replace it in providing other media services, such as arranging meetings and tours. Thus, it filled the vacuum the state had left in its relations with the foreign press. To raise money in the United States, the organization purchased airtime and ran commercial advertising campaigns on television. The Foreign Ministry, which refrained from spending funds on advertising campaigns, was not pleased by the Israel Project's activity in this area: "They generated hysteria surrounding Israeli public diplomacy, which caused us enormous damage in the Jewish community. You wouldn't believe what things came out of their activity. From the State of Israel's perspective, this was an irresponsible and reckless step."[3]

•

The prevailing view in the Jewish world vis-à-vis coverage of the Mideast conflict—that it is biased and unbalanced—led to the growth of *media-monitoring NGOs*. In many cases, this activity helps to correct biases and, in turn, influences policymakers. Some of these organizations focus on the Western press. CAMERA (Committee for Accuracy in Middle East Reporting in America), founded during the first Lebanon War, was one of the first to do this. It seeks to generate public pressure on the media to force it to correct the imprecise facts it publishes. Over the years, it also became active on American campuses. In March 2008, the organization exposed problematic coverage on the BBC,[4] compelling the network to admit its errors and apologize. CAMERA also expanded its activity to include the Spanish language (Revista), with the aim of addressing the large Hispanic population in the United States—about 30 million people.

On Yom Kippur 2000, just as the second intifada erupted, the Honest Reporting organization was founded. Like CAMERA, this organization sprang from frustration with media coverage of Israel. Three months after its inception, the founders approached the Aish Hatorah Foundation for assistance in building an Internet site, developing *hasbara* materials, and boosting the number of subscribers. Two years later, a similar organization arose in Canada, followed by another one in Britain in 2006. In practice, the organization monitors reports in the media and asks the reporting agency to correct any bias or inaccuracy it detects.

Another group of NGOs, including MEMRI (Middle East Media Research Institute) and PMW (Palestinian Media Watch), monitors the Muslim and Arab media. Yigal Carmon, a former IDF intelligence officer, founded MEMRI in 1998 with the aim of "bridging the language gap between the West and the Middle East." After defining the region to monitor (Egypt and North Africa, Iraq, Saudi Arabia, Iran, Syria, Lebanon, the Palestinian Authority, Turkey, Libya, and Sudan), Carmon established offices in London, Berlin, and Moscow. The NGO translated its research materials into additional languages and later opened an office in Iraq too. All funding for MEMRI's activity comes from donations and from selling services; its requests for government support or assistance from other institutional bodies have been rejected. Carmon notes, "I realized I had no one to speak with, it was simply a waste of time. The Foreign Ministry—I don't want to hear about it. They give money to 'Aish Hatorah.' No one helps me, I wouldn't accept it, but I can't even say that someone offered."[5] Carmon and Itamar Marcus, the founder of PMW, do not merely communicate the material directly or via networks; they launch *hasbara* campaigns and meet with decision makers and opinion makers.

PMW was founded in 1996, after the Oslo Accords, with the aim of exposing Palestinian duplicity: talking peace to the world while spewing incitement in Arabic. When the second intifada erupted, the organization revised its mission. Instead of speaking to policy makers in Israel in Hebrew, it started to publish in English and direct its activities toward audiences outside of Israel. It connected to large networks of Israel supporters and reached millions of people. Marcus deploys spokespersons outside of Israel, provides them with *hasbara* materials and information, and asks them to make an impact on the local level.[6] MEMRI and PMW are again two examples of private initiatives that replaced official state activity.

•

Private initiatives and NGOs arose in response to the dearth of *Israeli state broadcasts in the international arena* and Israel's failure to utilize this significant tool in new public diplomacy. In contrast, there is a wealth of Arabic-language networks and channels. In March 2008, Israel Radio canceled its shortwave broadcasts, except for those in Parsi, and English broadcasts were incorporated in the REKA (IBA International) network, which broadcasts mainly in Russian. The only remaining option for overseas listeners was the website of the Israel Broadcasting Authority (IBA), which had a limited capacity.

The new initiatives all seek to provide broadcasting content from Israel, and most are based on the Internet and new media. The privately owned i24news began broadcasting from Israel in July 2013 in Arabic, English, and French. As noted earlier, i24 began cable broadcasting in Israel in 2018 after the enactment of an amendment I sponsored. The new public broadcasting corporation in Israel includes a plan for an Arabic-language channel, but its broadcast range is not required to cover the entire Middle East.

Earlier initiatives include The Israeli Network, which began broadcasting in September 2001 and today reaches several tens of thousands of paying subscribers—mainly in the United States but also in Europe, Canada, Australia, and New Zealand.

The Jewish Life Television Network (JLTV) is an initiative by the American television producer Phil Blazer. "It's an educational and entertainment channel aimed at inspiring the Jewish community and teaching the non-Jewish community, not in a missionary or fundamentalist way, about Israel and about Judaism, for example, soft (Jewish) power. An example of this power is the broadcast of the Nobel Prize award ceremony from Sweden: This is a 'Jewish event' because a high percentage of Nobel Prize recipients are Jews; or, alternatively, programs that illustrate the contributions of Jewish athletes to American sports."[7]

Infolive TV provides information and content at no cost via the Internet, funding itself through sponsorships and advertisements. Olivier Rafowicz, founder and CEO of Infolive TV, offers two news programs a day, news bulletins, in-depth reports, and interviews with Israeli figures.

Jerusalem Online is an Internet news service in English. The site was launched in August 2005 and has tens of thousands of subscribers, according to its managers. Unlike other sites, the channel receives prepared television materials and edits them in English translation for its viewing audience. It is funded by donations, advertisements, and sponsorships.

•

The GPO bears the primary responsibility for providing services for the foreign press. After Ehud Barak cut its budget, it retained mainly technical roles, issuing visas and press credentials. However, Israel cannot afford to neglect the important task of cultivating relations with the foreign press. Four Jerusalem-based NGOs stepped in to fill this vacuum.

Media Central was founded in 2006 by Honest Reporting to deal with the community of foreign correspondents. It offers a site in central Jerusalem where journalists can come to receive information services, lectures by experts, translations, technological infrastructure, and briefings.

The Israel Newsmakers Forum (INFO) also works with foreign correspondents. The organization is located in the Mishkenot Sha'ananim cultural center in Jerusalem, funded by the Jerusalem Foundation, and offers the foreign press tours and meetings with Israeli figures. The model for Mishkenot Sha'ananim, according to its director Uri Dromi, is the American Colony Hotel in East Jerusalem, where Palestinians conduct *hasbara* among foreign reporters. INFO is designed to serve as the Israeli counterpart.

Media Line is a unique news NGO that seeks to encourage balanced media coverage, strengthen independent reporting from the Middle East, and remove cultural barriers between Israeli and Arab journalists.

A fourth NGO that operates in this field is the Israel Project, described earlier.

•

American campuses have become a central front in public diplomacy. Veteran institutional organizations such as Hillel and B'nai B'rith have always operated on campuses. Many of the organizations that arose in the 21st century have focused their activities on campuses, based on the assumption that people shape their worldviews during their college years and that the students they influence will someday fill key roles in American society. The increasing importance of molding public opinion led to the formation of organizations such as Israel at Heart. This organization, the personal initiative of New York businessman Joey Low, began operating in 2002 in the wake of Operation Defensive Shield. At first, Low invited to the United States two Israeli combat soldiers who had participated in the fighting in Jenin. Later in 2002, he brought 16 groups for tours at American universities. He has continued to finance this activity from personal funds and from contributions by his friends. "I looked for Israelis who live regular lives and can find a common denominator with American counterparts. It is now conventional to talk about 'Israel beyond the conflict,' and I think that I clearly had an impact in this direction, of looking differently at Israel and at its successes in various fields."[8]

Stand With Us is an international educational organization founded in response to the second intifada. It seeks to ensure that Israel is properly presented in communities, libraries, campuses, and the media. The organization has branches in a number of major U.S. cities and in Israel. Its activities include fundraising, sending gift packages, blood donations, visits, and promoting Israel's interests in the media.

The American-Israeli Cooperative Enterprise (AICE) engages in new public diplomacy at campuses throughout the United States. It provides content to students interested in Jewish history, culture, and politics, along with training on the use of this information. AICE offers a virtual Jewish library, publications such as *Myths & Facts: A Guide to the Arab-Israeli Conflict*, advocacy training, and a program that brings about 25 lecturers from Israel to teach for one year at American universities. This program, funded by the Charles and Lynn Schusterman Family Foundation, is a response to dozens of Arab-funded Middle East research institutes that engage in Arab public diplomacy at American universities.

These multiple activities created the need for coordination. This is a familiar weakness of organizations in the United States, which often step on each other's toes. Consequently, the Israel on Campus Coalition was formed as an umbrella organization for most of the pro-Israel organizations operating on American campuses. The coalition, funded by the Schusterman Foundation and the Hillel organization, formulated three methods of operation: strengthening strategic cooperation, boosting Israel supporters on campuses, and coordinating and directing the efforts of pro-Israel organizations. The coalition united individual organizations into a network and lifted their activity from the local to the national level.

•

NGOs involved in Israel's public diplomacy brought this activity into new areas. During the past decade, this was particularly salient in the field of *humanitarian assistance*. The IsraAID NGO, comprising 35 Israeli humanitarian organizations, was formed in 2001 with the aim of providing urgent assistance during humanitarian crises in the world. This activity has a potent and long-term impact. In the past, during humanitarian crises, veteran organizations such as JDC, B'nai B'rith, the AJC, and JFNA have provided rapid monetary and other assistance. They are now joined by new organizations such as Medical Cadets, the Humanitarian Fund of the Kibbutz Movement, the Students' Association of Israel, and Aid Without Borders. "Our objective is to strengthen Israeli assistance, increase monetary resources, and expand the activity. If, as a result of this, the media in those disaster areas portray Israel in a different, positive light, that's good," says Shachar Zahavi, IsraAID's CEO.[9] The organization recently began activity in Germany, working to assist the many refugees arriving there from the civil war in Syria.

Israeli officials recognize the wisdom of humanitarian assistance and readily dispatch delegations during crises and natural disasters—including Haiti in 2010, Turkey and Greece in 1999, and Mexico in 1995. Israel offers proven capabilities in rapidly deploying field hospitals, as well as experience in rescuing the injured at sites of terrorist attacks.

•

International NGOs in the field of human rights intensified their involvement during the second intifada and generally adopted an anti-Israeli stance. In light of their high international standing, this had severe repercussions for Israel. Against this background, and in the wake of the 2001 Durban conference, Gerald Steinberg of Bar-Ilan University founded the NGO Monitor organization in 2002. NGO Monitor conducts critical research on publications issued by these organizations and offers its findings to the media, philanthropic institutions, diplomats, scholars, and the general public. NGO Monitor aims to expose bias in the work of human rights organizations and guide them toward a balanced approach to the conflict. In 2016, in part due to the NGO Monitor's activity, the Knesset enacted the NGO Law, designed to closely examine the international funding received by Israeli NGOs. The legislation stirred strong criticism in the United States and in Europe, but the government of Israel dismissed this criticism.

Additional initiatives during this period include the creation of the Israel 21C organization, which focuses on commercial diplomacy, particularly in the United States, and Israfest, an organization that promotes *cultural diplomacy*. Israfest seeks to introduce American audiences to the social and cultural diversity of Israel.

•

The second intifada sparked significant changes in Israel's official and unofficial public diplomacy. While the official entities adapted themselves to the new public diplomacy and its tools, a large group of NGOs mobilized in a range of pro-Israel activities. In the context of the new public diplomacy and low-intensity violence, *hasbara* activists had to reorganize to operate at the pace of the new media technologies and in accordance with globalization.

NGO activity includes both short-term efforts (such as the Israel Project) and long-term efforts (such as Israel 21C). The broad range of time frames, areas of activity, and target audiences is impressive. This activity provides a foundation for sustainable networks of new and more extensive public diplomacy, exploiting the potential of the latest communications technologies.

Chapter 11

"National Explainer"

The years 2000–2008 were critical in the formation of a centralized array of public diplomacy in Israel. The security events that occurred during those years—the second intifada, the Second Gulf War, the disengagement from the Gaza Strip, and the Second Lebanon War—forged a political consensus that led to the creation of the infrastructure of a national *hasbara* array. While not yet centralized, it was a crucial step, reflecting the lessons learned from these military crises.

On October 2, 2000, immediately after the start of the second intifada, the Foreign Ministry established a media center specifically designed to serve the foreign press. Foreign correspondents, unlike local journalists, lacked a central base of operations, and a meeting place was needed for joint activity with purveyors of public diplomacy. In the past, the Government Press Office (GPO) had been responsible for creating this type of hub, but this time the Foreign Ministry took the initiative and set up the center at the Isrotel Hotel in Jerusalem. The ministry offered other government ministries and the GPO to join it, and the GPO, IDF Spokesperson's Unit, Israel Police, and IDF Censor all set up operations there. Prominently absent was the Prime Minister's Office (PMO), where two senior positions remained vacant—head of the *Hasbara* Division and foreign media advisor.

The "national explainer" is an official state position that was always filled in the past by military or uniformed personnel. This position entails explaining the military situation to the public from an official perspective.

The media center in Jerusalem served about 2,000 journalists and conducted daily briefings as well as ad hoc press conferences as needed. Foreign Ministry overseas missions connected to it via the ministry's Internet site. The center formulated daily *hasbara* messages that were communicated to the foreign media and the ministry's overseas missions. Regretfully, due to the high cost of operating the center, it was soon shut down.

∼

Three days after the center was formed, Maj. Gen. (ret.) Danny Yatom, the head of the prime minister's political-security staff, asked me to coordinate Israel's *hasbara* during the outbreak of what came to be known as the second intifada. This request—backed by Ehud Barak, who served as both prime minister and defense minister, and Shlomo Ben-Ami, the foreign minister—came in the wake of what the press described as "the collapse of Israel's *hasbara* array."[1] Israeli spokespersons found it hard to contend mainly with the gruesome visual coverage of the intifada and the anti-Israel reactions broadcast throughout the world. I accepted the offer, but on the condition that I would not only coordinate public diplomacy but also actively guide and deploy the *hasbara* array. I began directing the media center, turning it into the headquarters of Israeli *hasbara*.

In addition to conducting daily press briefings, the center built a flexible system to rapidly respond to unanticipated events, such as the abduction of three soldiers at Har Dov on October 7, 2000, or the lynching of IDF soldiers in Ramallah on October 12, 2000. First, I appealed to Israel's police commissioner to loosen restrictions and allow the media (and television crews, in particular) to cover the scenes of terror attacks. A similar call went out to the IDF chief of staff, which also included a request to deploy operational documentation photographers.

The center served as a one-stop shop for inquiries from the public, as well as serving the Israeli and foreign media. It facilitated an ongoing exchange of information among the official entities engaged in public diplomacy. Nonetheless, as customary in Israel, every political figure tends to respond to news events in his or her own way. There was no coordination to begin with. A daily page of messages the center issued was intended to help the "explainers" but could not force them to speak in the same spirit and create a uniform message.

Disseminating a uniform message is one of the fundamental challenges in a *hasbara* campaign. At the beginning of the second intifada, for example, a disagreement arose between Prime Minister Ehud Barak and two of his ministers (Shlomo Ben-Ami and Shimon Peres) about how to interpret the Palestinian violence: Did the Palestinian Authority initiate the violence or did it erupt spontaneously? In turn, this raised the question of whether Israel should direct its criticism at Arafat and pin him with responsibility for the events. The prime minister decided to commission a white paper that would describe in detail the Palestinians' acts of violence and Arafat's direct involvement in terror. He convened a taskforce chaired by Yatom and guided its work. As the team collected the incriminating material, it quickly became apparent that the PMO and Foreign Ministry were at loggerheads over its content.[2] The rapidly gathered material included documents and photographs that proved Arafat's role in terrorism and described how he had violated agreements and encouraged violence. When the report was complete, the PMO instructed the Foreign Ministry to distribute it to its missions, but the ministry announced that it did not intend to do so. "We had a big argument about the white paper: Barak and Danny Yatom were in favor of disseminating it, but Shlomo Ben-Ami forbid this. This was another small disagreement between Barak and Ben-Ami: Should we discredit Arafat?"[3] After the bombing of a bus carrying children from Kfar Darom on November 20, 2000—and despite opposition from the Foreign Ministry—the Israeli public's anger and frustration pushed the PMO to distribute the document.

A second dispute arose between Prime Minister Ariel Sharon and Foreign Minister Peres during Operation Defensive Shield regarding Arafat's responsibility for the outbreak of the intifada.[4] There was not always consensus in the PMO either—for example, contradictory statements were issued by PMO officials concerning the Arab summit conference in Cairo in late November 2000.[5] Conclusion: Lack of coordination.

In the field of governmental strategic thinking, four teams worked without any connection or coordination among them, other than the occasional exchange of working papers. Three of them operated within the IDF Spokesperson's Unit, and I, in my new position, convened a fourth team of media experts, retired diplomats, reserve officers, academics, and businesspeople with extensive experience in the international arena. The Foreign Ministry also conducted strategic thinking of this type. When the media interviewed the state's leaders, the disagreements between them were plain to see. Unlike the chaos on the Israeli side, the Palestinians had a small number of spokespersons who adhered to uniform *hasbara* guidelines in their public appearances.

I asked the prime minister to participate in the cabinet weekly meetings and in the special meetings of the defense cabinet, explaining that it was vital for government ministers to receive a public diplomacy professional's assessment at the decision-making stage and not only in the aftermath. My request was approved—though with some limitations—and I was indeed given the opportunity to present the full array of public diplomacy considerations on the topics under discussion. Unfortunately, I was not invited to all the meetings.

Conclusion: The public diplomacy dimension was missing.

Due to the high cost of operating the media center, it was decided to move to Beit Agron, where the GPO is located. However, two weeks later the center and the entire *hasbara* array were completely shut down. Thus, the same old mistake was repeated. In the absence of a media center and *hasbara* array, coordination among the various players diminished, while the intifada, on the other hand, raged with increasing intensity, demanding greater coordinated efforts in the field of public diplomacy.

Conclusion: Lack of resources.

At this stage, I decided to end my temporary service as the head of the *hasbara* array and return to my previous position.

When Sharon became prime minister, his bureau chief, Uri Shani, reached the conclusion that Israel needed a *hasbara* ministry. As noted, a ministry of this sort had been created several times in the past, but each time it was eventually eliminated. Sharon, prodded by Shani, tried at least to appoint a minister to coordinate *hasbara* affairs, and he asked Minister Tzipi Livni to take on this responsibility. Livni agreed and began to study her new and unfamiliar role. Four months later, she finally announced that she had defined the nature of this role in consultation with the prime minister: "There is a supreme need for overall government guidance on the issue of *hasbara*, but we need to determine who is responsible for Israel's *hasbara* policy. This is not only the question of who will manage the *hasbara*; it's also a question of what the policy is and how to coordinate among the different players."[6]

As usual, the Foreign Ministry, this time under Shimon Peres, rejected any reform in the *hasbara* business and preferred to keep the status quo. As a result, Livni's new role was completely neutralized.

~

Efforts continued, and the next stage was a project initiated in 2002 by Brig. Gen. (ret.) Israela Oron, the deputy director of the National Security Council. Oron composed a groundbreaking and revolutionary document on the State of Israel's political, military, and security *hasbara*: "Proposal for a *Hasbara* Array." For the first time since the failed attempts to establish a *hasbara* ministry, there was a working paper on the table that included strategic vision and organizational structure, calling for the creation of a centralized array for public diplomacy. After thoroughly examining all the options, Oron recommended that the array be subordinate to the prime minister. However, much to her chagrin, Oron's recommendations were shelved. She explains: "Due to both political and personal considerations, the ministers rejected my proposals. In my view, the fact that the Foreign Ministry is deployed throughout the world does not necessarily mean that it should be the supreme and exclusive authority dealing with Israeli *hasbara*."[7] Despite the setback, Oron's efforts marked another stage toward establishing a centralized array of public diplomacy.

~

For years, the state comptroller has called for establishing a central *hasbara* array. On October 7, 2002, he released a new report, stating: "The lack of a supreme authority to guide and coordinate all of the governmental *hasbara* entities has been a main cause of the failures in this area over the years. . . . The recurring effort over the years to provide a suitable solution for this problem in the Prime Minister's Office did not succeed, and efforts to establish a center of professional knowledge in the Prime Minister's Office failed."[8] From 1985 to 2002, the state comptroller submitted four reports pertaining to public diplomacy: Three focused on the Foreign Ministry and one on the IDF Spokesperson's Unit. Each report highlighted the flaws in *hasbara*, despite the repeated critiques, particularly the lack of a supreme and a professional authority.

Maj. Gen. (ret.) Yaakov Orr was the official in the State Comptroller's Office responsible for scrutinizing the defense establishment. Orr, an experienced and highly regarded officer, concluded that the government would remain unable to advance this issue until it designated a supreme authority to guide and oversee a uniform, integrated, and coordinated *hasbara* policy spanning the entire government. He explicitly called for the establishment of a national *hasbara* array, because "there has been no regular and orderly response to the urgent need for an integrated and coordinated *hasbara* array at the national level."[9]

∼

Prior to the Second Gulf War, Israel prepared for potential Iraqi missile strikes, as it had done during the First Gulf War. Again, Israel was particularly concerned about biological or chemical weapons. The government debated whether to adopt strict precautions that required public preparation, or to maintain a low profile and wait to see if and how the threat developed. Prime Minister Sharon chose the strict approach, taking no risks, and again ordered the formation of a national *hasbara* array, this time led by a former IDF spokesperson, Maj. Gen. Amos Gilad. The security cabinet approved Sharon's request to appoint Gilad as the "national explainer." This appointment immediately stirred opposition and turmoil both within the government ministries and the IDF.[10]

In the end, Israel was not dragged into the Second Gulf War, though on two occasions the citizens of Israel were indirectly involved. On February 18, 2003, the IDF spokesperson, on his own initiative, advised the public to immediately purchase essential items and to prepare sealed rooms; on March 19, the IDF spokesperson again instructed the public to carry their gas masks with them until further notice. The second directive came in response to confusion created by contradictory television news reports: Channel 2 mistakenly reported that the IDF Home Front Command had ordered the citizens of Israel to open their gas masks, while Channel 10 and Channel 1 instructed their viewers to refrain from doing so. The conflicting reports forced the PMO to issue an order: The residents of Israel should open and carry their protective kits.[11] This typical series of events underlined the lack of coordination among the different *hasbara* authorities and vis-à-vis the media. The *Haaretz* daily noted the difference between the First Gulf War and the Second Gulf War: "While in 1991, there was one IDF spokesperson and an electronic media whose broadcasts were forcibly merged. This time, there will be a wealth of 'explainers' without any clear hierarchy among them, who are already engaged in a free-for-all of mudslinging."[12]

Public diplomacy during the war left a number of open questions. For example, who was supposed to instruct the civilian population? It turns out that both the IDF Spokesperson's Unit and the IDF Home Front Command, in parallel, set up emergency studios designed to perform the same role. More crucial was the question of who was authorized to interrupt regularly scheduled radio and television broadcasts to instruct the population how to act in emergency situations. The various radio and television channels, which had grown in number, were unwilling to yield airtime to the state. The confrontation reached the Supreme Court, which accepted the state's arguments and confirmed the state's option to interrupt routine broadcasts. However, the court prohibited the state from interfering with foreign news broadcasts. Thus, it was clear that the new media reality of multiple channels in Israel and abroad made it harder for the government to disseminate different information through local and foreign channels. A third issue was the appointment of a "national explainer" to speak on the government's behalf. As noted, the appointment of Sharon's confidante, Maj. Gen. (ret.) Amos Gilad, to this position was not well received in the IDF and civilian authorities. A report by the Knesset Foreign Affairs and Defense Committee on the Iraq War stated: "The committee believes that the appointment of a 'national explainer,' as authoritative and talented as he might be, to centralize and coordinate the *hasbara* strategy, was wrong. . . . In practice, the appointment of the national explainer became the fifth wheel on the *hasbara* cart, resulting in a lack of clarity and even sowing confusion among the public."[13]

On December 7, 2003, following deliberations about the Foreign Ministry's budget, the government assigned Cabinet Secretary Israel Maimon a challenging task—to study and formulate recommendations on how to reinforce Israel's *hasbara* array. Forty-five days were allotted for this task, but four years would pass before Maimon and his team finally presented their recommendations.

During this four-year period, two major developments occurred, underlining the need for a centralized array. In March 2005, after 38 years, Israel decided to disengage from the Gaza Strip, and Sharon again appointed one of his advisors, Brig. Gen. (ret.) Eival Gilady, to lead national *hasbara*. Gilady was instructed to mobilize all government ministries, but, as usual, disagreements arose between the PMO and the other ministries, and between Gilady and the IDF Spokesperson's Unit, the strongest entity in Israel's public diplomacy.

The second development occurred during the summer of 2006. Hezbollah ambushed an IDF patrol, killing three soldiers and taking two others captive. This led to a major confrontation between Israel and Hezbollah. In contrast to the second intifada, a typical case of low-intensity warfare, the Second Lebanon War was a conflict of high intensity between a state's large military force and a paramilitary organization operating within a neighboring state and exercising greater force than a guerrilla organization.[14] That is the primary difference between Israel's first war in Lebanon, in 1982, when the IDF defeated the PLO, driving it out of Lebanon, and the Second Lebanon War. Other aspects of the war in 2006 were similar to the second intifada: a basic clash of asymmetric forces,[15] a massive assault on the home front, and a blurring of the terms "defeat" and "victory" at the end of the conflict.

Again, in this war, the State of Israel failed to deploy a central public diplomacy array, despite the state comptroller's multiple reports on *hasbara* and the fact that a draft version of Maimon's recommendations was already available. The government met on July 12, 2006, and voted to go to war, and Olmert appointed his media advisor, Asaf Shariv, to coordinate the national *hasbara* effort. Three weeks later, Shariv asked to be relieved due to an overload of work and was replaced by Maimon. Nonetheless, it again became apparent that, in practice, the IDF Spokesperson's Unit was the national spokesperson, only it had the extensive organizational apparatus and comprehensive planning capability and vision required for public diplomacy in a war of this scale.

Numerous reports were submitted after the Second Lebanon War, and about 10 of them addressed public diplomacy. Together, the reports present an almost complete picture of the war outcome, though a precise account will be available only 50 years from now, when war documents are released. Four of the main reports—the Winograd Commission Report, the State Comptroller's Report 58A, the Gellert Committee Report (an internal committee of the IDF Spokesperson's Unit), and the report of the Knesset's *Hasbara* Subcommittee—thoroughly addressed key public diplomacy issues.

∼

The reports said that Israel's public diplomacy failures in the Second Lebanon War were similar to previous flaws, which came as no surprise to anyone familiar with this history. Though the Israeli-Palestinian conflict takes place in the Middle East, it is affected by the four components of the new international arena—globalization, technology, diplomacy, and war.

These four components create a new environment that dictates new rules of engagement vis-à-vis the media. The new conflicts are small in scope; however, thanks to the new technology, every local incident quickly turns global. Representatives of both the new and traditional media report live from the scene of every incident, sharing it immediately with the entire world. In general, the Middle East today contains a number of limited conflicts and intensive terror activities. It is a sort of laboratory of present and future wars. The salient conflict is between Israel and the Palestinians, but there are other low-intensity conflicts in other junctions in the Middle East, such as the struggle of Kurds in Iraq and in Turkey and the international struggle against ISIS. Thus, in conducting war, states should be prepared for the media's presence everywhere and at all times and should allocate resources and means to win this battle too.

∼

The Israeli political and social environment creates the atmosphere and conditions in which Israeli public diplomacy operates. Policymaking in this field is not different from other strategic organizational processes of planning, implementation, and follow-up. Five components of public diplomacy have been identified to verify its effectiveness and success: overall strategy, strategic planning, operative preparations, implementation, and assessment/monitoring/research.

Public diplomacy is a component in every diplomatic or military decision in which economic and legal aspects also play a role. Israel has failed to place public diplomacy at the forefront, alongside other top-priority fronts.

Thus, Maimon concluded that an overall vision was needed for public diplomacy, unlike the present situation, where each entity addresses a different target audience: "No single entity sees the complete picture of the *hasbara*. In fact, there is no one to dictate *hasbara* policy. Only one entity in the State of Israel is able to do so—the Prime Minister's Office. The overall policy originates from the PMO and therefore they need to explain it too."[16] The foreign minister at the time, Tzipi Livni, unlike her predecessors, was the first to support Maimon's view that the PMO is the place where overall strategy should be formulated.[17]

The *hasbara*-media aspect was lacking not only at the initial strategic level but also when planning diplomatic and military operations. Advanced planning is required in Israel due to the ongoing state of emergency and the rapid transition from routine to emergency. The IDF has contingency plans that enable it to rapidly respond to terror attacks and other security events, and it should be similarly prepared to act vis-à-vis the media. Public diplomacy should be an integral part of the entire process, starting with the planning stage. "If there is no serious entity that works routinely, continually, with in-depth thinking, which engages in ongoing assessment—it won't work in times of emergency,"[18] concluded Gadi Eizenkot, a future IDF chief of staff, a year after the Second Lebanon War.

In the tactical dimension, when preparing for a military operation or diplomatic activity, public diplomacy must be a full partner. Precise planning should already include the role of the media—before, during, and after the event. Since the media will sooner or later report each incident, planners must take into account the *hasbara*-media consideration during the planning stage. Former diplomat and MK Colette Avital emphasizes: "If we want to embark on an operation or refrain from it, the government must consider in the decision-making process how this aspect will affect Israel's image, how the countries of the world will react, what will return as a boomerang and what the price will be. Only then will the correct decision be made."[19] Maimon, the former cabinet secretary, believes that the proposed National *Hasbara* Forum should prepare action files for emergency situations in advance: "When needed, we'll pull them out. *Hasbara* comprises the essence, the policy, the messages, and the tools. We have to prepare the tools of *hasbara* and not only the essence."[20]

The flaws increase as the process moves toward implementation. The weaknesses of the government and public system combine with the lack of strategic thinking at both the tactical and strategic levels. All of this affects the implementation of policy in the following areas:

1. The need for both *speedy and credible* responses becomes more acute in the wake of technological developments and the nature of warfare, which create new situations, such as harm to noncombatants: "We need to immediately respond to all of the accusations directed against us and provide the media with precise and rapid answers,"[21] asserts the veteran American Jewish leader Malcolm Hoenlein.

2. The *multiplicity of state entities* that engage in public diplomacy is a welcome phenomenon in itself, but there is a need to coordinate them in order to communicate a uniform message. The message does not represent only one way of thinking, but rather a range of expressions that converge around a shared policy. The lack of multiple voices dims the uniform message and detracts from its public presentation. It is customary to explain the diversity of voices in Israel's public policy as evidence of its democratic political system.

However, that is only a partial answer. Many politicians express their views on foreign and security matters without coordinating this with the entities responsible for public diplomacy and without the requisite information. While the media is happy to be able to draw from a variety of statements, it is difficult for an outside observer to discern a clear and coherent policy of public diplomacy.

3. Public diplomacy is conducted on two levels: at the elected echelon—by politicians from the government and the Knesset; and at the professional echelon—by professional spokespersons. Both levels should be *up-to-date and precise*, should be closely familiar with the media arena, and should cultivate public-speaking skills.

4. Israeli public diplomacy responds slowly to *technological innovations* that offer new possibilities and can boost the effectiveness of *hasbara*. The Internet, for example, is a central means of communication in the world today, offering a wealth of tools for the new public policy—tools that span borders and are accessible to many. It is the central platform for two-directional communication between the state (and its agencies) and each of its target audiences. The Maimon team totally ignored technological issues at first, but the government later recognized the essential role the Internet plays, and a special team was assigned to study how to utilize the Internet in public diplomacy.

5. In light of this data and the research the Maimon team conducted, as well as Israel's experiences in the Second Lebanon War and the disengagement, Maimon recommended the creation of a national *hasbara* array. The government would later adopt his recommendations, with some revisions, as explained later. Still, we return to the budget issue: "When the *hasbara* budget of the Foreign Ministry is $8 million, including the salaries of *hasbara* attachés, clearly this is zero," says former Foreign Minister Silvan Shalom. "Just for comparison—the advertising budget of the Pelephone cellular company is $15 million."[22] After discussing the recommendations of the Maimon team, the government decided to increase the Foreign Ministry's *hasbara* budget, but the increase was earmarked for the

branding project only and not for the ministry's public diplomacy activity.

⁓

Recent years have underlined the vital need for a centralized array of public diplomacy and tipped the scale in its favor. It is gradually becoming apparent that Israel followed a winding path of public policy during its first 60 years and is now transitioning from a decentralized system to a centralized array. Public diplomacy is struggling to gain a leading role in the national decision-making process. All solutions so far were based on reaction and response to a given crisis situation. The system should produce an optimal organization, designed for the Israeli case and parallel to the existing systems in other states operating under similar conditions.

Chapter 12

Blood on Their Hands

The lynching in Ramallah is first a shocking human drama, but it also reflects severe flaws in the decision-making process in Israel, including the indifference toward public diplomacy. In the wake of the lynching, Israel was swept by a mood of incitement at home and failed to exploit an opportunity to create legitimacy in world public opinion.

•

On October 12, 2000, Vadim Nurzhitz and Yossi Avrahami, IDF reservists, drove in a private vehicle toward the military base where they served, near Ramallah. They lost their way and wound up in the city itself. The two were arrested by Palestinian police at a checkpoint by the entrance to Ramallah and taken to the police station for questioning.[1] The news of their arrest and associated rumors quickly spread, drawing thousands of people to the station demanding that the two soldiers be handed over to them. When the police officers refused, the mob broke into the station. They pushed the Palestinian police officers aside and went up to the second floor, where the soldiers were held. The police officers fled and the mob attacked the soldiers, beating them viciously. One of the soldiers was thrown from the second-floor window and beaten to death by Palestinians who had gathered outside the building.[2] "The event is a result of the incitement broadcast on the Palestinian media," said the head of the Operations Directorate, Maj. Gen. Giora Eiland. "Yesterday they saw on Palestinian television a training exercise on a model and today they did it 'live.'"[3]

In the afternoon, the bodies of the two soldiers were transferred to the IDF coordination and liaison base. "There's no longer anyone to save," said the physician who examined them.[4] Journalists reporting from the Palestinian police station initially said that three soldiers were involved but then correctly stated: Two soldiers had been murdered. Israel debated whether to publicize photographs of the dead soldiers. The policy was not to publish pictures of terror victims to protect their privacy and dignity, but the *hasbara* interest took precedence this time.[5]

The IDF spokesperson at the time, Ron Kitri, was one of those who wrestled with this question: "The bodies came back to us mutilated. We photographed the bodies and prepared 70 copies at the IDF Spokesperson's Unit. The photographs were horrific. The chief of staff decided we shouldn't use them. Due to the sensitivity, the intention was not to disseminate them to the media, just to show the photographs to the decision makers. The proposal was rejected."[6] Then-minister Dan Meridor thought the pictures shouldn't be shown: "Their impact is short-term at most, and their damage is long-term."[7] On the other hand, the deputy defense minister, Dr. Ephraim Sneh, explicitly asked the defense minister to use photos of the bodies for *hasbara* purposes: "I told him to convene all of the ambassadors, and in the second round the senior foreign correspondents, without cameras and to send them right away to Abu Kabir [the forensic institute where the bodies were held]. He asked me whether I was saying this as an expert in pathology. No, as an expert in *hasbara*, I responded. Of course, nothing was done. This is an example of the lack of conceptual readiness for this. I think this changed a bit later in the intifada."[8] Maj. Gen. (ret.) Uzi Dayan thinks the dilemma stemmed primarily from Israel's shame and discomfiture over what had been done to its soldiers.[9]

Ehud Barak, serving as prime minister and defense minister, was in his office meeting with representatives of the Yesha Council of Jewish Settlements when the news arrived about the lynching in Ramallah. Yehoshua Mor-Yosef, one of the Yesha Council leaders at the meeting, recalls: "'If the reports coming in now are indeed correct,' Barak said, 'then everything will look different starting this evening.' We expected to seize control of Ramallah at least."[10] The television reporter Shlomi Eldar heard Barak's advisors trying to convince him not "to go crazy,"[11] but they also explained that public opinion in Israel expected a response. "Even before the lynching in Ramallah, most of the public said in surveys that Barak was showing excessive restraint. The IDF deployed combat helicopters and its soldier fired in all directions, but the public's message to the prime minister was that from its perspective he was not in control, was not in the know, wasn't fulfilling their wishes. . . . Barak felt pressed. In the discussions, he kept demanding that the army provide him with targets, and when there were none, he called for attacking buildings, Palestinian Authority institutions, whatever."[12]

Barak instructed the air force to present him with targets for attacking in Ramallah and Gaza. Gadi Baltiansky, Barak's media advisor, noted that President Bill Clinton tried to reach Barak on the telephone to dissuade him from retaliating, but the prime minister didn't answer the call in order to avoid a confrontation.[13] "The lynching occurred at noon. At 4:00 p.m., we decided to attack. The defense minister conducted a very short discussion and gave the order to attack a maximum number of targets in the Palestinian Authority, from Jenin [in the West Bank] to Jabaliya [in the Gaza Strip]."[14] The IDF spokesperson was not invited to the operational discussion, so he was not able to express his view on the proposed plans.[15]

The IDF responded quickly by deploying helicopters to fire at targets, some of which were unrelated to the lynching. Israeli diplomat Gideon Meir called this response "Pavlovian." His Foreign Ministry colleague Meir Shlomo described it as "real estate attacks," a phrase also used by Avi Dichter, the Shin Bet chief at the time.[16] This pattern was repeated a month later, when a bus carrying children was bombed in Kfar Darom, a Jewish settlement in the Gaza Strip: "That evening, there was a hysterical attack, fifteen targets in Gaza. . . . When this works to your benefit, you quickly hit back, based on internal considerations, on Barak's considerations of political embarrassment," says *Haaretz* correspondent Amos Harel.[17]

Barak convened the Ministerial Committee on National Security Affairs that evening, after the IDF's first attack and after pictures of the lynching had already appeared on television. "I remember the expressions of horror and pain, and the feelings of vengeance among the most senior people in the state, as they came to the government meeting at the Defense Ministry in Tel Aviv," says Gilead Sher, Barak's bureau chief at the time. "When the ministers enter the government session enraged and with completely human feelings of vengeance, you're convinced as a semi-active observer that a very big operation will emerge from here."[18]

The ministers expressed approval for the initial attack and authorized Barak to order additional air assaults in the West Bank and Gaza Strip.[19] However, *hasbara* considerations were again ignored in their decision making.[20] Dichter, the Shin Bet chief, who had participated in the discussions, instructed his subordinates to make a special effort to apprehend all of the Palestinians who took part in the lynching and to bring them to Israel.[21] "We'll settle accounts with those who perpetrated the murder,"[22] Barak vowed at a press conference.

In the discussions preceding the IDF response, a disagreement arose between the Central Command and the General Staff. The Central Command's chief intelligence officer, Col. Yossi Kuperwasser, called for deferring the response to take full advantage of the media impact, while Brig. Gen. Amos Gilad, head of Military Intelligence's Research Department, believed that an immediate response was needed. As one senior intelligence officer explains, "The feeling at the Central Command was that a severe mistake was made here, the media aspect of the lynching was not exploited as a factor to balance the story of Muhammad al-Dura, and the focus was on the military action in the territories."[23]

In the first wave, Israel attacked three targets in Ramallah: the police station in El-Bireh (the site of the lynching), the central broadcasting antenna of Voice of Palestine radio, and the command headquarters of the Palestinian security forces. *Haaretz* commentator Ze'ev Schiff defined the action as "one of the most peculiar operations the IDF has ever conducted."[24] Maj. Gen. Eiland said that in an effort to prevent Palestinian casualties, Israel provided advance warning of the attack.[25] The warning had a media-related motive: "Carnage in the streets of Gaza and Ramallah would provide Palestinian propaganda with counter photographs, which would balance the strong impact of the photographs of the murder and abuse of Israelis."[26]

In the second wave, helicopter gunships attacked targets in Gaza: rubber boats of the Palestinian naval force, the headquarters of the Force 17 commando unit, and a police station.[27] This marked the first time since the Oslo Accords that Israel deployed helicopters to attack Palestinian territory.[28] The IDF spokesperson explained that the assaults were limited and designed to communicate a clear message to the Palestinian leadership to immediately halt the violence. In a third wave, air force helicopters continued nighttime attacks, this time against targets in Nablus, Hebron, and Jericho.[29]

•

Now we turn from the operational details to the media-*hasbara* aspect of the incidents.

Early in the morning of October 12, rumors began to spread about an attack against IDF soldiers in Ramallah and later about a lynching. Radio and television channels shifted to an emergency broadcasting format of continual news updates instead of regular programming. By the afternoon, Channel 1 and Channel 2 were already broadcasting initial pictures from the scene of the lynching, along with the reactions of political figures, who were quick to condemn the shocking murder. "The media's decision to repeatedly broadcast pictures of the lynching accorded strong legitimacy for intensive military action, and even provided an international advantage for Israel's *hasbara* in the world. On the other hand, there was a fear that broadcasting the pictures over and over might incite violence and attacks in the Israeli street against the Palestinian public,"[30] notes media expert Udi Lebel. The helicopter attacks in Ramallah and the Gaza Strip were featured in the direct broadcasts of Israeli and international channels. Global networks, including CNN and Sky, repeatedly interrupted their regular programming with news flashes. "This dilemma arises a great many times," Gadi Eizenkot explains. "The Israeli media showed the Palestinians with blood on their hands on the balcony, but the story in both the Arabic media and the international media was primarily the Israeli attacks in the Palestinian cities and not the lynching."[31]

The first pictures from the site of the lynching showed the Palestinian mob besieging the police station, with police officers entering and exiting. The camera focused occasionally on a second-story window and showed people waving their hands triumphantly. This clip was the only footage from the scene and aired many times during the course of the day. Rumors of an extraordinary incident at the police station drew several journalists to the site. One of them was Eti Wieseltier, a producer and film editor for Italy's Channel 5, who arrived that morning with two camera crews. The photographers had heard that two Israeli undercover soldiers had been captured and were being held at the police station. One of the photographers, a Jordanian, held his camera up high, broke through the crowd, and filmed what was happening. "The first thing I saw was them tossing a body from the window. At that moment, a woman came out of the gate, pulled us aside, and asked us to hide. All around us, the police officers were shouting, 'Don't photograph, don't photograph!' We were the only crew. . . . It was very frightening."[32] Another eyewitness to the lynching was Mark Seager, a 29-year-old British photographer who happened to be in the area. He saw a group of Palestinians walking from the police station, dragging a body. He tried to take a picture, but was punched in the face. The mob snatched the film from his camera, so important evidence was lost.[33] Other material photographed by journalists was also destroyed by the Palestinian crowd.[34] With the exception of a few pictures from an unknown source that were broadcast that morning, the pressure of the crowd prevented photographers and journalists from doing their job and pushed them away.

It is doubtful whether the Palestinians were mindful of the incident's *hasbara* implications at that moment. What worried them more was that the Palestinian police or Israeli security forces would identify and arrest the murderers.[35] The Palestinian media refrained from reporting the incident for many hours, but the Jordanian photographer working for Italian television was able to film the incident through the fence; he gave the tape to Wieseltier and urged her to leave the site immediately. She brought the tape, which turned out to be the most important documentation of the incident, to Jerusalem Capital Studios and transferred a clip of two and a half minutes to Italy's Channel 5. Wieseltier also contacted the American TV networks and offered to sell them the footage. The Italians set a price of $1,200 per broadcast minute but subsequently decided to disseminate the film at no cost.

I was on my way to the media center in Jerusalem when the prime minister called me with a directive to give maximum exposure to the incident. Barak emphasized that it was an important story that could balance other news stories, such as the al-Dura affair. After receiving this directive and in light of the *hasbara* potential, I decided to present the ghastly pictures to the media. The media center prepared to exploit the *hasbara* potential to the fullest. Ilan Sztulman of the IDF Spokesperson's Unit, who was at the media center, learned that Italy's Channel 5 had documented the lynching and sought to obtain the film so that the IDF could "identify what happened there."[36]

Sztulman and the Foreign Ministry's deputy spokesperson, Noam Katz, asked the Israeli Embassy in Rome for assistance. Ambassador Yehuda Milo, and the embassy's spokesperson, Ofer Bavli, immediately went to the offices of Channel 5, which agreed to provide the footage as soon as it was broadcast. Israeli journalist Nahum Barnea recalls: "Only toward the evening, the Israelis realized that the footage from Ramallah was a lifesaver for *hasbara*, the Israeli answer to Muhammad al-Dura, the boy from the Netzarim Junction. The Israeli pressure reversed now—they demanded broadcasting as much as possible, everywhere, preferably in slow motion."[37] Israel received the film, which was simultaneously released for broadcast in Israel, Italy, and the world media. "They [Italian TV] did a smart thing—instead of broadcasting the tape exclusively and then exposing themselves to possible revenge, they gave it freely, at no charge, to all of the channels that wanted it,"[38] says Foreign Ministry official Meir Shlomo. The film showed a body being tossed from a second-floor window and the mob abusing it; a few of the rioters looked out from the window, and one of them waved a pair of hands stained with blood. "This was an important success of the Israeli information apparatus, which was able to very effectively portray the Palestinians as bloodthirsty monsters, as demonic and unbridled murderers,"[39] says Dr. Ron Schleifer, an expert in psychological warfare.

•

The public followed the drama for many hours, starting in the afternoon and continuing with the aerial attacks on the Palestinian Authority later in the day. The IDF spokesperson waited before issuing an official announcement about the lynching, in accordance with the IDF's policy of withholding comment on IDF casualties until their families receive official notice. However, the news is often reported in foreign or Israeli sources before the families are notified, and this is what happened here. The wife of Yossi Avrahami, one of the lynched soldiers, phoned her husband and one of the murderers answered the call and informed her: "We're killing him now." Nonetheless, the IDF spokesperson's official announcement was only issued after examining the bodies and informing the families. There was also a need to quash rumors about additional casualties. Meanwhile, the spokesperson reported about the IDF's attacks in Ramallah and Gaza. The order of the announcements was not chrono-logical—that is, the spokesperson announced the attacks first and only later issued a statement about the murder of the two soldiers. From a *hasbara* perspective, the IDF spokesperson was unable to present the attacks as a response to the lynching.

The media center operated in two channels that day—military and diplomatic. In the military channel, the head of the IDF Opera-tions Directorate, Maj. Gen. Eiland, briefed reporters on the lynching and the IDF operations conducted in retaliation. The IDF spokesperson made a special effort at the media center: "I mobilized 10 reservists for the media center, and we tried to aggressively exploit the incident vis-à-vis the media. We tried to 'pitch' the story—placing spokespersons and continuing to focus on the lynching."[40] In the diplomatic channel, Foreign Ministry officials Gideon Meir and Meir Shlomo invited the producer Eti Wieseltier to present her story to the media. "After I saw CNN broadcast the entire Israeli attack, suddenly only this picture remained, of the Israelis attacking from the air in Ramallah. It really infuriated me and seemed wrong. After all, something terrible had occurred, and no one was talking about it," she says.[41] At the press conference, she told how the Palestinians had prevented her crew from approaching the police station, except for her photographer who managed to film for a few minutes. She had qualms about her involvement in *hasbara* as a journalist but decided to give her testimony at an official state event. The press briefing included a screening of the film her photographer had shot in Ramallah.

In parallel to the special array of spokespersons orchestrated by the IDF spokesperson, there were also unofficial spokespersons who acted on behalf of the Prime Minister's Office and IDF. "After the lynching, we were instructed to raise the volume of the incident as much as possible and as much as needed," says David Baker, who worked at the PMO. "The idea of 'marketing' was born there—not in the way that I disseminate information via email on a daily basis, but in an effort to reach more and more media outlets and initiate interviews. The lynching drove us to speak more. At the moment, I became the national marketer of the IDF and Foreign Ministry, and I marketed the authorized spokespersons of the PMO, even though they were not civil servants or uniformed personnel. I worked intensively in this way for quite a few years, and was very successful."[42]

Other activities were conducted in writing and orally. Foreign Minister Shlomo Ben-Ami and Maj. Gen. Eiland made the rounds of TV studios in Jerusalem, denouncing the lynching and Yasser Arafat's regime. In this way, they prepared public opinion for Israel's response. According to Ben-Ami: "What should a government do in response to the chilling lynching of two reservists in Ramallah? Submit a protest? Continue business as usual? The tragedy lies in the fact that we knew, and I personally said this dozens of times, that no military response of ours would solve the problem. But at the time, we were compelled to respond. A state cannot remain idle in the face of such bloodshed."[43]

During that day and the next, the media combined the two news stories, but Israel's retaliation was the main story. The *New York Times'* coverage included quotes from the prime minister's press conference, as well as a report on the disappointment of peace activists over the deterioration of relations between Israel and the Palestinians.[44] The newspaper also reported on a demonstration of solidarity with Israel staged across from the Israeli Consulate, where Nobel Prize laureate Eli Wiesel spoke, expressing his shock over the lynching. On October 13, an article in the *Washington Post* opened with an account of the attack on Palestinian facilities by Cobra gunships and only afterward told about the murder of the IDF soldiers in Ramallah.[45] Despite the *hasbara* efforts, it seems that the aerial attacks completely undermined the Israeli message: "In the initial hours after the incident, it seemed that Palestinian *hasbara* was achieving a victory in the battle for American public opinion," the Israeli daily *Yedioth Ahronoth* reported. "The impression from CNN broadcasts from Ramallah and Gaza was that the helicopters were indis-criminately bombing these cities. For many hours, the American news network became 'a Palestinian stronghold'; there was no senior Israeli spokesperson present, not in Israel and not in New York, to explain which targets Israel was hitting."[46]

Palestinian and Israeli spokespersons competed for airtime in the international media. The Foreign Ministry was peeved about the sym-pathetic coverage the Palestinians were receiving, and Gideon Meir, the deputy director-general for media and *hasbara*, sent a letter of complaint to CNN. "We're not asking that CNN become an agent of the Israeli government," he told the *Jerusalem Post*. "What we're asking from this important media organization is to be honest and to be even-handed. Right now, we don't see it."[47]

The Israeli complaints against the international media intensified after the *Al-Hayat Al-Jedida* newspaper published a letter on October 16 from Riccardo Cristiano, a representative of Italian state television (Rai) in Israel. Cristiano explained in the letter that Italian state television was not responsible for broadcasting the footage of the lynching and that the film was made by a private Italian station, Channel 5: ". . . we always respect the journalistic procedures with the Palestinian Authority for work in Palestine and we are credible in our precise work. We thank you for your trust, and you can be sure that this is not our way of act-ing. We do not do such things."[48] Cristiano apparently did not expect his letter to appear in the press, and it immediately drew an Israeli response. The IDF Spokesperson's Unit translated the letter and sent it to the Foreign Ministry. "We exposed the terror the Palestinians impose on the networks and on journalists. Foreign correspondents quibble with us about everything we allow or don't allow," says Arik Gordin of the IDF Spokesperson's Unit. "But when the Palestinians don't allow them to enter Palestinian territory or threaten them and they live in fear, and this affects their reporting—then it's okay, and they don't complain about it. This incident [the publication of the letter] largely reflected a particu-lar reality that existed in those days, so it worked in our favor."[49] The publication of the letter exposed the existence of an unwritten covenant between the foreign press and the Palestinian Authority, which defined what was permitted and what was forbidden in covering events in the territories under Palestinian control. Clearly, this agreement violates the rules of journalistic reporting, and it was kept secret since its exposure would damage the credibility of foreign correspondents. This was a rare incident—a journalist admitting that there were conditions for media coverage in the Palestinian Authority.

Following Cristiano's letter, the media center temporary revoked his press credentials and the Government Press Office emphasized that it would not accept such conduct by journalists. Noam Katz, the deputy spokesperson at the Foreign Ministry and former spokesperson at the Israeli Embassy in Rome, explained: "Italian state television acted wrongly twice, violating all of the rules of journalistic ethics. First, its declaration that there are things that it would refrain from broadcasting because they are damaging to the Palestinian Authority or liable to damage it—is, of course, contrary to all of the rules of journalistic ethics and the duty of reporting. Secondly, it points an accusatory finger at their Italian colleagues, exposing them to vengeance to some extent."[50] Ron Prosor, then the Foreign Ministry's spokesperson, regrets that the international media fails to appreciate Israel's openness in comparison to the restrictions imposed on press coverage in the Palestinian Authority: "With us, there is full accessibility for representatives of the world's media. They can obtain reliable information from many sources, and crosscheck it. They travel freely; there is almost no censorship. On the other hand, their activity in the territories is subject to the good graces of the terrorist organizations, which provide them the information. This connects to the lynching in Ramallah—we were very lucky that the Italian crew actually revealed the tape and paid a price for this."[51]

While Claudio Accardi, the director of Italian state television's office in Israel, tried to repair the damage, Cristiano's employers in Rome did not wait long: On October 18, the channel's general manager, Pier Luigi Celli, announced the decision to immediately recall Cristiano from Jerusalem.

Other cases of threats against journalists and abductions reinforce the view that the Palestinians maintain a regime of intimidation vis-à-vis the foreign media.[52] Ron Schleifer believes that this is not the only reason for anti-Israel coverage and that it should be viewed in a broader context: "In the past too, the foreign media had been accused, whether implicitly or explicitly, of anti-Semitism (as in its coverage of the lynching in Ramallah) as a central motive in covering the Arab-Israeli conflict. Even when the reporters or editors or owners are Jews, Israelis have a ready explanation centering mainly on their constraints as 'assimilating Jews.' "[53]

•

Several of the Palestinians involved in the lynching were arrested a few days after the incident. During the following months, the Shin Bet succeeded in apprehending all of them.[54] As the Shin Bet director had publicly promised, the organization disseminated a picture of Abd al-Aziz Salha, the terrorist who had raised his bloody hands triumphantly during the lynching—this time raising his hands chained in handcuffs. The Shin Bet, applying the principles of public diplomacy, took action in the media arena to fully exploit the effect of apprehending the terrorist. The photograph was published in Israel's three major newspapers on June 26, 2001. Publication of the photograph was intended to boost public morale and fulfilled the Shin Bet's commitment to eventually catch anyone perpetrating such crimes.[55]

Salha's arrest did not end the hunt that started on the evening of the incident. On June 29, 2005, it was announced that a Palestinian police officer involved in the incident had been caught in a combined operation of the IDF and Shin Bet.[56] The Shin Bet's persistence brings to mind the Mossad's mission in the wake of the murder of Israeli athletes at the Munich Olympics in 1972. Acting upon a directive from Prime Minister Golda Meir, the Mossad eventually tracked down the terrorists responsible for the Munich killings.

The end of the story is typical of the Israeli-Palestinian conflict: Abd al-Aziz Salha, the terrorist who was photographed with bloody hands and later in handcuffs, was released to Gaza in the deal that freed Israeli soldier Gilad Shalit in October 2011.

•

Within 12 days, two pictures were published in the world that shaped the Palestinian-Israeli conflict for a long time. The prominent media coverage of the two incidents—the death of Muhammad al-Dura and the lynching of two Israeli soldiers in Ramallah—can be attributed to the similarities between them and the new media environment. Both events were extraordinary—cameras rarely document the moments of death. Israelis and Palestinians alternated as the strong and weak side; Israel ostensibly killed al-Dura, and the Palestinians slaughtered two Israeli soldiers in Ramallah. In the asymmetry of low-intensity violence, Goliath (Israel, the strong side) assumed the role of David (the underdog) for a short period of time.

Israel's retaliation undermined the attempt to create symmetry between the al-Dura incident and the lynching in Ramallah. As soon as Israel resumed its aerial attack (for the first time after a long interlude) and fired missiles into Palestinian population centers, the balance of forces also shifted: Israel was again the powerful side with advanced technological capabilities and the Palestinians were again perceived as weak and helpless victims. "The incident exposed Israel to an expression that was always associated with it—the 'cycle of violence,'" says Alon Pinkas, a former Israeli consul general in New York. "That's the worst, it takes the moral idea away from us. A person sits in New York, sees the news, and indeed sees a 'cycle of violence.' You lose him from a *hasbara* perspective if you start to preach to him that the Palestinians already showed their true colors in rejecting the Peel Commission's partition plan in 1937; he sees al-Dura and the lynching, the Dolphinarium,[57] the Ghalia family,[58] and children killed in Sderot."[59] This is how the cycle of violence is viewed.

•

When the second intifada erupted, the only public diplomacy systems operating in Israel were the permanent ones in government ministries and in the IDF. At the end of the Rosh Hashanah vacation week, even those curtailed their activity. Immediately after the al-Dura incident, a media center was established in Jerusalem, at the Foreign Ministry's initiative. Several days later, the prime minister and foreign minister decided to create a superstructure for *hasbara* to contend with the defense situation and media circumstances. The idea was to bring together all the *hasbara* entities to form a shared technical-physical center that would coordinate and even instruct them. This marked an innovation in Israeli public diplomacy.

The media center offered journalists a consistent and regular address, and it served as a venue for convening the media for joint *hasbara* events. This capability was translated into local and international *hasbara* initiatives and utilized to monitor the media, to receive feedback from diplomatic missions and official Israeli overseas entities, and to immediately apply lessons in the ongoing work. Around-the-clock activity, seven days a week, is required to meet the media's endless demands for information.

•

The primary shortcoming in the media strategy vis-à-vis the lynching incident was the disregard for public diplomacy at the critical junctures of decision making. The prime minister was aware of the *hasbara* value of the incident, but the decisions he made during those hours did not take this factor into consideration in a practical way. There is no point in maintaining organizational systems such as a *hasbara* array or media center if they are not an integral part of the decision-making process, presenting the public diplomacy implications. The head of the *hasbara* array should participate in policymaking discussions and explain the media-*hasbara* considerations. Additional public diplomacy entities should be mobilized for the stage of implementing the decisions.

Other conclusions from the lynching incident pertain to the media's impact on decision-making processes. The nonstop news coverage on radio and television created pressure on Israel's leaders and pushed them toward more extreme decisions. The media reflected the public's mood and even magnified it. The CNN effect and the Al Jazeera effect reinforced the international disapproval of Israel's retaliatory response to the incident. The lynching in Ramallah and the extensive media coverage sparked a dramatic change in the relations between Israel and the Palestinians. For the first time since the Oslo Accords in 1993, Israeli helicopter gunships attacked targets in the Palestinian Authority. This perhaps signaled the beginning of the collapse of the Oslo Accords, which culminated in Operation Defensive Shield in 2002 and today are practically a dead letter.

The lynching incident marked another step toward establishing a centralized array of public diplomacy. A series of initiatives by the media center during the hours following the incident created a coordinated *hasbara* campaign. However, the *hasbara* officials were disappointed to discover that they were excluded from the centers of decision making during the critical hours. A sense of missed opportunity and failure grew after the media center was closed weeks later and after I resigned from my position as head of the *hasbara* array. All at once, Israel returned to the routine pattern of public diplomacy, with special adaptations for times of emergency. This is not enough during a period of terrorism that goes on and on. Nonetheless, this incident was another milestone in the long journey of Israeli public diplomacy, from a decentralized system to a centralized array.

Chapter 13

Was There a Massacre?

The establishment of an international media center in Jerusalem was an important act in itself, but it was primarily a technical one and did not address the absence of public diplomacy considerations in the decision-making process. Israel deployed its military might in Operation Defensive Shield and soon dealt a fatal blow to the centers of terrorism in the West Bank. But it erred in not combining this hard power with components of soft power, including the media, the international front, coordination with NGOs (Israeli, Jewish, and international), and humanitarian assistance. All these could have created smart power, an appropriate mix of the two types of power.

∾

The "massacre" in Jenin was one of the tumultuous episodes of Operation Defensive Shield, involving military, diplomatic, legal, and other fronts. Above all, it reflected the problematic nature of *hasbara* and the battle for consciousness.

Operation Defensive Shield was a turning point in the second intifada, coming after 19 months of violent incidents and 12,380 terror attacks. By May 1, 2002, the death toll had reached 318 Israeli civilians and 154 security personnel, and 2,708 Israeli civilians and 1,138 security personnel had been injured.[1] Palestinian terrorism primarily targeted the civilian population, focusing on schools, restaurants, nightclubs, shopping malls, buses, and other public places with large crowds.

In March 2002 ("Black March"), the worst month since the start of the second intifada, 135 Israeli were murdered in terror attacks and 687 were injured.[2] The deterioration in the security situation and the surge in terror attacks peaked on Passover Eve, March 27. A terrorist from Tulkarem, Abd al-Basset Odeh, disguised as a woman and carrying a forged Israeli ID card, entered the Park Hotel in Netanya and blew himself up among the guests assembled for the Passover seder. The bombing killed 29 people and injured about 150. The desecration of the holiday forged internal cohesion and consensus in Israel, providing legitimacy for military retaliation.

In the wake of the attack, the government of Israel decided to change its policy toward the Palestinian Authority in the West Bank and instructed the IDF to reoccupy areas that had been transferred to Palestinian control. To ward off international pressure,[3] Prime Minister Ariel Sharon announced from the outset that Israel would withdraw to defined security zones after completing the operation. Defensive Shield was a formative event. It succeeded in dramatically reducing the Palestinians' ability to mount terror attacks, suicide bombings in particular.[4] A survey conducted by the University of Haifa found that Operation Defensive Shield significantly reduced the level of fear in the Jewish public.[5]

The operation reflected the IDF's new strategy, which combined a number of measures, including incursions into Palestinian territory, targeted killings with advanced technologies, and construction of the separation fence. Shmuel Nir, a senior intelligence officer, defined the operation as "another stage in the ongoing effort to wear down [the Palestinians], which has not ended."[6]

The operation began on March 29 in Ramallah, seat of the Palestinian Authority (PA) and Yasser Arafat's headquarters. The IDF imposed a siege on the Muqata building, the PA's headquarters in Ramallah, but refrained from entering the building and directly harming Arafat. To ease the pressure, Arafat was forced to transfer the murderer of Minister Rehavam Ze'evi from the Muqata to a prison in Jericho. Among the most-wanted terrorists apprehended in Ramallah was Marwan Barghouti, the commander of the Tanzim organization, who was later brought to trial in Israel and sentenced to life in prison. The IDF occupied most of the main cities in the West Bank, including Nablus and Tulkarem, which were considered hotbeds of terrorism. Three other centers of fighting remained: the Muqata in Ramallah, the Church of the Nativity in Bethlehem, and the refugee camp in Jenin, where Odeh's handler lived.

〜

The fiercest battle in Operation Defensive Shield was in Jenin, which the IDF had described as "the capital of suicide bombers." This applied primarily to the refugee camp attached to the city, which had already become famous as a center of terrorism in the 1980s. Three organizations operated in the camp: Palestinian Islamic Jihad, Hamas, and Fatah. They exploited the city's proximity to population centers in Israel and dispatched suicide bombers on 31 attacks, killing 121 people (including the carnage at the Park Hotel) and injuring 643.

The city of Jenin stretches over nearly 4,500 acres, including the refugee camp (about 110 acres). Of the city's 37,000 residents, 13,000 lived in about 1,900 homes in the camp. Activists in the three terrorist organizations were well prepared for the IDF operation, aided by extensive physical and human infrastructure, thanks to close cooperation from the camp's residents. The commander of the camp, Hazem Qabha, deployed hundreds of armed fighters in 15 subsectors. "They went with a strategy there that said: We're turning the refugee camp into Stalingrad—we're fortifying it, planting mines," says Shaul Mofaz, the IDF chief of staff at the time. "We decided to enter the camp because that was the main habitat of the terrorists and wanted men."[7]

According to the testimony of Tabet Mardawi, an Islamic Jihad commander, his men planted about 1,000 explosive devices aimed at preventing IDF vehicles and infantry troops from entering sites in the camp. The bombs were placed along three lines of defense and were the principal obstacle the IDF faced.[8] Sheikh Abu al-Hija, the commander of Hamas's Izz al-Din al-Qassam Brigades in the camp, describes the situation: "We planted explosives on the roads and in houses. Surprises awaited the occupying forces. In a number of places, there were clashes between the mujahideen and the occupation forces. The mujahideen use automatic weapons, explosives and hand grenades."[9]

A reserve division commanded by Brig. Gen. Eyal Shlein was assigned the mission of occupying the camp. Under Shlein's command was an infantry brigade, a Golani battalion, a Nahal battalion, and crews from the naval commandos and Duvdevan unit. The forces were not trained or prepared for the media aspects of the operation. According to one soldier who participated in fighting: "We didn't receive instructions in writing or orally—not about the media and not about things they photograph in the media. In the brigade, there was no one to speak with about things pertaining to the media. I looked for personnel from the IDF Spokesperson's Unit. I could have interviewed the commanders of the bulldozers. I could have interviewed the commanders of the tanks. I could have spoken with the brigade commander. I could have spoken with everyone. Even disposable cameras or things that could have helped us coordinate all sorts of things among us, were not provided."[10]

The IDF reported impressive achievements; it discovered laboratories for producing weapons and found Qassam rockets, explosive belts, car bombs, and roadside IEDs. However, it was less successful in apprehending wanted persons who were hiding in the camp.[11] The operation in the Jenin refugee camp dragged on. The soldiers advanced on foot and required aerial and engineering support. "The bulldozers simply 'shave' the homes, inflicting horrible destruction. When the world sees the pictures of what we did there, it will be enormous damage for us."[12]

On April 9, Israel announced it was pulling back from the cities of Tulkarem and Qalqiliya, while stepping up its efforts in the Jenin refugee camp.[13] That same day, an infantry platoon entered a courtyard of a building and was trapped between explosive devices and crossfire by terrorists. Thirteen IDF fighters were killed. It was the highest number of IDF casualties in a single day of combat in many years. A wave of rumors circulated until the IDF Spokesperson's Unit issued an official statement.

The defense minister and IDF chief of staff considered deploying the air force and artillery. However, fearful of harming noncombatants, they preferred to operate on the ground and dispatched D9 armored bulldozers to the camp.[14] "Bulldozers produced by Caterpillar, weighing 50 tons, crossed the streets of the camp and detonated bombs planted along the route. In some cases, infantry troops followed them in armored vehicles in order to carry out their mission."[15]

The use of bulldozers was designed to clear the way for the soldiers in the narrow alleyways and to neutralize booby-trapped homes by demolishing them.[16] Lt. Col. Adir Haruvi, the head of the Media Branch in the IDF Spokesperson's Unit, explained the need for the bulldozers: "The homes were booby-trapped. There were many explosive devices there, and it was difficult contending with this. The bulldozer can do this easily. It's bulletproof. It comes, knocks down the home, and the explosive device goes off. There were places when the bomb that exploded first set off a series of bombs, and three homes fell at once. The bulldozer could do all this without the soldiers getting hurt."[17]

The last of the armed Palestinians surrendered on April 11. Of the 1,900 homes in the camp, 134 (6.8 percent) were razed. The refugee camp, besides the damaged section, remained mostly intact.

～

Following the fierce battle and closure of the refugee camp to the media, rumors spread about the number of Palestinian casualties and the circumstances of their deaths. The IDF entered the Jenin refugee camp on April 2; after 48 hours of fighting, official Palestinian spokespersons already began to claim that the IDF had carried out a massacre in the camp. The first to speak in these terms was the PA's cabinet secretary-general, Ahmed Abdel Rahman, who denounced the world's silence about the "massacre" committed against the Palestinian people. Two days later, Nabil Sha'ath, another Palestinian Authority leader, reported in a meeting of the Arab League that Israel had conducted a massacre in the Jenin camp.[18] The Palestinian Authority's representative to the United States, Hassan Abdel Rahman, told CNN that Israel was planning to annihilate the Palestinian people. "There is a blanket bombing today of the cities of Nablus and Jenin,"[19] he declared. Some 250 Palestinians had already died in the bombings, he said, including many women and children.

From April 6 and onward, the Palestinians disseminated reports about a massacre in the camp. The *New York Times* reported on April 7: "Palestinian officials warned of massacres. But reliable tallies of the dead were not available, because ambulances were not able to pass through the battle zones to the dead and wounded."[20]

The source of rumors was the arrest of suspects, who were taken from the camp to neighboring communities.[21] In the daily press briefing at the media center in Jerusalem, the IDF spokesperson expressed concern that the Palestinians were planning a media narrative: "We have information that they [the Palestinians in the refugee camp] were ordered to leave in order to create manipulation and sell a story that a massacre had been committed."[22]

Foreign Minister Shimon Peres expressed a similar view: "I'm worried that Palestinian propaganda is trying to accuse Israel of a massacre in the city of Jenin, while it actually is a battle against well-armed terrorists."[23]

At this stage, the number of casualties in the camp began to grow. The IDF spokesperson estimated a total of 200 dead and injured.[24] *Haaretz* correspondents Ze'ev Schiff and Amira Hass reported: "There is a lot of talk about an enormous number of Palestinian casualties, about many who were injured by gunfire and are lying in the streets, in alleyways and homes without receiving medical treatment, and about the rotting corpses of the dead because most have not been evacuated for several days."[25]

The rumors intensified on April 10, when the IDF began a massive deployment of bulldozers. Nabil Sha'ath raised the number of casualties to 300,[26] and Saeb Erekat spoke of 500 in his interviews with CNN: "I'm afraid to say that the number of Palestinian dead in the Israeli attacks has reached more than 500 now. And I think the number may increase once we discover the extent of the damage and the massacres committed—particularly in the Jenin refugee camp and in the whole city of Nablus."[27]

∼

The Palestinians and international aid organizations raised accusations about the humanitarian situation in the refugee camp, including fears that Israel was trying to conceal the real number of Palestinian casualties.[28] The Israeli human rights organization B'Tselem also described the humanitarian distress in the camp: "During the course of the operation, kidney patients could only get to the hospital after many efforts to coordinate their passage. There were cases of patients dying before an approval was obtained. Protecting the sick and injured is one of the basic principles in international law. This principle too was violated during Operation Defensive Shield."[29]

Israel understood that Palestinian propaganda was focusing on the humanitarian misery. Therefore, the IDF spokesperson promised journalists that they would be allowed to enter the camp as soon as possible to gain an impression with their own eyes.

One of the issues brought before Israel's High Court of Justice during the fighting pertained to the evacuation and burial of bodies. Turning to the judicial system in Israel to demand action (or cessation of an action) by the executive branch was a relatively new phenomenon, inspired by the legal remedy the High Court had awarded in previous security incidents. The Adalah NGO submitted eight petitions: "The nature of the petitions, the immediate submission date and the way they were submitted stirred interest in the local and international media, and their attention turned to the court's hearings and rulings. The local and international interest grew from one petition to the next. The hearings were held in the main hall of the Supreme Court. The hall was packed and there was a strong presence of the local, Western and Arab media."[30]

The public dimension of the Adalah petitions was no less important than the legal one, and there was an implicit threat to also appeal to international tribunals.[31] The NGO revealed its strategy: to pressure Israel and lift the blockade of the camp through legal proceedings and media exposure, and by mobilizing international legal organizations and other NGOs in this effort.

The discussions in the High Court led the parties to agree to mount a joint operation by the IDF, International Red Cross, and local entities to find, evacuate, identify and bury the dead. The information on humanitarian damage reached the High Court together with reports about the "massacre" in Jenin. On April 14, the court issued its ruling: "Petitions claimed that a massacre had been committed in the Jenin refugee camp. Respondents strongly disagree. There was a battle in Jenin, a battle in which many of our soldiers fell. The army fought house to house and, in order to prevent civilian casualties, did not bomb from the air. Twenty-three IDF soldiers lost their lives. Scores of soldiers were wounded. Petitioners did not satisfy their evidentiary burden. A massacre is one thing; a difficult battle is something else entirely."[32]

NGOs and international organizations like UNRWA and the Red Cross demanded that Israel allow them to enter the refugee camp in order to perform their jobs. Terje Rød-Larsen, the UN's Mideast envoy, echoed this demand: "What we are seeing here is horrifying—horrifying scenes of human suffering . . . Israel has lost all moral ground in this conflict. They [the dead] are not only fighters. We've seen kids. There was a 60-year-old woman who was found, . . . What is really shocking beyond belief is that the Israelis have not conducted a search-and-rescue operation in 11 days."[33]

Rød-Larsen made similar statements to the *New York Times* and complained to Israel's foreign minister that there were "hundreds killed and thousands missing" in the camp.

〜

Journalists were allowed into the entire camp on April 14, and foreign military attachés were invited to visit on April 18. They met with the commander of the operation, Brig. Gen. Eyal Shlein, and with Col. Miri Eisen. "Eyal spoke in Hebrew, and I translated him," Eisen recalls. "But not word for word. He was arrogant and condescending, toward the attachés too. . . . He used words he should not have used. He explained the battle, the operations, the limitations. If in the battle of Jenin we had 23 killed and they had 50, it's hard to say it was a lethal blow and certainly there was no 'massacre.' We later took 20 foreign attachés and took them into the refugee camp. The 'massacre' was constantly on the agenda. We didn't call it a massacre, but rather a 'harsh battle.'"[34]

The placement of Eisen, as a woman, at the forefront of *hasbara* was important and refreshing. She had already appeared in the media as a professional and articulate intelligence officer, presenting captured documents at the media center in Jerusalem. Now she was dispatched to Jenin to brief the media. "The IDF Spokesperson's Unit should remove all of the generals who stammer in English and immediately appoint one spokesperson to speak on its behalf on television. The ultimate candidate is that colonel from military intelligence. I don't know what she does on a daily basis or at this moment, that's not important at all. She needs to appear all the time on all the global television networks on behalf of the IDF. The fact that she's a woman representing an army will arouse empathy."[35]

The humanitarian distress and the "massacre" continued to echo in the media, and the United Nations and Secretary-General Kofi Annan began to address this issue. The UN Security Council was requested to commission an international investigation of the incidents in Jenin.[36] At first, Israel raised no objections, and in a telephone conversation between the foreign minister and the UN secretary-general on April 19, Peres declared that "Israel has nothing to hide." Peres emphasized that any information requested would be provided to the UN representative when visiting the area.[37] The same day, the Security Council approved an initial resolution (1405) that addressed the "dire humanitarian situation" and supported the UN secretary-general's initiative "to develop accurate information regarding recent events in the Jenin refugee camp through a fact-finding team."[38]

After the composition of the committee was announced, however, Israel changed its stance and refused to assist it.[39] This was in light of statements made by its members—Terje Rød-Larsen, the UN's Mideast envoy ("humanitarian crime"), Peter Hansen, commissioner-general of UNRWA ("it would not be an exaggeration to say a massacre was committed"), and the UN's human rights commissioner Mary Robinson ("there's a parallel between the IDF's actions and Palestinian suicide bombers")—which clearly indicated they had formed an opinion in advance.

Annan announced a change in the composition of the committee on April 22, appointing Martti Ahtisaari, the former president of Finland, as chairman. Israel still rejected the committee, and Prime Minister Sharon decided to delay its arrival: "It's better to attack the matter now at the price of a difficult moment in the world media than to later face a report that would be intolerable from our perspective."[40]

The change in Israel's stance followed a memo submitted by Daniel Bethlehem, an expert in international law and advisor to the prime minister. His assessment was that Israel had not sufficiently considered the potential consequences and damage of the committee's investigation.[41] During the following days, Israel did everything it could to delay the start of the committee's work. On April 30, the cabinet convened and decided that conditions were still not ripe to allow the committee to visit.[42] The real turning point occurred after a meeting between Annan and the U.S. secretary of state, Colin Powell. At the end of the meeting, the UN secretary-general decided to disband the committee. Underlying this decision was an agreement between Israel and the United States that committed to impose an American veto of any Security Council resolution on Jenin.[43]

The United States, as usual, was alone in supporting Israel. Many other countries—including Austria, Belgium, Portugal, Spain, Sweden, China, Cyprus, and France—denounced the operation in Jenin.[44] The topic eventually returned to the General Assembly, which asked the secretary-general to present it with a report based on "all available resources and information." On August 1, 2002, Annan submitted a report that drew from Israeli and Palestinian sources, though Israel had not cooperated with this UN effort. The secretary-general noted that 52 Palestinians were killed in the camp ("up to half may have been civilians"), along with 23 Israeli soldiers. There was no evidence of 500 fatalities: "The UN report on Israel's military incursion into the refugee camp in Jenin did not find any evidence supporting Palestinian accusations that Israel massacred civilians. However, the report cited accusations that Israeli soldiers used excessive force and prevented medical treatment for injured or sick Palestinians."[45] Annan determined that both the Palestinians and Israel had used the civilian population as human shields. *Time* magazine conducted an independent investigation and reached a similar conclusion: There had been no massacre in the Jenin camp.[46]

Even before the UN secretary-general published the summary report, the NGO Human Rights Watch cleared Israel of accusations of a massacre (though it still harshly criticized IDF activity in the camp). The organization "found no evidence to sustain claims of massacres or large-scale extrajudicial executions by the IDF in Jenin refugee camp."[47] Israeli human rights organizations such as B'Tselem also published daily updates and provided other information that served as the basis for reports by Amnesty International and other international groups.[48]

~

The UN report did not bring closure, and the Jenin controversy continued to simmer. The actor Mohammad Bakri produced a documentary film entitled *Jenin, Jenin,* based on research he conducted in the refugee camp after the end of the operation. When he tried to screen the "documentary" film in Israel, the Israeli Film Council refused to grant approval.

Bakri petitioned the High Court and the attorney general defended the council's decision.[49] Over the course of a year, starting in October 2002, representatives of bereaved Israeli families and IDF soldiers waged a public campaign against screening the film and received support even from Defense Minister Shaul Mofaz: "The film is deceitful, tendentious and inciting, purporting to ostensibly provide a documentary description, but the events it describes are false and imaginary."[50]

Captain Dr. David Zangen, the physician of IDF Reserve Brigade 5 during Operation Defensive Shield, led the campaign: "I saw the film . . . and I want to tell you: We did not destroy and did not shell the hospital in Jenin. We did not take children and use them as forced laborers. We did not smash children's heads against a wall or shoot children in the head. We did not fill pits with the corpses of Palestinians, which have never been found. We did not shoot a toddler, as described in the film, with the bullet entering from the front and exiting from the back. No such body was found and there is none. We did not demolish homes with their residents inside them, and we did not commit those loathsome war crimes that people in Bakri's film testify about."[51]

During and after the fighting, Zangen emerged as the leading spokesperson for the fighters. This is another example of the ability of individuals to lead a public campaign, mobilizing close friends as well as the government and entire public. (We witnessed this in the role of Philippe Karsenty in the case of al-Dura.) Zangen collected the documentary material, was interviewed, delivered lectures in Israel and abroad on the true story of Jenin, and appeared in court during Bakri's appeal. Despite the soldiers' requests, the High Court accepted the appeal. Justice Dalia Dorner ruled: "There is no way to escape the conclusion that the decision not to allow the screening of the film unlawfully infringes the freedom of expression of the petitioners. The film 'Jenin, Jenin' should be permitted to be screened in theaters, and the viewing public should be allowed to judge it for themselves. The order nisi should be made absolute, the decision of the [Israel Film] Council should be reversed, and the screening of the film should be allowed."

The ruling includes important remarks on the closing of the camp and the "massacre": "During the warfare and for several days following, journalists were forbidden from entering the camp. It was only possible to learn what had occurred by seeing the battlefield itself, and from testimony of the people involved. This media blackout contributed to the conflict regarding the events." Concerning the "massacre," the High Court cited the report by Human Rights Watch, which like other international reports, repudiated the charge that "the IDF had slaughtered the residents of the camps and carried out systematic executions."[52]

~

The Jenin events are significant not only from the operational perspective (the question of whether there was a massacre or not), but also in their media coverage. Within 48 hours of the start of Operation Defensive Shield, the number of foreign correspondents in Israel doubled, reaching 700.[53] For the second time since the beginning of the intifada, Israel opened a media center. The Foreign Ministry and IDF Spokesperson's Unit launched the center on March 29 at the International Convention Center in Jerusalem, and they were joined by representatives of the PMO, the Defense Ministry, the Coordinator of Government Activity in the Territories unit, the Ministry of Public Security, the GPO, the Military Censor's unit, and, for the first time, the Shin Bet.[54]

Journalists arriving in Israel were requested to report to the center to receive press credentials. The center provided visual and written information to them and their colleagues stationed in Israel, and it made spokespersons available to them in various languages during most hours of the day.[55] The director of the media center on behalf of the Foreign Ministry was veteran diplomat Aryeh Mekel. "I drew several lessons from the first media center at the beginning of the intifada, primarily in regard to the scope of activity. This time it was more organized. One of the lessons was that every day at 4:00 p.m., the journalists would receive a briefing. I made the briefing very significant since it always included a diplomatic briefer and a military briefer," Mekel recounts.[56]

~

It is important to study the *hasbara* aspect of Operation Defensive Shield. The decision to launch the operation was made quickly, without integrating the *hasbara* aspects during the planning stages. The head of the IDF Operations Directorate was supposed to represent this aspect in the decision-making process: "The IDF should have a media strategy that will be part of the overall strategy and will make things easier for us. It's much harder to repair damage after the fact than to develop a strategy in advance. [But] in Defensive Shield, there wasn't time to think about the media. We ran right in."[57]

Before the operation began, the defense minister at the time, Ben-Eliezer, prohibited reporters from entering the territory. This marked a deviation from the openness policy that had recently developed in the IDF. "The chief of staff and his team didn't really intend to wage a media campaign and allow the media access to the West Bank," says former IDF Spokesperson Kitri. "We went into Judea and Samaria without the media, the media pressured for greater access mounts, and all of our requests were repeatedly denied again and again."[58] Ben-Eliezer rejects this account: "I did not prohibit the media from entering."[59] But the directive the IDF received was clear and, in practice, the fighting in the Jenin refugee camp was conducted without media coverage. While the Israeli side prevented access, the Palestinians sent reports from the camp via telephone and other means, but without visual material.

"The prohibition on including the media in Defensive Shield came from the chief of staff and was based on a directive from the defense minister following a report broadcast on Israeli television two weeks earlier, showing IDF soldiers searching homes and making arrests in the territories."[60] It was harsh footage showing soldiers bursting into Palestinian homes, turning them upside down, and leaving destruction behind. The controversial report was filmed by a Channel 10 television crew that provided pool coverage for the Israeli media. An editor at Channel 2 recognized the potentially problematic and exclusive content in the footage and decided to broadcast it. The IDF Spokesperson's Unit was unaware of the broadcast: "It created a boomerang and terrible reaction. The decision was to keep the media away. They asked me, who released the footage? Who is to blame? Let's find the culprits. And no one spoke up. Consequently, they didn't allow journalists to enter the territory with IDF forces."[61]

Reporters did not join the IDF forces, but they traveled independently in rural areas and sometimes even managed to enter some of the besieged cities. Three main battlegrounds were completely sealed off, with no one able to approach them: the Muqata in Ramallah, the Church of the Nativity in Bethlehem, and the Jenin refugee camp.[62] Lacking access, foreign reporters used local Palestinian stringers who knew how to circumvent IDF checkpoints.[63] The outcome of course was anti-Israeli.

❧

In a fierce battle on April 9, 13 IDF soldiers and an unknown number of terrorists were killed, and a flurry of rumors ensued. "It turned out that the rumors circulating on the Internet were stronger than the censorship and the efforts to guard the information," says *Haaretz* reporter Amir Oren.[64] At least nine Internet sites published unofficial information on Jenin that day.[65] "That event, in my view, was a complete victory of technology over all of the conventional means of reporting," says Rafi Tadhar, a senior Shin Bet official who accompanied IDF activity in the refugee camp. "All of the information got out first thanks to the Internet and telephony, and we could only respond after the fact."[66]

There was a media vacuum in the Jenin refugee camp, which the Palestinians succeeded in filling. Their stringers navigated the friendly and familiar territory and found bypass routes to the heart of the media. Their fictitious version made waves and, in the absence of a rapid response, silence was tantamount to an admission of guilt. The fact that Israeli spokespersons were not on the ground undermined their efforts; they provided erroneous information on the number of casualties, thus reinforcing the myth of the massacre that never took place.

The rumors of the massacre already began on April 4, but the battle on April 9 and the massive deployment of bulldozers the next day helped it to proliferate. The television reporter Shlomi Eldar watched the broadcasts and was impressed by the Palestinian *hasbara*: "They started to present all of the official spokespersons, like Hanan Ashrawi, Saeb Erekat, and others. Their English was good and their explanations fluent. And then the Israeli spokespersons appeared. I heard them. Even when we should have had the upper hand, the inability to speak English hurt us. The broadcasts continued for eight hours straight until they were cut off. Eight formative hours."[67]

At the media center in Jerusalem, Mekel watched the broadcasts. "A dynamic developed in which Palestinian spokespersons like Erekat and people in Jenin continually appeared on CNN and for hours told all sorts of stories about what was happening there, while there were no objective journalists there to refute them. We did the best we could, but it was clear that testimony from the field was more convincing to CNN than all of the Israeli spokespersons."[68] Israeli reporters were also angry: "If the media had been present, bringing the true pictures, and photographing things, which is the only true testimony, you could have very quickly quashed the story of the massacre. When there's no media, it's possible to concoct stories. And which story gets more attention? The more dramatic story, of course."[69]

The refugee camp remained closed, but the IDF held briefings for the media and military attachés on a hilltop adjacent to the camp. Miri Eisen argued with reporters who sought to enter the camp—for example, a correspondent from the *Sunday Telegraph* claimed that Israel had no right to close the area because in any case it was an occupied area.[70]

In retrospect, the head of the Operations Directorate at the time, Maj. Gen. Dan Harel, admits that the IDF's media policy was wrong: "My decision to close Jenin to reporters was a mistake. I had an inaccurate picture of the battle and thought there really were a very large number of people killed. According to military reports, there were hundreds of bodies in the streets. When I realized there was no massacre, it was too late because by then they had already managed to build the false story about the massacre in Jenin."[71]

Reports from the hospital in Jenin spoke about hundreds of fatalities. The foreign media accepted these numbers. "For three days, the arena was open to tales of a horrible massacre, about bodies dumped in the street and rotting,"[72] journalist Ron Ben-Yishai notes. "It was foolish to believe we could contend with the rumors about the massacre from the media center," Kitri says.[73] Together with Foreign Ministry officials, Kitri lobbied to open the camp. The defense minister's advisors also convinced him of the need to overturn the decision to hermetically close the area.[74]

On April 11, the last terrorists hiding in the camp surrendered, but the IDF was still hesitant about opening it to the media. The first group of journalists, accompanied by Yaakov Dallal, an officer in the IDF Spokesperson's Unit, entered the refugee camp on April 14. "The journalists who had begged for access to the arena the previous week, came with only one objective: to check the Palestinians' claims of a massacre."[75] The journalist Amos Harel notes: "The visit the army allowed after a critical delay of three days from the end of fighting in the camp did not provide an unequivocal solution to the question that leaders and spokespersons, Israelis and Palestinians, had been disputing for nearly a week—how many dead bodies of Palestinians were in the refugee camp? All of the army personnel who spoke with us in Jenin, both officers and soldiers, categorically denied the accusations of massacring civilians; the Palestinian residents who fled from the camp told the reporters a completely different version."[76]

~

With the IDF's withdrawal from Jenin, the media's focus shifted from the camp to the diplomatic arena, the United Nations. The secretary-general's report ostensibly closed the discussion on the question of a massacre. Nonetheless, the myth of a massacre persisted. Operation Defensive Shield was a military success, significantly reducing the number of terror attacks—though terrorism continued at low intensity during the following years. The operation in the Jenin refugee camp is not considered a military success—the IDF cannot bear a balance of 23 fatalities among its soldiers versus 52 Palestinian fatalities, most of them terrorists. The important achievement of Defensive Shield was the intelligence advantage the IDF acquired in the West Bank, which became the key to fighting terror in later years.

The episode in Jenin is well remembered in Israel, among the Palestinian public and in world public opinion. An Internet search for "Jenin" and "massacre" yields well over 100,000 results, some of which still give the impression that a massacre indeed occurred there in April 2002. A massacre in Jenin is imprinted in the world's memory and will apparently remain there. Israel's military achievement in the overall operation is overshadowed by this impression. The "massacre" in Jenin not only lives on in Palestinian mythology but also remains documented in Western media files. "We are talking here of massacre, and a cover-up, of genocide," a British columnist wrote in the *Evening Standard*. Another British newspaper, the *Guardian*, asserted that what happened in Jenin was "every bit as repellent" as Al-Qaeda's terror attack on September 11.[77]

~

Looking back years later, several key lessons emerge regarding Israel's public diplomacy approach. While Israel displayed operational initiative in Defensive Shield, its public diplomacy was reactive. The IDF's preparation for the operation did not include the component of public diplomacy—contrary to the IDF's combat doctrine, which mandated the inclusion of the media in operational planning and explicitly defined the spokesperson's role and the place of journalists. "For years, we've been preaching to the IDF that it should change its basic situation assessment to also include the subject of *hasbara* as a component in the operational assessment, such as, the enemy and the territory and even the weather. This has still yet to be really implemented. The case of the massacre in Jenin that never occurred is an example of how Israel's reputation is stained, even when it wins in battle."[78]

Yet Israel did make a sound tactical decision in establishing a media center, which proved itself throughout the operation but was obviously not enough. Dozens of interviews were conducted at the center and it distributed a great deal of information to the media. However, its distance from the combat arena diminished its ability to contend with pictures from the Muqata in Ramallah, the Church of the Nativity in Bethlehem, and, especially, from the Jenin refugee camp. Dan Meridor, a former justice minister, says: "Today's war is a war of pictures; we no longer listen to the story, but just look at the pictures. The new kind of war is continually waged in two places—on the field and on the screen. If you lose the screen, you might have also lost the war."[79]

In the case of the Jenin refugee camp, the IDF chose to completely seal off the area. Between full and open coverage, on the one hand, and absolute closure, there is an intermediate option—operational documentation. The IDF understands that it should document its actions for internal and external needs. This did not occur during the fighting.

$$\sim$$

Several public diplomacy fronts came together in the Jenin affair. First, the operational military front influenced the diplomatic activity at the United Nations and internationally. On the legal front, petitions for the High Court's intervention in IDF activity were made, particularly from the humanitarian perspective. There was also a threat to appeal to the High Court of Justice at The Hague. On the economic front, churches in the United States threatened to divest from the Caterpillar company, which produced the bulldozers that razed homes in Jenin. On the public diplomacy front, the Palestinian strategy drove Israel to a defensive stance, trying to repeal the accusations of war crimes. Israel erred in not embedding the media in a reasonable and measured way in IDF activity to proactively refute the anticipated campaign of rumors.

Both sides regarded the battle of Jenin as a turning point in the war for consciousness. The Palestinians were looking for an opportunity to create a myth of heroism, glorifying their battle. Israel, on its part, was determined to uproot and destroy terror cells in the West Bank to deter future terrorism, as a symbolic act. But we should remember that the battle took place in a post-heroic era that emphasizes the sensitivity of a liberal-democratic state to casualties on both sides. Consequently, when the fighting in the camp intensified, Israel refrained from deploying powerful weaponry like artillery and the air force, which would have caused massive casualties, and chose to use bulldozers on the ground instead. This is a typical post-heroic war consideration.

Maariv's correspondent in London, Shaul Sadka, summed up the entire operation from his perspective: "The terrible failure . . . is attributable to the amateurish Israeli *hasbara*. Not only did Jerusalem initially admit to over 100 Arab fatalities, it revealed its nakedness to the entire world when it was unable to fend off the diplomatic and media attack that compared the Jewish state to the Nazi regime. It did not confront journalists who spoke of hundreds of dead bodies in Jenin; it refused to consider legal measures against journalists who saw 'with their own eyes' nothing short of 'mass graves'; it did not defend the honor of IDF soldiers in the political corridors; and it even refrained from challenging the UN, whose camps continue to host terrorist organizations that turn them into breeding grounds for suicide bombers."[80]

Chapter 14

Deploying a Public Diplomacy Network

What is the best model for public diplomacy in liberal democracies in an era of low-intensity warfare? The battle against international terror is being waged simultaneously on several fronts, including the public diplomacy arena. The optimal model employs tools of public policy in confronting terrorism on the consciousness front. This chapter will present several innovations for creating a global array of public diplomacy that operates in the new age of technology and globalization, branches out to local spaces, and adapts to local conditions.

Israel's war against Arab terror continues within the territory of the State of Israel, in the West Bank, and on the global front. In 2005, Israel unilaterally disengaged from the Gaza Strip, withdrew its military forces, and dismantled its civilian settlements there. The expectations for an end to Palestinian violence failed to materialize; instead, Israel's exit from Gaza intensified the terrorism from the Strip. In 2006, after Hamas attacked an Israeli post and abducted an IDF soldier, Gilad Shalit, Israel launched an extensive military campaign (Operation Summer Rains) against Hamas. Two years later, on December 27, 2008, in the wake of ongoing shelling of Israeli communities from Gaza, the IDF invaded the Strip and remained for about two weeks. In this operation (Cast Lead), 13 Israeli civilians and soldiers were killed, along with about 1,300 Palestinians, including some 800 armed combatants. Two other rounds of clashes between the IDF and Hamas followed, including a 51-day war in the summer of 2014. That last round of warfare demonstrated that Hamas had significantly upgraded its capacity to become a paramilitary force with both offensive and defensive capabilities.

The acts of violence in the West Bank intensified in October 2015, around the time of the Jewish New Year. As occurred 15 years earlier, the

Temple Mount, sacred to both Jews and Muslims, was the focal point of tension and the catalyst for the rioting. A new wave of terrorism killed dozens of Israelis and injured hundreds. Most of the attacks were with "cold" weapons—knives and vehicles (deliberate attempts to run down pedestrians or people waiting at bus stops). Officials in Israel prefer to define these incidents as a "wave of terror" and adopt the Arabic word (*hiba*) "awakening" rather than "intifada." The incidents correspond completely with the model of low-intensity violence—that is, a series of attacks that lead to a cumulative number of casualties. This is one arm of the assault on Israel.

The other arm is diplomatic. In international arenas, the State of Israel's right to exist is sometimes called into question, without eliciting a swift and sharp response by Israel. Declarations challenging a UN member state's right to exist, and which are not categorically rejected, encourage the delegitimization of Israel. This also applies to UN agencies. For example, in October 2016 UNESCO approved two separate decisions that challenged the historical connection between the Jewish people and the Temple Mount. These decisions, while absurd and lacking any historical foundation, illustrate the anti-Israel bias that exists in international organizations.

The challenge facing Israel is unique. It must continuously and relentlessly fight on both the military and diplomatic fronts. Other countries in the world are also threatened by neighboring states or by terrorism; from this perspective, Israel's situation is similar. But Israel is an extreme case, facing a combined threat ranging from unconventional weapons, missiles, and suicide bombers, to riots and a popular uprising. It is doubtful whether any other country in the world is exposed to these dangers daily, while continuing to conduct its normal affairs. A prolonged conflict has repercussions not only on Israel's international standing, but also on its internal way of life, economy, society, and culture.

The questions before us also pose a challenge to other liberal democracies that have encountered similar situations. Small-scale wars or low-intensity warfare have proliferated since 1945 and comprise the overwhelming majority of military confrontations in the world today.

•

The Israeli system includes the principal government ministries, led by the Prime Minister's Office, government authorities dedicated to public diplomacy, and organizations that support *hasbara*—within or outside of the government. Two new entities have joined the state's system of public diplomacy—the Shin Bet and the IDF Home Front. The Shin Bet has undergone a fascinating process of gradual exposure, from a clandestine organization whose very existence was kept secret to a state agency that openly and consciously conducts public relations. The IDF Home Front faces many challenges and encompasses both civilian and state entities, with the latter including both uniformed and nonuniformed personnel. This complex mix is unwieldy in times of quiet and even more so in emergencies. During the second intifada, the Second Lebanon War, Operation Cast Lead and later, in conditions of low-intensity fighting, the home front was the primary target of terror attacks. Clearly, the state's high population density and its narrow and long borders are an invitation for targeting the home front, as indeed occurred incessantly during 2000–2005 and beyond.

One of the characteristics of the public system in Israel is to improvise solutions due to a lack of long-term planning. Israel tends to let things develop until a critical moment arrives, and then it quickly formulates responses that bypass the bureaucracy and other government shortcomings. In this spirit, Israel's public diplomacy agencies have responded to the challenges of Palestinian terror and the new media environment with hasty and improvised organizational changes.

One after another, Israel has added new tools of public diplomacy to the existing ones. Their adoption and implementation have reinforced the recognition that a patchwork policy is insufficient and that an overall strategic approach is needed. Nonetheless, Israel still lacks a supra-system to coordinate the use of these tools in a comprehensive and long-term perspective. There is also inadequate funding for exploring innovations in the field of the new public diplomacy and for teaching them to public diplomacy professionals in Israel, who complain, justifiably, about meager budgets that are incomparably smaller to those invested in bolstering hard power.

Throughout its history, Israel has searched for organizational solutions for the public diplomacy system, using a trial-and-error method. This has ranged from weak ad hoc mechanisms during times of national crisis to the establishment of a government ministry devoted to *hasbara*. None of these solutions were sustainable, but common patterns of action gradually emerged, such as opening a media center during emergencies or communication protocols among the entities.

The second intifada accelerated the transition from a decentralized system of public diplomacy to a centralized array. In an effort to institutionalize this process, Israel decided to examine the organizational tools available for deployment in the battle for consciousness and the best way to integrate them. It required another series of reports and working papers, primarily by the state comptroller, and, unfortunately, another war (the Second Lebanon War, which also culminated in a sense of failure), before reaching a consensus on establishing a national *hasbara* array.

•

Israel lacks a strategic approach that views public diplomacy as a central component of equal weight to political and security considerations. This approach must incorporate public diplomacy in every diplomatic or military action. All the events examined earlier are characterized by a palpable lack of overall strategy from which tactical and operative decisions could be derived. This lacuna in Israeli policy is nothing new, but this does not justify the absence of a public diplomacy strategy in the decision-making process.

Public diplomacy should be an integral part of strategic thinking from the outset, and it should be fully implemented at each stage. The initial response sets the tone and determines the long-term perception of an incident. Nonetheless, decision makers do not devote sufficient attention to public diplomacy considerations.

Since these aspects are not accorded their due weight in the decision-making process, public diplomacy officials are not regularly invited to preparatory meetings and forums of decision makers. Many organizations operate in the public diplomacy arena without a strategic approach, central direction, or implementation tools at a national level, and the coordination among them is based solely on personal relationships. Each organization serves a different partisan-diplomatic-political entity, and these considerations underlie each of their professional actions. The balance of power among the components of Israeli public diplomacy is unequal, and the IDF has a significant advantage over the Foreign Ministry, Government Press Office, Israel Police, and even the Shin Bet.

Public diplomacy officials, as professional and thorough as they may be, lack a central entity to *integrate* their separate programs into a single one, and to formulate and disseminate a *uniform message*. Without this, official Israeli spokespersons will present different and even contradictory positions, thus weakening the overall policy impact.

Public diplomacy officials compete among themselves. In the past, the competition was primarily between the Foreign Ministry and the IDF, while today the IDF also competes with the Shin Bet. One central entity would be able to curb this competition and channel it toward the shared objective.

•

The *international media* operates throughout the Middle East and dictates the global picture of the events in the region. Israel must allocate suitable resources for fostering professional relations with representatives of media outlets and should establish an entity to deal with the foreign media and assist it in fulfilling its missions.

A correct strategic approach toward the *foreign media* would create sound working relations and even foster a positive attitude toward Israel by the media. A positive connection with foreign correspondents is a first step in ensuring fair coverage. An effort should be made to confirm that violent incidents are covered by media outlets that subscribe to accepted journalistic rules and ethics.

Operational documentation is designed to provide a response, even if only a partial one, to Palestinian cameras or the complete absence of media coverage. To counter Palestinian coverage, the IDF and the State of Israel must fully deploy operational documentation during ongoing security incidents, such as drone attacks or land-based combat.

The Palestinians have also expanded their influence in *satellite broadcasts*. Israel is missing an opportunity to exploit its technological advantage for purposes of public diplomacy and to disseminate its messages of soft power to Arabic speakers. The cost of these systems is negligible in comparison to the human and financial price of combat.

The new technology has completely changed the traditional division of roles between broadcasters and receivers. The public, which only received information in the past, primarily via the media, is an active participant in the new array: It generates content on the Internet and bypasses the traditional media. The hierarchical approach, based on the one-way streaming of information from the media to its consumers, became a horizontal, flat, and two-directional system, operating according to new rules and relying on the new power of the individual. Civil society draws from the power of the individual or individuals who collaborate in the new frameworks of NGOs. These organizations have created networks that operate on the sub-state and supra-state levels.

Starting from the Durban conference, Israel has learned the hard way about the hostility of *NGO empires*. Operation Defensive Shield triggered a comprehensive change by engendering pro-Israeli NGOs, which leveraged the new technologies to enter the international arena. Motivated individuals mobilized to lead public campaigns via these NGOs, which act independently to promote Israel's interests without any direct organizational link to Israel.

The conflict between Israel and the Palestinians is a testing ground for media innovations and challenges. National systems of *information technology and research* are essential tools for contending with the challenges that emerged in the second intifada. Monitoring the media provides vital information on how events are reflected in the media and is critical to formulate a response or initiative. A late response entrenches the Palestinian narrative in global consciousness.

To learn how the world regards Israel and its actions, an orderly process of assessment and monitoring is needed. Surveys, which are not always reliable, are not enough. There is a need to enhance some of the assessment tools to obtain a clearer picture.

The National *Hasbara* Headquarters

In July 2007, the government decided to establish the National *Hasbara* Headquarters in the Prime Minister's Office, based on the recommendations of the cabinet secretary, Israel Maimon. It was a first and important decision in Israel's transition from a decentralized system to a unified array. The decision stated: "The National *Hasbara* Headquarters will coordinate all of the *hasbara* entities in the State of Israel in order to present a credible, uniform and consistent *hasbara* policy."[1] This was welcome progress, but still only an interim step toward a centralized array of public policy that Israel needs more than ever. The government decision concluded the work of Maimon's team, which had begun prior to the Second Lebanon War. The State Comptroller's Report (58A) and the war itself accelerated the pace of the team's work, which spanned three and a half years.

Three documents represent milestones in the decision to establish the National *Hasbara* Headquarters: the Maimon team's draft report (April 2006), the PMO's response to the State Comptroller's Report (April 2007), and the government decision itself (July 2007). After years of deliberations over the desired organizational structure, Maimon concluded that conditions were ripe for establishing a centralized national *hasbara array*, but later softened this definition to a national *hasbara headquarters*.

Vision: The Maimon team's draft report proposed establishing a centralized body that would guide and coordinate all of the *hasbara* entities. From the first moment, Maimon had no doubts about the need for a central *hasbara* body: "There is no entity that sees a complete picture of the *hasbara* policy. In fact, no one is dictating *hasbara* policy. Only one entity in the State of Israel can do this, the Prime Minister's Office. The policy emanates from here, so it needs to be explained from here."[2]

It was important for Maimon to note that he was not inventing a new *hasbara* mechanism; rather, he called for integrating the existing one. He proposed a headquarters entity rather than an executive one to avoid "politics," he said.

Status of the head of the hasbara *headquarters*: It was agreed that the director of the headquarters should be a professional with an understanding of diplomatic and military affairs, as well as expertise in the media and *hasbara*. There was also a consensus that the director should be appointed by the prime minister and directly report to him, and should be included in all of the forums that shape government policy in the diplomatic and security fields. The government decision also noted that the director should be involved in all discussions with *hasbara* implications.

The government decision thus stipulated that the head of the *hasbara* headquarters fills two roles: director of the headquarters and media advisor to the prime minister. It reinforced the direct connection between the director and the prime minister and prevented the division of these roles between two people.

Two forums for hasbara were formed: a National *Hasbara* Forum and an Emergency National *Hasbara* Forum. The former convenes regularly to shape Israel's public diplomacy strategy, in accordance with decisions by the prime minister and the government, and there is no disagreement about its role. The latter is a subgroup of the National *Hasbara* Forum and is active during times of emergency. The Foreign Ministry was assigned exclusive responsibility for guiding the *hasbara* activities of Israel's representatives abroad. "The Foreign Ministry wanted it to be clear that it remained solely responsible for *hasbara* overseas. How do you reconcile 'exclusively responsible' with 'a coordinating, integrating, and guiding entity'? This was the art of formulating the wording and years of experience in the profession. In the end, you can live with the wording and in essence you're not changing anything."[3]

Hasbara *considerations during security events*: Maimon also proposed including *hasbara* strategy in security-related initiatives, which are generally conducted without receiving assessments of the potential *hasbara* implications. Minister Tzipi Livni, who was responsible for coordinating *hasbara* at the time, explains: "If we had known in advance how the events would develop and if we had worked systematically, we could have prepared the key diplomatic messages."[4]

Media Monitoring Center: In Israel, there are several information technology and communication (ITC) arrays operating separately, without sharing information. The government decided to establish a national ITC array and assign it responsibility in this field vis-à-vis the Israeli and foreign media.

National Media Center: The government stipulated that the Foreign Ministry would be in charge of the center, with assistance from the GPO and IDF Spokesperson's Unit.

Unfortunately, the government refrained from setting a real *budget* for *hasbara*, and sufficed with defining the need to identify monetary sources for establishing the *hasbara* headquarters and boosting overseas *hasbara*.

Nonetheless, six months after submission of the Maimon report, the government finally appointed a director for the National *Hasbara* Headquarters, and thus took a significant step forward.

What Is the Best Organizational Model for Public Diplomacy?

This is the key question this book raises, and here we will draw from political theories and Israeli practices to suggest a model that will help in coping with the challenges of a period of low-intensity warfare. To answer this question, we need to review models of information flow, from classical diplomacy to the new public diplomacy; describe an organizational structure of a public diplomacy headquarters and its integration in the array of new public diplomacy; and suggest a contemporary organizational solution for the new dimensions of public diplomacy, such as two-directional communication, direct and indirect access, new players, and the use of communications technologies.

The basic structure of information flow includes three entities: the public, the government, and the media. It is customary to regard mass media as playing a mediating role between the public and the government/head of state. According to Itzhak Galnoor, "The use of the media as a mediating agent between the government and the public is ancient, and so is the basic need for dialogue between the two sides. From the government's perspective, this dialogue has far-reaching significance; it can be used to communicate information, messages and instructions to broad audiences. For those under its rule, it can be used to monitor government policy, while also communicating protests, agreements and demands to the rulers."[5]

The media is an active and influential agent in transferring information and messages from the government to the public. Initially, the media's role was limited to that of a mediator, but it gradually took on additional roles and became an arena in itself. The basic components of this model—government, media, and public—are also incorporated in later models, adapted to new eras and technological changes.

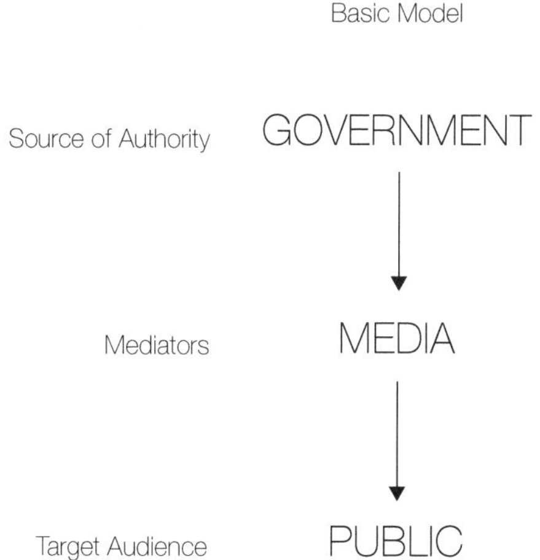

Figure 14.1. The Role of the Media: Basic Model.

The Voice of America (VOA) model was appropriate for the World War II era and the ensuing Cold War. VOA radio began broadcasting in 1942 and became the most prominent instrument of American public diplomacy during that period. It was part of the U.S. Information Agency and participated in the psychological battle against the Soviet Union and its allies. Other government entities in the United States, such as the CIA and Department of Defense, engaged in similar activity.[6]

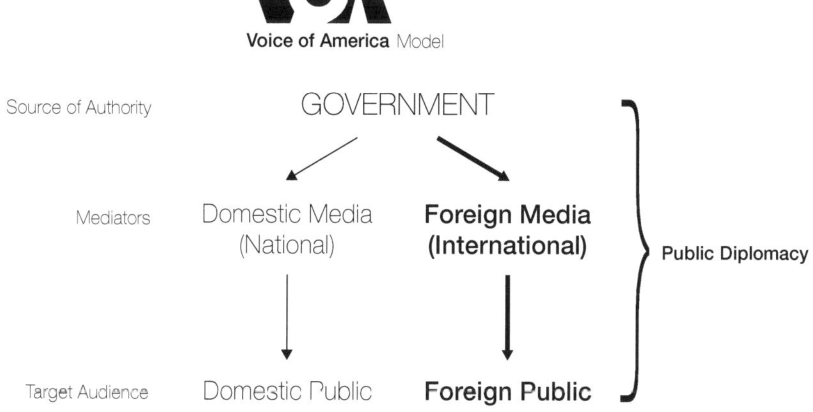

Figure 14.2. The VOA Model.

This model divides the public into two target audiences, domestic and foreign, each targeted by a different broadcasting system—the internal media serving the national audience and the external media directed at the international audience. According to American law, international broadcasting networks in the United States were not allowed to broadcast to the United States itself. In other countries, too, including Germany, England, and France, there was a complete separation between the different target audiences and the media designated to serve them.

•

CNN International's model of information flow suited the late Cold War period (1989) but also continued into the early 21st century. CNN, the first global broadcasting network, began broadcasting in 1980 and, together with other global networks such as the BBC, helped to accelerate the collapse of the Soviet bloc and remove the barriers between East and West. These networks tore down the walls separating internal and external broadcasts and exposed additional political and geographic regions to Western culture. Domestic audiences in various countries watched the same broadcasts at the same time, and the satellite networks influenced changes in political, economic, social, and cultural systems. With the ascendancy of the CNN International model, the government and its official agents were no longer the exclusive source of authority;

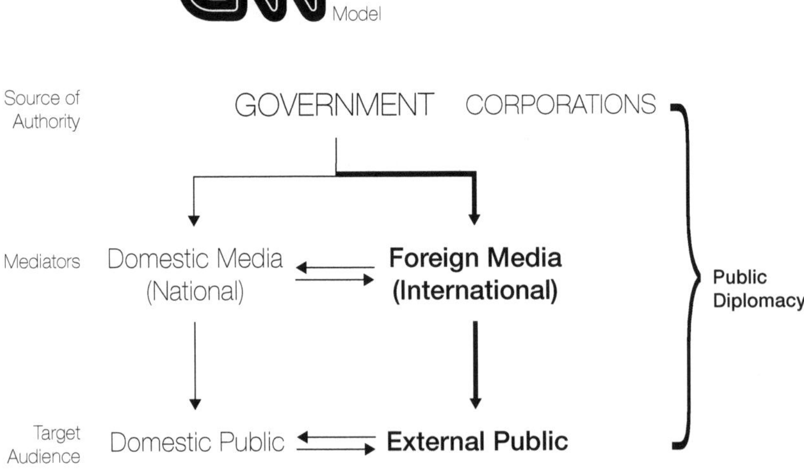

Figure 14.3. The CNN Model.

they were joined by privately owned corporations. This loss of exclusivity reduced the government's sway over the new private-commercial broadcasting. The media, the principal mediating agent, now operated in a mixed arena, internal and external, and it was no longer possible to separate target audiences who viewed the identical broadcast. The new private networks initially addressed the world as a single unit and broadcast the same programming everywhere. Gradually, an opposite process occurred: The global broadcasts split into regional broadcasts according to geographic cross-section and language.

•

The information flow model of Google, the world's most popular search engine, was introduced in 1998 and represents the new media in general and the Internet in particular. Google fits the era of new public diplomacy: The government monopoly no longer exists and official broadcasts have

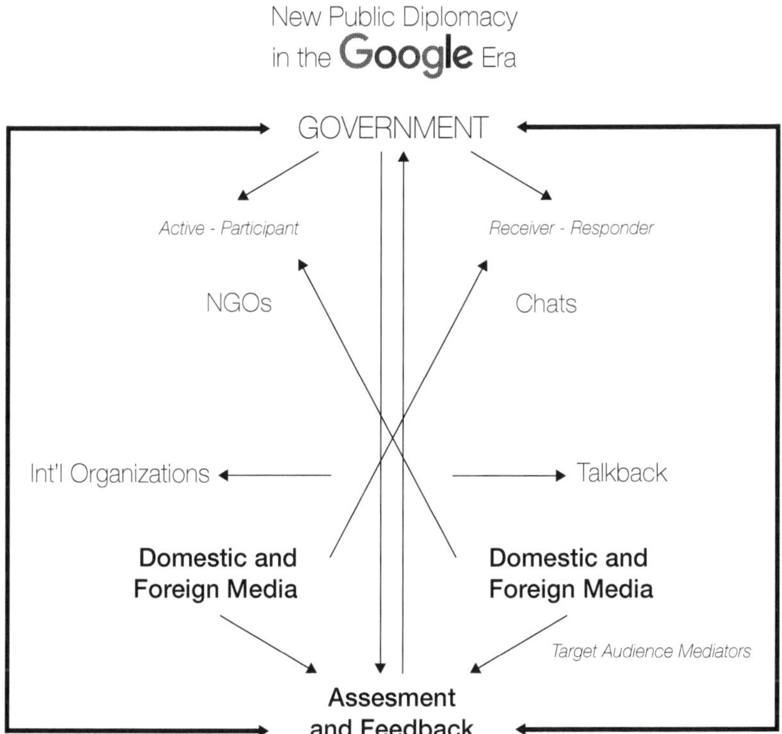

Figure 14.4. New Public Diplomacy in the Google Era.

become a part of the international broadcasting map, which includes private networks. New direct and two-directional channels were opened between the government and the public. The government could assess the public response to its official messages and policies via these channels. The new media joined the conventional mediator, the traditional media, and they compete against each other. The new media offers a range of possibilities, but is not replacing the traditional media, which continues to play its role. The public, the target audience, can directly respond to the government's messages and can become involved in social, political, and economic processes. Google is also involved in the impactful field of virtual social networks, whose power is growing in all areas of life.

The online social network Facebook is based on content Internet users create and share with other users. After launching in 2004, it conquered the entire world within a decade. As of the second quarter of 2016, Facebook had 1.71 billion active users (logging in at least once per month), a 15 percent increase over the previous year, and 1.13 billion people were logging in on a daily basis. Already in 2013, users were generating 4.5 billion "Likes" per day.[7] These numbers represent a nearly inconceivable scope of Internet use, reflecting how deeply the Internet affects our lives today.

Facebook represents a group of flourishing social networks that share similar characteristics. All of them excel in enabling their users to create and exchange content—and affect reality. The Internet magazine *eBizzMBA* ranks the leading social networks today as Facebook, YouTube, Twitter, LinkedIn, and Pinterest.[8] We should also note the capabilities of smartphones. In various blogs and forums on the Internet, users create virtual communities and make an impact on the world around them.

The Facebook model is direct and indirect, hierarchical and horizontal, one-directional and two-directional—all at the same time. Therefore, it is significantly different from the first basic model, which was direct, hierarchical, and one-directional. In the past, the government was the exclusive provider of information and later was still the primary one. In the Facebook model, it is becoming just one of many equal providers in the information system. It holds the greatest amount of data and the most important information, but the new entities are chipping away at its power. To engage in dialogue with these new entities, the government must make the conceptual and technological adjustments to remain relevant in the process.

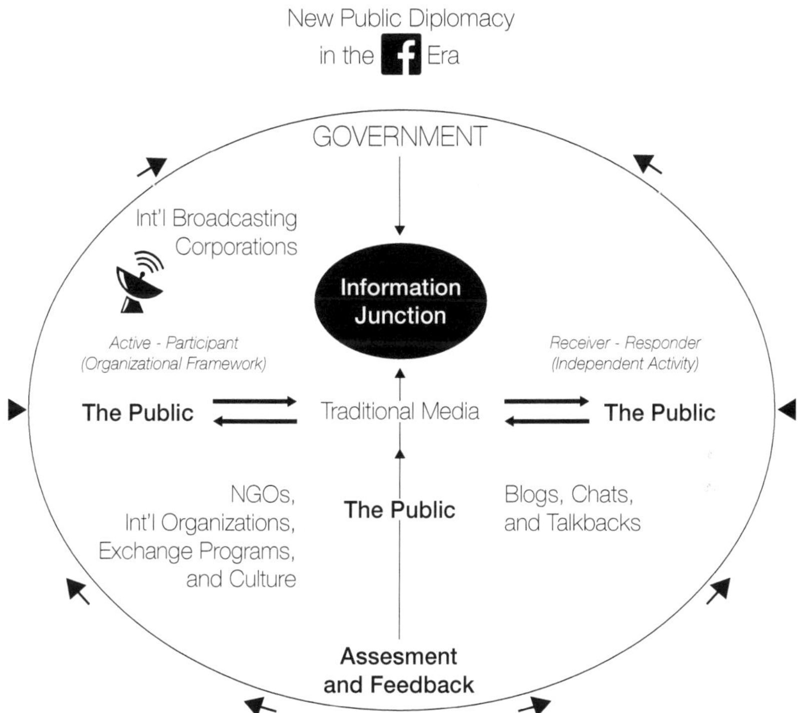

Figure 14.5. New Public Diplomacy in the Facebook Era.

The flow of information is the key to the sound operation of public diplomacy. The past decades have witnessed a historical development from the initial and simple model to the one prevalent today—Facebook and the social networks. In the past, the media was the primary mediator. In the Facebook model, the traditional media still exists, but it is weaker and must compete to survive in light of economic pressures. The new media changed the balance of power between the government and the public, undercutting the former's traditional role. The flow of information became horizontal and two-directional, and it is conducted between the government and public, and among the public itself. If the government wishes to remain relevant in the process, not to speak of retaining its senior standing, it must adapt itself conceptually and technologically to the new channels of information flow.

Empowering the individual in the media process. The public is composed of individuals, but today individuals can choose the public with which they wish to affiliate. They can communicate with others and create new social networks. The new public is no longer a "general" public. It includes subgroups and small communities that divide into new and old categories, such as areas of interest, age, gender, and personal history. Addressing a generally defined "public" is no longer possible and is ineffective. Dialogue with the "public" focuses on specific subgroups, and even directly on the individual.

The individual as an initiator and creator. In the Google model, the individual already acquired the ability to actively participate and respond. The Facebook model adds the ability to initiate and create. These capabilities change the array of relations between the government, media, and public. The public employs its newfound media capabilities to create messages that it shares horizontally or sends vertically to the government. The government lost its monopoly over the media to the large privately owned networks, and they both lost the monopoly over media content. Today, there are three entities operating in the media field with similar capabilities: the government, the media, and the public.

•

Based on the new model and the new capabilities it offers, I recommend three practical steps, which constitute milestones for establishing a diplomatic array that will adapt itself to the Facebook era. The first step is to deploy a "public diplomacy molecule." This is an innovation in the field and is based on the world of networked communication. The second step is to create a Public Diplomacy Authority in Israel to support and assist the new world of molecules. The third step is a specific recommendation to establish a global broadcasting network that will combine satellite broadcasts, cable, and Internet and disseminate information on Israel in various languages.

These steps are tailored to fit Israel but also are apt for addressing the global challenge in this area.

Molecules of Public Diplomacy

The public diplomacy array will be based on the model of "public diplomacy molecules." The term "molecule," borrowed from chemistry, refers to connected atoms that constitute the smallest unit of matter. The choice of this term signifies that the tiny units faithfully represent the center that operates them. The idea is to deploy a network of public diplomacy molecules throughout the world to perform ongoing missions in this field. The center will instruct the molecules and direct them toward activity in their regions. The molecule's personnel will work as volunteers, motivated by a desire to help Israel.

The idea of deploying a molecular array is based on the world of networked communication. Salient examples of this are the smartphone and iPad, small portable systems capable of receiving and sending information via a range of communication technologies. These systems serve functions that were performed by large stationary systems in the past. Thanks to similar devices, these molecules can disseminate messages in a much greater scope than ever before. The molecules engage with the new human networks of the virtual world and translate connections among individuals and between individuals and organizations. At the state level, government ministries—led by the Foreign Ministry and its overseas missions—are responsible for public diplomacy. In the world of the Internet and social networks, at the sub-state and supra-state levels, NGOs perform these missions. The molecules offer a new definition of the relations between a state and an individual or individuals located outside its territorial borders, who are nonetheless carrying out roles of public diplomacy on the state's behalf.

Individuals in cyber space, equipped with new abilities, exert influence on geographic and social spaces through connections and networks that stretch beyond their close environment. Israel can conduct a strategy of Diaspora diplomacy, drawing upon a global network of Jewish communities, large and small, in nearly every corner of the world. The communities maintain ties based on a religious and national connection—among themselves and with Israel. Organizations like the Jewish Agency, Keren Hayesod-United Israel Appeal, the Joint Distribution Committee, the Jewish Federations of North America, Hadassah, B'nai B'rith, and the World Jewish Congress create and expand networks. "The Jewish organizations can be excellent *hasbara* ambassadors of the State of Israel if the government will know how to guide and train them for this mission."[9]

Exclusive reliance on the "Jewish connection" is natural, but it risks stirring anti-Semitic overtones as evoked, for example, in the *Protocols of the Elders of Zion*. Jews in the Diaspora have often been accused of dual loyalty—to their country and to the Jewish people / State of Israel. Therefore, Israel must moderate its expectations from the Jewish community and can mitigate the problem by massively recruiting non-Jews who feel an affinity with Israel and the Jewish people for its array of public diplomacy. In the United States, for example, there are a growing number of Christians, evangelicals and others, who express strong support for Israel. I propose calling this network "Friends of Israel" so that it can include both Jews and non-Jews. The goal is to combine the circle of pro-Israel Jews with mixed and diverse groups, as the American Jewish Committee has done in Europe. The International Fellowship of Christians and Jews, established by Rabbi Yechiel Eckstein, is another example of mobilizing pro-Israel non-Jews and has recorded impressive accomplishments. The fellowship focuses on Christian lovers of Israel and channels its philanthropy to weak populations in Israel. Such networks have existed in the past and advocated for the State of Israel at every diplomatic and military junction in its history. The difference is that now they can utilize the new communications technologies and work much more effectively.

Economic diplomacy and cultural diplomacy also offer new networks of people active in the business world, academia, and culture. Colleagues from a range of fields conduct discourse via these networks, and sometimes they translate into meetings at conferences and international events.

In their book *Diffused Warfare*, Haim Assa and Yedidia Yaari analyze low-intensity warfare and conclude that asymmetrical conflict and global terror will continue to plague the world and Israel: "This means that the very concept of 'national security' is about to significantly change. The transition from contending with threats from states to contending with threats from organizations scattered among a sympathetic or hostile population, far or near, and which possess a real capacity for disrupting the everyday life of a state system, is fundamentally changing the way in which states perceive their security."[10] The authors propose a military solution based on the global network, utilizing it "to replace the central [military], expensive, complex and human-driven platform with many small, relatively inexpensive and autonomous munitions platforms that will be no less effective. A real possibility has developed for an alternative built upon multiplicity and relative simplicity. That is: many, small and simple."[11] Diffusion and decentralization of power are responses to the asymmetry of terrorism. The molecules deploy in enemy territory and act against it. They are all linked to one center, but operate independently. *My proposal is to shift the military strategy in asymmetrical conflict to the world of public diplomacy. Ultimately, both work in the same way.*

In the era of all-out warfare, traditional diplomacy was appropriate; public diplomacy emerged during the Cold War and further developed in the era of global terrorism to become the new public diplomacy. The current stage of the war on terror and the new public diplomacy is being waged in the arena of consciousness. Terrorism and guerilla warfare avoid direct and focused conflict and spread hostilities to many points in the enemy's territory. The use of information technologies, including international broadcasting and the Internet, amplify terrorism beyond its gains on the ground. The state responds in the same language. It proposes a war for consciousness that is also based on decentralized activity and that mobilizes the media as a force multiplier. This activity is built upon molecules of public diplomacy the state operates in the distant arenas.

The concept of molecules as long-term external branches, tiny but capable, adds new global dimensions to public policy. This is the strong side's response to the weak side in asymmetrical conflict. Now, the strong side can use the molecules to deploy small forces over a large territory in unexpected ways, while adapting to the specific conditions of each environment.

Israel should make use of the support networks that exist on the Internet and also create new global networks. The proposed network of molecules is built upon this conception. Each molecule is connected to the network, while representing the country of origin in at least four fields: media, third sector (NGOs), business sector, and academia. In this way, it operates four significant tools of public diplomacy.

The molecules are connected to three networks: local, regional, and national. All of the national networks are to be combined in a global

Public Diplomacy Model

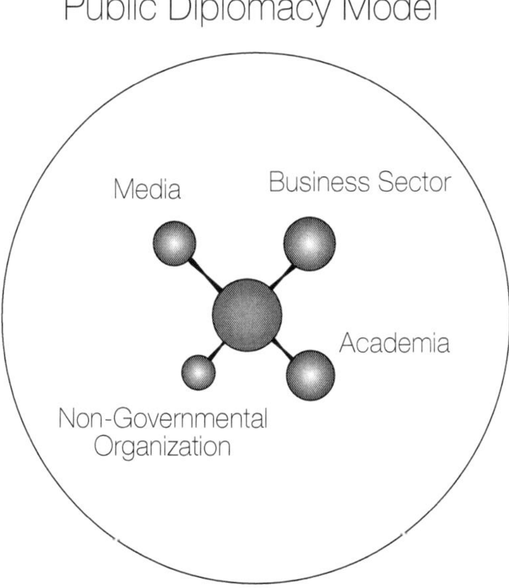

Figure 14.6. Public Diplomacy Model.

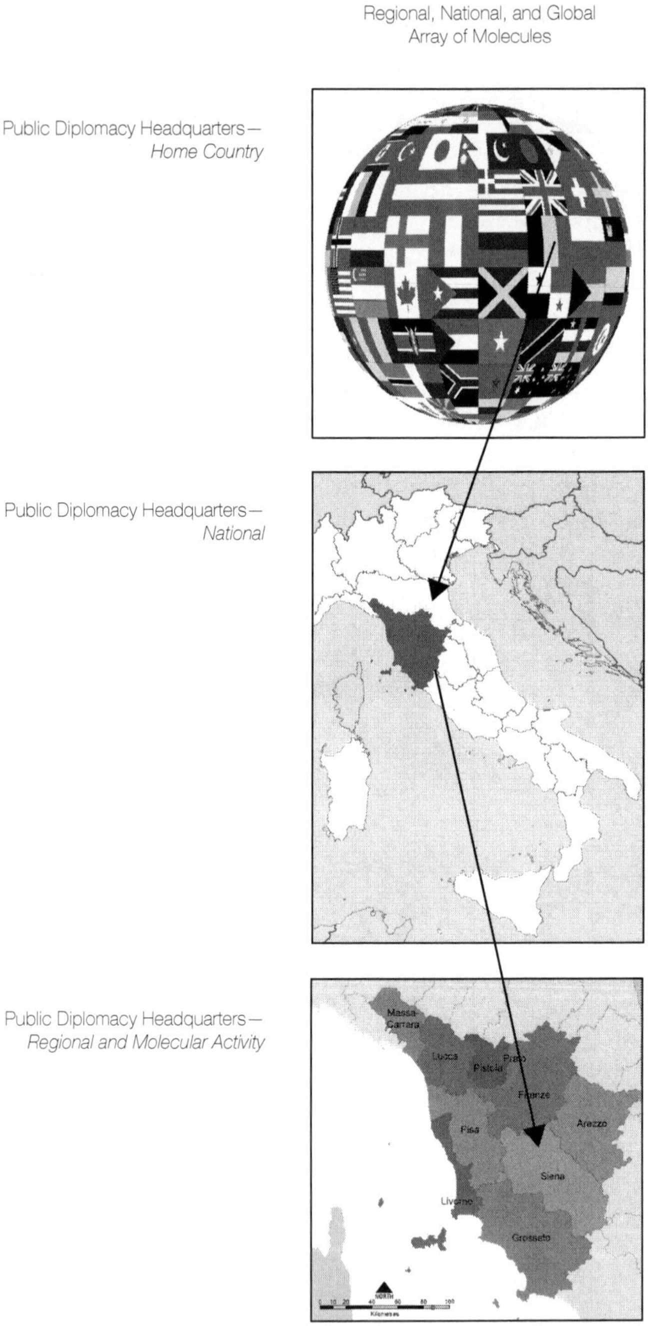

Figure 14.7. Regional, National, and Global Array of Molecules.

array centered at the proposed Public Diplomacy Authority, which will send messages and information to the molecules, and the molecules will then adapt them to a specific language, culture, and arena. The molecules will enjoy relative freedom of action, considering their distance and the special conditions of their respective arena. They will coordinate their activity with neighboring molecules and later report back to the headquarters on the results of their activity, according to evaluation criteria defined in advance. There will be two-way communication between the molecules and the Public Diplomacy Authority: the authority provides instructions, but it also listens and uses the information it receives to formulate an assessment of the media and overall policy.

This optimal model for public diplomacy is generic. Although based on Israel's experience, it developed during a period and in circumstances similar to those of other liberal democracies. Terrorism threatens the entire Western world, and liberal democracies are searching for effective patterns of counterterrorist action. The optimal model combines general components and Israeli components and thus can be adapted to other liberal democracies because the technological world and the processes occurring in it (such as globalization) are common to all. The tools of public diplomacy are shared by all states, as are the circumstances of low-intensity warfare, the prevalent type of conflict today. Thus, the optimal Israeli model can be applied in other states and arenas.

Public Diplomacy Authority

A centralized array of public diplomacy in the form of a state authority is a national need in Israel. The proposed array comprises the Public Diplomacy Authority (PDA) and additional governmental and nongovernmental agencies. The PDA includes the Center for Public Diplomacy (discussed later) and representatives of the various agencies, and it proposes joint methods of operation and the use of public diplomacy tools.

The new authority's unique contribution lies in centralizing all public diplomacy activity under a single organizational roof. This is a significant change designed to maximize and focus the efforts in this field. These efforts are fragmented today, and even when they are conducted successfully, there is a lack of synergy with other areas of activity. Establishing this type of authority requires a strategic organizational approach and readiness to contend with the political and organizational pressures that are rampant in the Israeli environment.

The director-general of the PDA is the top professional responsible for public diplomacy and should accompany the minister of public diplomacy in all consultations and meetings with the prime minister and his staff, the cabinet, and the government plenum in which the prime minister's media advisor is present—with the exception of political or personal consultations. The director-general of the PDA is a partner in shaping policy and executing it via the PDA and represents the public diplomacy aspect in decision-making processes, based on situation assessments regarding the media and public opinion. He or she must present these assessments in the decision-making process. The director-general's role is also to predict how the media and public opinion will react to decisions and events, and to suggest paths of action.

At this level, there are three roles that can be performed separately or jointly: 1) advisor to the prime minister and government on planning and executing public diplomacy policy (this is the primary role of the director-general of the PDA); 2) government spokesperson, who regularly appears before the media and the public to directly explain government policy and decisions; 3) a national explainer who communicates with the public during times of crisis or emergency, explaining the situation and instructing the public how to act.

The heart of the PDA is the Center of Public Diplomacy, which serves 24 hours a day as the *media situation room*. The center includes representatives of the main public policy entities: the PMO; Foreign Ministry; Defense Ministry; the Ministry of Industry, Trade, and Labor; the IDF Spokesperson's Unit; and intelligence agencies. In times of emergency, the representatives of the Public Security Ministry and Israel Police join the deliberations at the center, along with personnel from the National Emergency Authority, the IDF Home Front Command, and national rescue organizations. The center operates continuously throughout the year and is connected to situation rooms in the IDF, Shin Bet, and Foreign Ministry.

The national Media Monitoring Center monitors the Israeli and foreign media and sends regular reports to the Center for Public Diplomacy. The center periodically produces media assessments, primarily entailing an analysis of Israeli and international media, based also on public opinion surveys, discussions in international forums, decisions by international bodies, declarations of leaders, and other indexes pertaining to Israel's standing in the global arena. The director-general of the PDA presents the situation assessment in diplomatic and security forums.

In its role as a media situation room, the center collects information published about Israel in the media and on the Internet. It does this on a routine basis because policymakers are constantly interested in this information. The situation room intensifies is efforts during times of emergency, producing output more frequently and providing it to the relevant government officials. This output also serves as raw material for the PDA in formulating recommendations and plans.

The Center for Public Diplomacy operates 10 branches of the new public diplomacy, addressing a range of fields, from the immediate to the long term. Branches and professional fields that focus on the short term include media and public relations, international broadcasting initiatives, online diplomacy, Diaspora diplomacy, and international law. A second category includes nongovernmental activity of all time frames: short term, medium term, and long term. A third group encompasses four branches dealing with long-term activity, including humanitarian assistance, cultural diplomacy and exchange programs of delegations and individuals, economic diplomacy, and branding.

Alongside the PDA, there is also a Public Advisory Council of representatives from the public, the private sector, academia, and the third sector. The primary role of this apolitical council is to provide nongovernmental public support for the PDA. The council aims to assist the PDA and contribute input from various fields of civil life. The government will appoint the council but must allow it maximal independence and authority to boost its credibility and public standing. The council employs tools of public diplomacy, such as various forms of economic diplomacy, internal and external NGOs, international law, public relations, cultural diplomacy, foreign aid, and Diaspora diplomacy.

What is the preferred place of the public diplomacy array in the government system in Israel? Throughout the book, we have noted the salient advantage of having the array directly report to the prime minister and integrating it into the PMO. Indeed, as of 2016, the National *Hasbara* Headquarters, which acts as the national coordinator of public diplomacy, is directly subordinate to the prime minister, in part due to the prime minister's penchant for centralization. Nonetheless, in light of past experience, and in order to underline the importance of this subject, I propose that at least a deputy prime minister head the PDA, or a senior minister in his absence.

International Broadcasting Network

This third step in establishing a public diplomacy array also has strategic importance, but of much smaller dimensions. The emergence of Arabic television networks in the Middle East and worldwide demands an Israeli response. An *international broadcasting network*—privately owned and subject to public supervision—should be established. The government will grant a license to broadcast in Arabic, English, and other languages, in Israel and abroad. The broadcasts will be digital and transmitted via satellite. The network will be funded through advertisements, sponsorships, and donations. A government-appointed public council will award the broadcast license and supervise its use. The channel will reach Arabic-speaking target audiences in Europe and in other parts of the world via satellite broadcasts, the Internet, and other ways. The use of the two languages—Arabic and English—is essential and will enable reaching a wider audience.

In regard to broadcast content, my proposal calls for a mix of news/current events programs (for short-term purposes) and programs about Israel and Israeli life, which will build mutual trust (a long-term investment). Public diplomacy will find its place in medium-term and long-term subjects, laying a foundation of information and in-depth familiarity with Israeli society and its values. It is no coincidence that these subjects are components of soft power, which a state should exercise to win support and change opinions in the target country.

Chapter 15

Countering the BDS Movement

Israel is again immersed in war, a new war, a war against BDS—boycott, divestment, and sanctions. The level of violence in 2016 is low. True, a new wave of violence began in September 2015, inflicting a substantial number of casualties. Israelis argue whether this wave constitutes a real intifada, or just an "awakening." Of course, this is also a political argument, between the government and the opposition. The Palestinian camp is also experiencing a similar dispute. Hamas sees this as a third intifada, while the Palestinian Authority has refrained from entering this dispute about how to define the surge in violence. In any case, more than ever before, the wave of terror is characterized by low-intensity and sustained violence, leveraged in the political, legal, economic, and public diplomacy spheres. Israel is learning to overcome the new terror but is confronting the global BDS phenomenon that poses a formidable and unprecedented challenge.

The aim of the BDS movement, as expressed in social networks and traditional media, is to undermine the international legitimacy of the State of Israel and to establish a Palestinian state in the entire territory of Mandatory Palestine. In this new battle, Israel and Palestine are vying to shape the world's consciousness and views of their long and bloody conflict in two stages. First, they are fighting through public diplomacy for the hearts of civil society. Second, they seek to translate public support into policy changes by pressuring elected officials.

Israel was slow in formulating a situation assessment for the new battle. At first, Israel ignored the dangers posed by BDS, perhaps because the state was primarily focused on the Iranian nuclear threat. However, after the deal with Iran was signed, Israel halted its public and secret efforts to stymie Iran's nuclear aspirations and turned its attention to the new challenge. The seminal decision came on October 13, 2015, when the government assigned the Ministry of Strategic Affairs to lead the battle against the BDS movement, marking the beginning of an open campaign against it.

The director-general of the Strategic Affairs Ministry, Sima Vaknin-Gil, appeared before the Knesset's Transparency Committee and acknowledged that Israel is regarded internationally as a "pariah state" and set a goal that by 2025 no one in the world would still think of questioning Israel's right to exist.[1] Gilad Erdan, the strategic affairs minister, thus chose a very ambition goal: to end the battle over Israel's legitimacy, a battle that began even before the state was founded. Indeed, since November 29, 1947, when the UN General Assembly voted to establish two states in the territory of the British Mandate, Arab states have attacked the decision itself and its underlying logic and have adopted various means to isolate Israel, including economic boycott. As researchers Pnina Sharvit-Baruch and Kobi Michael explain: "The delegitimization phenomenon relies on a conceptual infrastructure and a network of groups and activists located in many countries around the world. It is marked by sweeping criticism of Israel's policies as well as political, cultural and economic activism against Israel."[2] In this context, the "Zionist is racism" resolution approved on November 10, 1975, was a very important milestone.[3]

The launching point for renewing the historical campaign was the World Conference against Racism, Racial Discrimination, Xenophobia, and Related Intolerance that convened for the first time in Durban in September 2001 (see chapter 2). The location of the conference in Durban and the atmosphere there naturally invited a controversial comparison between Israel and South Africa. The world had mobilized against South Africa's apartheid policies by isolating and boycotting the country until it finally moved to majority rule in 1994. The South African precedent became the battle plan for those seeking to delegitimize Israel, and this engendered the BDS movement. The Durban conference, which came a year after the outbreak of the second intifada, included an unprecedented attack against Israel, primarily by NGOs from around the world. Israel was referred to in the discussions and decisions as a colonialist, racist, and imperialist state.[4] The NGO Forum called upon the international community "to impose a policy of complete and total isolation of Israel as an apartheid state . . . which means the imposition of mandatory and comprehensive sanctions and embargoes, the full cessation of all links . . . between all states and Israel."[5]

Amir Ofek, head of the Foreign Ministry department dealing with civil society, described the diplomatic era ushered in by the Durban conference: "This is a battle for consciousness that focuses on civil society, and its central objective is to smear Israel and portray it as an apartheid state and lawbreaker in order to distance it from the international community and facilitate a change in official policy, which is perceived as too positive and supportive of Israel."[6]

•

After the second intifada ended in clear defeat for the Palestinians in 2005, they adopted the tactic of BDS. In November 2007, representatives from 170 Palestinian NGOs met in Ramallah at the first Palestinian BDS Conference and established the BDS National Committee (BNC). The BNC is the Palestinian coordinating body for the global BDS network of anti-Israel activists, primarily in Western countries, based on a strange but effective coalition of radical leftists and Islamists. The goals of the BDS campaign include opposing recognition of Israel or any negotiation with it, ending the occupation, demanding the rights of Palestinian refugees, rejecting the concept of two states, and advocating a vision of one state under Palestinian control.[7]

Omar Barghouti, who earned a master's degree in philosophy from Tel Aviv University, is the most prominent BDS leader, traveling frequently throughout the world. In 2011, he published a book entitled *Boycott, Divestment, Sanctions: The Global Struggle for Palestinian Rights*. Michael Deas is another high-profile BDS leader who appears often at conferences to recruit new members. Deas serves as the BNC's coordinator in Europe and represents ECCP (European Coordination of Committees and Associations for Palestine), an organization of BDS supporters in 22 European states.

Nonetheless, it is difficult to identify a global organizational structure for the BDS movement or a central headquarters. It operates as a networked movement, expanding its influence via social media. The "cells" of BDS supporters develop similar initiatives, each adapted to their different local settings. The state comptroller addressed the BDS phenomenon in a report released in May 2016: "Since 2005, Israel has been subject to incessant attempts by certain nongovernmental organizations abroad to incite against it and position it in public consciousness as a violent state and serial violator of international law. These organizations portray Israel in the global media, inter alia, as an isolated apartheid state, and they encourage various target audiences overseas to impose an economic, academic, cultural and diplomatic boycott on organizations, institutions, and individuals from Israel."[8]

Here are a few examples: supermarkets in Luxembourg boycotted Israeli products; the UN Human Rights Council published a blacklist of companies operating in Jewish settlements; the multinational G4S security services company left Israel; the KaDeWe department store in Berlin removed from its shelves eight types of wine produced in West Bank settlements and in the Golan Heights; Walmart stopped selling a costume of an IDF soldier; a caricature in Germany compared purchasing oranges from Israel to buying from the Nazis; a decision was made in Iceland's capital to boycott products from Israel; the European Union decided to label products from West Bank settlements; the pension fund of the United Methodist Church in the United States is boycotting Israeli banks; SodaStream was pressured into moving its factory inside the Green Line; the Sainsbury chain in Britain reduced its orders from Israel; two banks in northern Europe—Nordea (Sweden) and Danske Bank (Denmark)—announced their intention to boycott banks in Israel; the Dutch pension fund PGGM decided to stop investing in five Israeli banks; the president of South Africa called for a boycott of goods from Israel; Germany's national railroad company decided to stop participating in a high-speed rail project linking Tel Aviv and Jerusalem; Starbucks defended itself against calls to boycott the coffee chain and denied that it was financially supporting Israel; a Turkish-German website declared its unwillingness to sell merchandise to Israelis; the Presbyterian Church in the United States decided to boycott HP, Motorola, and Caterpillar, all suppliers of equipment to Israel; Deutsche Bank declared that investing in Bank Hapoalim is immoral; Germany threatened to suspend grants to Israeli high-tech projects if transferred to the settlements; the European boycott delivered a severe blow to Israeli farmers in the Jordan Valley; the largest water company in Holland severed its ties with Israel's Mekorot water company.

A typical example of economic boycott is the decision by the Orange cellular company to cut its economic ties with Israel. The company's CEO, Stephane Richard, announced the decision during a visit in Cairo, explaining that business potential was greater in Egypt than in Israel. This statement elicited an angry response in Israel and the government officially demanded that the French government, which owns part of the global Orange company, take action to stop the boycott. Orange indeed retracted the public statement but soon afterward went ahead with its plan to sever ties with Israel.

In 2013, the minister of finance at the time, Yair Lapid, announced that his ministry had prepared a report estimating the economic impact of the growing European boycott movement on the Israeli economy, but he refused to divulge the figures. Only after appealing to the Supreme Court was it revealed that the blow to the economy could range from 1.5 billion shekels to as much as 40 billion shekels per year.

In 2015, two senior economists at the Finance Ministry expressed their view that the European Union's labeling of products was a "turning point" that could lead to "a cascade of norms in which states adopt the new norm at an increasing rate until it is completely internalized by most of the international community."[9]

The BDS campaign led to a *legal war* ("lawfare") against Israel. Already in 2001, an arrest order was issued in Belgium against then–prime minister Ariel Sharon, and this was followed by other attempts to indict senior Israeli government officials and IDF officers for alleged war crimes. For example, there was a move to arrest Avi Dichter and Dan Meridor in Spain in 2013—Dichter due to his involvement in the targeted killing of terrorist Salah Shehade, and Meridor because he was a member of the cabinet at the time of the Marmara raid. In 2014, a court in Istanbul asked Interpol to arrest Gabi Ashkenazi, Eliezer Marom, Amos Yadlin, and Avishai Levy because of their roles as senior IDF officers in the Marmara affair. That same year, Minister of Justice Tzipi Livni was forced to accept immunity from prosecution so that she could meet in London with the U.S. secretary of state. Also on the legal front, the Palestinians decided to join the International Criminal Court (ICC) in The Hague and sought to apply the ICC's authority to the West Bank. Israel, incidentally, is not a member of the ICC, as such membership would open the door to lawsuits against Israel. The Comoro Islands requested the ICC's intervention in the Marmara affair since the ship was registered in the Comoros and flew its flag at the time of the incident. In 2004, the International Court of Justice in The Hague ruled against the separation fence in the West Bank, a ruling of declarative-recommendatory import.

The *academic boycott* of Israel encompasses three categories: central organizations, local activities, and an unseen "gray" boycott. The Israeli Academy of Sciences reported explicit boycott initiatives in recent years in Britain, Canada, Ireland, and the United States, but an unspoken boycott is reflected in the cancellation of visits by foreign scholars in Israel, and in the rejection of grant applications by Israeli researchers or their candidacies for university positions.[10] For example, the Modern Language Association (MLA), an umbrella group for linguistics and the instruction of English and English literature, passed a resolution censuring Israel, and the American Studies Association (ASA) voted in favor of an academic boycott of Israel. *Haaretz* commentator Chemi Shalev wrote that the ASA's decision "marks a significant and symbolic landmark for the Palestinian-led BDS movement. It should also be viewed as a serious cause for alarm by policy-makers in Jerusalem as well as by Israel's supporters."[11] The American Anthropological Association (AAA) decided to support a boycott of Israel but later withdrew this support. The largest academic union in Britain, the University and College Union (UCU), and the National Union of Students (NUS) adopted similar anti-Israel positions. The famous physicist Stephen Hawking canceled his participation in the Presidential Conference in Jerusalem to express solidarity with the Palestinians.

Another aspect of the academic fight is on the campuses, primarily in the United States, that became a battleground after the Durban conference. Students are a very important target audience and represent the future American leadership. The Students for Justice in Palestine organization leads the BDS movement among students and is active on about 150 campuses. About 20 branches of the Jewish Voice for Peace organization also lend support to the BDS efforts. Palestine Week is an accepted event at many universities, despite protests from some student groups and Jewish communities.

The *cultural aspect*, one of the three dimensions of soft power according to Joseph Nye, is a central tool in public diplomacy. The BDS campaign decided to pursue two strategies: pressuring artists not to perform in Israel, and obstructing and disrupting the appearances of Israeli artists overseas. For example, BDS activists implored Bruce Springsteen not to come to Israel; the Brazilian singers Caetano Veloso and Gilberto Gil announced they would appear in Israel, despite pressures from the BDS movement; a public campaign was mounted against the actress Scarlett Johansson because of her participation in advertisements for SodaStream; the appearance of the singer Matisyahu at a reggae festival in Spain was canceled; Roger Waters, a vocal advocate of the cultural boycott of Israel, told Robbie Williams that performing in Israel means supporting the murder of children; Bon Jovi resisted calls to cancel his performance in Israel; the Louvre Museum refused to arrange a tour for Israeli students; the singer Lauryn Hill canceled her appearance in Israel; moviemakers called for the Locarno Festival to cancel the screening of a special program on Israel; in 2015, hundreds of British artists declared a boycott of Israel until the occupation ends; the Tricycle Theatre in London announced that it would not host a Jewish film festival; and there were calls to block Israel's participation in the Edinburgh Festival.

Sports are supposed to be detached from politics, but even there a front opened against Israel. Recently, at the Rio Olympics, the Israeli delegation was booed at the opening ceremony and an Egyptian judoka refrained from shaking the hand of his Israeli opponent. Athletes from Israel are accustomed to such receptions when competing overseas.

A prominent incident was the attempt in 2015 to expel Israel from membership in the FIFA international soccer federation. The chairman of the Palestinian Football Association, Jibril Rajoub, complained that Israel was discriminating against Palestinian players, preventing access to playing fields, and blocking tournaments between the West Bank and Gaza. Rajoub called the Israel Football Association an instrument of apartheid and demanded that FIFA expel Israel from its ranks. This battle lasted for weeks, and extensive and vigorous action by the Foreign Ministry was needed to narrowly thwart the Palestinian initiative. Rajoub decided to withdraw the request at the last moment, without explaining the reason, and he came under harsh criticism in the Palestinian Authority and in Jordan. The Foreign Ministry expressed satisfaction over the failure of the Palestinian initiative but warned that it could not always mount such an extensive diplomatic effort, and it noted that anger toward Israel is easily translated into the language of sports.

The relations between the Palestinian Authority (PA) and the BDS movement are complex. Their respective objectives and methods are ostensibly different. The PA officially accepts the concept of two states and does not endorse the idea of bringing about Israel's collapse via a total boycott, as the BDS movement seeks to do. The PA does not propose a direct boycott of Israel; rather, it primarily opposes Israel's actions in the West Bank, which, in their view, hinder progress toward an accord. In light of the PA's international obligations, it must exercise caution. Since the BDS movement operates in the arena of civil society and not on the state level, the PA can keep its distance while still reaping the fruits of the BDS campaign. In September 2015, the Palestinians won the support of 119 UN member states in a successful campaign to fly the flag of Palestine outside the organization's headquarters in New York. This was an important achievement in the battle for consciousness, promoting the Palestinian cause in the international arena. Such symbolic achievements in public policy carry great weight.

·

The escalating fight against the BDS movement can be examined along four axes: covert-overt, direct-indirect, frontal-flanking, reactive-initiating. The first wave of activity was overt, direct, frontal, and reactive.

At first, the Foreign Ministry addressed the BDS phenomenon as part of its overall responsibility for Israel's international activity. Israel had yet to see the complete picture, just the various components. It succeeded in blocking a variety of extradition requests and fought openly against boycotts, but it lacked a comprehensive approach from the outset.

In 2010, three years after the BDS campaign was launched, the Strategic Affairs Ministry recommended that the prime minister create a dedicated headquarters in his office to formulate policy on the battle against delegitimization. A dispute immediately arose between the Strategic Affairs Ministry and the Foreign Ministry; the latter rejected the recommendation and opposed any interaction by the Strategic Affairs Ministry with the Foreign Ministry's regular partners. The National Security Council intervened and attempted to divide the roles between the two ministries. But the Foreign Ministry also opposed this effort, arguing in early 2012 that Israel should not create parallel units or duplicate activity. An agreement between the directors-general of the two ministries on a division of authority and responsibilities was never implemented.

In the meantime, the Justice Ministry quickly established a special taskforce and took action in the lawfare arena to protect its citizens, especially senior officials, from attacks by international organizations when traveling overseas. The aid flotillas to Gaza, and the Marmara in particular, surprised Israel, which was able to intercept them but found itself under increasing international scrutiny. Thus, despite their failure, the flotillas helped to boost international campaigns against Israel. BDS activists also came to Israel to be arrested and draw attention to their cause. Indeed, public opinion in the world became aware of Gaza's distress.

The question of how to respond to the BDS movement became a bone of contention between the Foreign Ministry and other state authorities. The Foreign Ministry traditionally preferred to maintain a low profile (see the discussion of the al-Dura affair in chapter 1), since open activity would provide greater exposure for the BDS movement and encourage it. Others within and outside of the government argued that the BDS phenomenon would not disappear on its own, and that appropriate resources would need to be invested to defeat it. But even within the Foreign Ministry, there was some disagreement over which *hasbara* approach to adopt. Israel's ambassador to the United Nations, Danny Danon, acted contrary to the ministry's position in initiating "the world's largest conference against the BDS movement" in 2016, thus providing extensive publicity for the BDS movement. "The initiative to act in the UN arena in the proposed format of a mass demonstration is a mistake," the researcher Michal Hatuel-Radoshitzky asserted. "In the UN arena, the effort to impose a boycott on Israel is not being promoted in a loud and demonstrative way. It is being done quietly by pro-Palestinian civil society organizations, thoroughly and systematically."[12]

While the state system was debating how to respond, with ministers and ministries each pulling in different directions, the IDF closely studied the new battleground. Three rounds of fighting between the IDF and Hamas and a second major war with Hezbollah in Lebanon taught the IDF that it must consider the factor of legitimacy in its military operations. The IDF realized that the duration of fighting in these types of small wars directly depends on their international legitimacy. As discussed in previous chapters, harming unarmed civilians ("collateral damage" in military lingo) and civilian infrastructure shortens the duration of fighting. Within about a week, the international community reacts, pressured by the local population and NGOs. Media coverage, especially television, and activity on social networks contribute to the buildup of international pressure and hasten the end of fighting. The IDF decided to subject its operational planning to strict legal scrutiny. It is doubtful whether any other army in the world imposes such heavy restrictions on itself. Legal advisors who specialize in international law accompany the IDF in its operational planning down to the brigade level to ensure that each operational plan meets the criteria of international law. At the same time, the IDF trained officers for liaison work with the civilian population, thus enabling them to advise commanders operating in civilian battle arenas—again, to avoid harming noncombatants.

Three government ministries dealt with the different aspects of the BDS movement and were expected to prepare strategic plans. The Foreign Ministry identified the similarity between the BDS movement and modern anti-Semitism and concluded that BDS is the new vanguard of the old anti-Semitism. The main change was that the arena of events was civil society rather than states. This called for a strategy of broad worldwide response, an offensive initiative and not a defensive one, to regain influence in the civil society in target countries. The ministry focused on sullying the "clean" image of the BDS movement and portraying its activists as anti-Semites.

The Strategic Affairs Ministry revealed a similar plan to fight the BDS organizations at a secret and closed gathering of 150 Jewish leaders from around the world—the Global Coalition for Israel (GC4I). This coalition was designed to provide an international network to fight the boycott on the local level, as this book proposes. The Strategic Affairs Ministry, like the Foreign Ministry, chose indirect and secret methods of operation. Such methods were inadvertently exposed in a public tender the Strategic Affairs Ministry issued for a person to serve as "senior head of the discrediting [literally, "blackening"] arena." The tender explained that the candidate would be assigned "responsibility for conducting an initiated battle against organizers and promoters of delegitimization in all matters pertaining to consciousness and the media, with the goal of generating counter-delegitimization." The public tender reveals that an unidentified government entity was formulating a strategy for a consciousness and media battle against promoters of delegitimization, and that the person filling the position would develop and implement tools in communication channels, including indirectly and via nongovernmental bodies. Needless to say, it was unwise to expose this type of secret activity.

After the tender was exposed, a number of articles were published about cyberattacks against BDS websites. The BDS movement accused Israel of attacking its website six times in an attempt to shut it down by overloading its resources. Of course, no one claimed responsibility for these attacks, which were described in a report by the eQualit.ie online security service. The articles on cyberattacks mention efforts aimed at shutting down the websites and television broadcasts of terrorist organizations during the second intifada. Israel did not lead these efforts at the time, but a number of countries answered its call to shut down broadcasting facilities and websites operating from their territory.

The minister of strategic affairs, Gilad Erdan, made a public appeal to Facebook to monitor messages communicated on its website in order to curb incitement. Erdan and Justice Minister Ayelet Shaked had previously announced the formation of a joint taskforce to address the phenomenon of incitement to terrorism on social networks. Facebook rejected the Israeli demand, citing freedom of expression. The government began drafting legislation that would hold Facebook and other social networks accountable for the content communicated via their sites. The proposed legislation and the entire public system is poised to assist the efforts Israel is investing vis-à-vis the BDS movement. The two ministers, Erdan and Shaked, also announced that they would work in tandem to prohibit international BDS activists from entering Israel and to deport those who manage to enter.

Prime Minister Netanyahu was slow to act on the BDS issue. In January 2014, he convened a government forum to discuss the growing threat of boycotts and sanctions against Israel. He was propelled into action after the Dutch pension fund PGGM decided to divest from the five major banks in Israel. He viewed this as a strategic step that would cause more extensive harm to the Israeli economy than the punitive measures previously taken against Israel because of its activity in the

West Bank. As usual, a dispute among the government ministers soon arose—in this case, involving Naftali Bennett and Tzipi Livni. Bennett contended that Livni was exaggerating the threats against Israel in order to support her argument against construction in the settlements, while Livni accused Bennett of seeking to undermine any accord with the Palestinians. Several weeks later, the prime minister spoke at the annual AIPAC convention in Washington and, for the first time, enlisted the Israel lobby in the anti-BDS effort. In his speech at the convention, he mentioned the abbreviation "BDS" 18 times and emphasized the threat the movement posed: "But the BDS movement is not about legitimate criticism. It's about making Israel illegitimate. It presents a distorted and twisted picture of Israel to the naive and to the ignorant."[13]

In October 2015, the government officially made the Strategic Affairs Ministry responsible for handling the BDS issue. It decided that the ministry would coordinate, integrate, and monitor Israel's efforts in this area, providing professional guidance and up-to-date situation assessments in collaboration with the Economics Ministry, Foreign Ministry, and other government ministries as necessary. The government decision also stipulated that a nongovernmental entity might be employed to assist in this battle. Thus, Israel's approach shifted from one extreme to another: BDS, once regarded as a nonentity, was now recognized as a clear strategic threat.

The largest public event dealing with the BDS movement was a conference in Israel in 2016, sponsored by the *Yedioth Ahronoth* newspaper and its *Ynet* website. In the weeks leading up to the event, the newspaper and website greatly expanded coverage of the topic. Participants at the conference included the president of Israel, government ministers, and representatives from dozens of organizations in Israel and overseas.

Meanwhile, the Foreign Ministry saw that the scope of BDS activity was growing and that coordination among the various groups was improving. Moreover, anti-Israel groups and activists were joining the BDS movement, which served as a sort of anchor. What began as only an idea gradually became a legitimate movement with international status and broad influence. The Foreign Ministry learned that it could no longer control the height of the flames and formulated a plan to combat the BDS movement. As previously stated, the ministry's basic premise was that the new movement was a form of modern anti-Semitism operating in civil society. While recognizing the difficulty in influencing civil society and its organizations, the ministry formulated an aggressive strategy of initiative rather than a defensive stance and sought to repair the damage that BDS activity had caused to Israel's standing in civil society throughout the world. The ministry recorded some successes, primarily in what ministry officials call the "transition from defense to offense," by tarnishing the movement's image. A series of failures in national and international events, plus the labeling of BDS activists as anti-Semites, hampered their ostensibly "clean" conduct.

The government later allocated about NIS 130 million to the Strategic Affairs Ministry to combat the BDS movement, and the ministry began to hire employees to conduct anti-BDS activity in Israel and abroad. This sum was four or five times higher than the Foreign Ministry's *hasbara* budget. The rift between the two ministries was an open secret. However, with no full-time foreign minister (Netanyahu held the foreign affairs portfolio) and the prime minister's primary attention turned elsewhere, parts of the Foreign Ministry's activity were deliberately divvied up and awarded to other government ministers. The Foreign Ministry, which had always been responsible for these matters, expressed its frustration in various ways. The ministry presided over a network of more than 100 missions worldwide that dealt with BDS-related issues as part of their job; there was also a department at the ministry's headquarters dedicated to fighting the BDS movement. The ministry demanded more resources for its activity and argued that only a diplomatic-civil and *hasbara* response could foil the BDS movement. However, the ministry was shunted aside, and the leading role remained in the hands of the Strategic Affairs Ministry.

•

By late 2016, a united international front had formed against the BDS movement—for example, legislative initiatives on the state level in the United States. Dozens of states in the United States have adopted or are considering measures to prevent the state from doing business with entities that boycott Israel. South Carolina was the first state to adopt this legislative tactic, followed by Illinois and other states. In New York, Governor Andrew Cuomo used an executive order to the same effect: In June 2016, he issued an order prohibiting any state funds from going to entities that support BDS activity. The executive order is binding on all state agencies and authorities.

At the federal level, two Republican senators, Tom Cotton and Marco Rubio, sponsored legislation against the labeling of products and stated that products originating in the West Bank and Gaza could be labeled as made in Israel. Cotton said that this initiative was intended to counter the global attempt to deny Israel's legitimacy.[14] A number of congressional representatives sponsored an amendment to a law promoting U.S. trade with the European Union, stipulating that any EU member state seeking to engage in free trade with the United States could not be involved in political boycotts of Israel.

In Canada, the parliament united in passing a bipartisan motion sharply denouncing the BDS campaign. A similar measure was adopted in Britain, prohibiting acts of boycott against Israel. (Labour Party leader Jeremy Corbyn, known as a critic of Israel, did not support this measure.) Several parliaments in Europe have recently discussed the question of funding for BDS organizations. In June 2016, the Dutch parliament debated the government's financial support for organizations backing the boycott movement against Israel.

It is not surprising that the United States was the first to mobilize against the BDS movement, nor is it surprising that this is occurring in the political-legal arena, where the Jewish community can leverage its power to offset its numerical inferiority. It is possible to fight the boycott movement with many tools, but the most effective instrument is simply to fight back in the same arena. The State of Israel and its friends, in the United States and in other places, have legal and economic tools that can harm the boycotters and exert counterpressure on those who are considering joining the boycott. These tools can influence companies, but also states.

The fight against the BDS movement can be aided by official governmental initiatives, but this is not enough. At heart, this is a battle being waged in civil society, which advocates freedom of expression and independence in its views. Unlike companies or governmental bodies, private individuals are entitled to decide which product they want to purchase, which country to visit on vacation, and which cultural performance to see. This makes it difficult to contend with the boycott on the grassroots level.

Joining in the anti-BDS battle were existing organizations, such as the Hillel organization, and new organizations mobilized by two businessmen: Sheldon Adelson and Haim Saban. The two hold very different political views, but they are united in their support for Israel and decided to sponsor an initiative to fight the BDS movement. Saban said: "I don't want to get into what Israel's policy is or is not. One thing is for sure: We do have an anti-Semitic tsunami that's coming at us." Adelson added: "The moment we change the decision of the various student organizations to approve sanctions against Israel, we'll be able to turn our attention to all of the other anti-Semitic and anti-Israel organizations."[15]

The largest American Jewish organization, the Jewish Federations of North America, created a taskforce for the war against delegitimization, and Israeli lecturers and supporters of Israel active at universities formed a network to warn of and respond to anti-Israeli events.

Many in the Arab world were glad to adopt the BDS movement. Representatives at the Arab League summit in Mauritania in July 2016 encouraged the boycott of settlements and their products and resolved to explore ways to work in cooperation with the global BDS movement.

●

The BDS map is similar to the flow chart I presented in the previous chapter on information and the media today (see figure 14.6). Governments no longer have a monopoly over information, just as they can no longer impose their will on the public in the civil arena. This reality allows individuals to speak their minds and disseminate their ideas, as well as make their own decisions on all of the current issues. The success and wide deployment of the BDS movement rely precisely on this principle; BDS leaders exploit the advantages of an open society, the flow of information, and basic democratic values such as individualism and freedom of choice.

The organizational deployment against the BDS movement brings to mind the difficulty in developing a centralized array of public diplomacy in Israel. If there were such an array, perhaps things would look different. However, as already explained, Israel has yet to find the formula for overcoming personal disagreements, disputes over authority, ego and ambition, which all lead to the same place in the end: Each minister and each system wants to do the work, and do it alone. Two ministries are now competing over which will do more, pleading their case before the government, the Knesset, and even before the public, each in its own way.

The state comptroller was called upon to put matters in order. Just as the state comptroller had written in the past about the failure to create a centralized national *hasbara* array, he now cited the divisiveness in the anti-BDS battle. The state comptroller noted that as of late 2015 there was a lack of clarity concerning the allocation of authorities and resources between the Foreign Ministry and the Strategic Affairs Ministry, and that decisions on this matter from 2012 had never been implemented. His report also states: "Despite the decision of the security-diplomatic cabinet of October 2015 to authorize the Strategic Affairs Ministry to conduct and coordinate the interministerial fight against the phenomenon of boycotts, consideration should be given to the fact that it still lacks the inherent operational advantages the Foreign Ministry possesses."[16]

This same message can be found in previous reports on Israel's public diplomacy array.

The state comptroller provided a detailed and instructive account of the shortcomings of the two ministries and cited the problematic nature of the division of roles between them. In regard to the Strategic Affairs Ministry, the state comptroller wrote that it had failed to take full advantage of the budget it received, did not show significant achievements in the battle against the BDS movement, and failed to implement its strategic work plan in 2015. The state comptroller was also critical of the Foreign Ministry, noting that despite the efforts made by its overseas missions to fight the BDS movement, the ministry lacked personnel dedicated to conducting this fight. According to the state comptroller, the Foreign Ministry's public diplomacy array is incapable of countering the hostility toward Israel overseas, and this hostility is penetrating communities that had previous supported Israel wholeheartedly.

In his report, the state comptroller also noted a lack of strategic cooperation between the Ministry of Diaspora Affairs and the Foreign Ministry. Despite a rise in anti-Semitism, including physical attacks against Jews and Jewish institutions, these two ministries operate on separate tracks that have not produced significant achievements on this front, according to the state comptroller's report.

•

Nonetheless, Prime Minister Netanyahu is actually quite satisfied with how the anti-BDS battle is going. In a rare appearance as foreign minister, speaking to a Knesset committee, he boasted: "We defeated them. We're taking action against BDS and, therefore, boycott supporters are on the defensive. They're taking hits on many fronts." This was a surprising assessment, especially since Israel's campaign had barely gotten started, the Strategic Affairs Ministry had just launched its long-term strategy, and the ministry's director-general had stated that it would take 10 years to uproot the BDS movement. Oded Eran, a researcher at the Institute for National Security Studies (INSS) who formerly served as Israel's ambassador to the European Union, said that the prime minister's remarks were not "complete" or "precise." Danny Ayalon, a former deputy foreign minister, reacted: "To say that we defeated the boycott movement is an exaggeration and it's also dangerous because it could lead to complacence."[17] Incidentally, on the same day that Netanyahu made his optimistic declaration, the National Labor Relations Board in the United States affirmed the right of the United Electrical, Radio, and

Machine Workers of America to boycott Israel. And this came a few days after El Al announced it would not open a direct flight route to the Spanish city of Santiago de Compostela after the city council passed a motion in support of the BDS movement.

All signs point to the fact that the BDS movement is not going away anytime soon. Its roots are planted deeply in anti-Semitism and hatred of Israel, enabling it to gain new followers every day. Israel must take action to fortify fronts throughout the world. The networked solution is immediate and obvious; it is a battle of network against network. The question of course is how to use the network and who uses it. Power struggles within Israel's government make it hard to shape an agreed-upon policy and, of course, makes it difficult to implement. The goodwill that exists in the world's Jewish communities, which feel the anti-Semitic dimension of the BDS movement, is not being exploited due to internal arguments and competition for funding. The BDS movement will not defeat Israel and it cannot totally isolate Israel, as in the case of apartheid South Africa. However, it has potential to cause real cumulative damage and gradually isolate Israel internationally.

In this battle, Israel should rely on its reservoirs of soft power—its history, values, culture, and scientific and technological achievements. This is not self-evident. Unlike Israel's hard power, which has proved itself in the past, soft power literally does not know how to win; it operates over the long term and creates gradual and slow change. There is no photograph of victory here (though, admittedly, pictures of victory have also become rare in low-intensity violence). However, this does not mean that BDS cannot be defeated. To do this, Israel should highlight the Jewish people's place in human history and its contribution to human creativity, along with Israel's contemporary importance to the democratic world and the values it shares with liberal democracies.

Joseph Nye spoke in the past about smart power as a combination of hard and soft power. More recently, he added: "Contextual intelligence is needed to produce an integrated strategy that combines hard and soft power" and he described contextual intelligence as "an intuitive diagnostic skill."[18] Applying this to Israel, this means the ability to understand the international context in which the state operates. Netanyahu's objective is to ensure the existence (survival) of the State of Israel in a hostile environment with multiple threats. Therefore, his mission should be to eliminate or mitigate these threats as much as possible. The BDS movement is one of them. It can be eliminated via tactics that are sometimes successful (and sometimes not). But it is also possible to take diplomatic measures, such as discourse with the Palestinian Authority and steps toward a two-state solution. In this way, at least some of the forces driving the BDS movement would be diverted and the movement would be weakened. That is the right path to pursue, in my view.

When Peres Died

Shimon Peres, president, prime minister, and defense minister, one of the most prominent leaders of Israel during its first 69 years, passed away on September 28, 2016.

His death, at age 93, was a sad yet fascinating opportunity to examine the path of Israel's leaders from the defense-military realm to the diplomatic-political arena. In retrospect, Peres was the last Israeli prime minister to devote approximately half of his life to defense before shifting to the world of diplomacy. This list of leaders includes Menachem Begin (Camp David Accords, peace with Egypt, and the full withdrawal from the Sinai), Yitzhak Rabin (Oslo Accords and the division of the West Bank between Israel and the Palestinian Authority), Ariel (Arik) Sharon (unilateral disengagement from Gaza), Ehud Barak (withdrawal from southern Lebanon and negotiations with the Palestinian Authority), Ehud Olmert (proposal for a unilateral withdrawal—"realignment"—from the West Bank), and Peres (Oslo Accords, Peres Center for Peace). Yitzhak Shamir and Golda Meir were exceptions, each blocking diplomatic accords in their own way. Golda Meir stymied initiatives for an agreement with Egypt, which ultimately resulted in a horrific war between Israel and Egypt. Shamir reluctantly agreed to participate in the Madrid Conference in 1991, but that diplomatic initiative led nowhere.

Prime Minister Benjamin Netanyahu endorsed the two-state solution in a speech at Bar-Ilan University (June 14, 2009), but in practice his long tenure (comparable in duration to David Ben-Gurion's) has been characterized by military battles against Hamas in Gaza and diplomatic deadlock.

The transformation of Israel's leaders is fascinating and can be understood in light of the old and familiar adage: "Things you see from here, you don't see from there." That is, as long as you are in the opposition and are not in a position of leadership, you can embrace extreme and negative positions, but once you enter the prime minister's bureau, your perspective changes and from that moment your positions moderate and urgently shift toward diplomacy.

Peres was one of the architects of Israel's defense establishment, serving as Ben-Gurion's personal aide and later as director-general of the Defense Ministry. Peres led the effort to build the infrastructure for Israel's defense industries: Rafael, Israel Aerospace Industries, Israel Military Industries, and the nuclear reactors in Dimona and Nahal Soreq. The reactors constitute one of the important keys to the State of Israel's security, perhaps *the* key. They provide Israel with a maximal security zone in a region rife with dangers and threats, including a nuclear challenge posed by Iran during the past decade. Here it is important to note that Israel strictly maintains a policy of nuclear ambiguity and has never acknowledged military capabilities or provided details in this context. After his death, the government decided to name the nuclear reactor in Dimona after Shimon Peres.

In the 1980s, Peres embarked on his quest for an Israeli-Palestinian accord. This followed years in which he was active in building settlements in the territories, settlements that are considered obstacles to peace in the eyes of the world. However, with the help of his advisors, he began to negotiate with Jordan and the Palestinians on the future of the West Bank. Thus, he reached the London Agreement with King Hussein (April 11, 1987), which then-prime minister Yitzhak Shamir scuttled, and later orchestrated the Oslo Accords, enlisting an unenthusiastic Yitzhak Rabin. Even after the Oslo Accords fell apart, during the second intifada (2000–2006), Peres refused to give up, and during his years as president he became the main standard-bearer of a peace accord between Israel and the Palestinians. At home, he prodded the prime minister, Benjamin Netanyahu; and in the foreign arena, he traveled the world and met with the leaders of various states, trying to persuade them that not all was lost and that it was important that they continue to invest in promoting a diplomatic agreement. He never despaired and never stopped. Some called him a fantasizer or perhaps a visionary who refused to accept the depressing reality on the ground and worked relentlessly for a breakthrough.

Peres's work in building Israel's defense capabilities boosted his credibility. Those who come with a security background, like Peres and other prime ministers, do not need to prove their commitment to defending the state. The credit they accrued then serves them in their diplomatic efforts. This applies not only to prime ministers. The ability of leaders to promote an accord and execute controversial moves such as unilateral separation derives from their public status in general, but primarily from their security record. This provides immunity, at least in part, from criticism and from being pejoratively labeled as "leftists." This is the basis for the accepted thesis in Israel that it is easier for leaders of the political right (Begin or Sharon, for example) to promote peace because no one will challenge their fidelity to the values of Greater Israel, while leaders of the left can more easily wage war because they can rely on support from the right.

Toward the end of his life, Shimon Peres returned to the Peres Center for Peace in Jaffa and changed its name to the Peres Center for Peace and Innovation. Adding the word "Innovation" is profoundly significant. Peres realized that the chances of peace were dwindling and wanted to add another dimension to the vision of the State of Israel. As an advocate of public diplomacy, he adopted the prevailing theme in shaping Israel's new image—a land of innovation and creative people. He believed that innovation offers great advantages from Israel's perspective; a small country can do great things through innovation. Therefore, he became enamored with nanotechnology and other fields of technology and pushed as hard as he could to embrace them.

This reflected his desire to strengthen the State of Israel's soft power, which is a function of human capital, intelligence, and creativity—attributes that Israel fosters and through which it can distinguish itself in the international community. For Peres, this meant turning away from the exclusive focus on peace; peace and innovation would now go hand in hand. It should be noted that innovation is also a value of hard power, because it contributes to the state's strength, international ties, and economy and boosts its national resilience. Innovation increases deterrence and keeps enemies at bay, preventing potential wars. Peres could hold the stick at both ends.

The funeral of Shimon Peres in Jerusalem was a sad and spectacular display of affection for the man, and by extension, for the State of Israel, which seeks every bit of support in the international arena. Unfortunately, Jerusalem has not witnessed this type of support since the assassination of Yitzhak Rabin on November 4, 1995. In the terms of this book, which focuses on public diplomacy, this was "funeral diplomacy." This relatively new term, derived in part from globalization, defines and ranks funerals. About 90 delegations from 70 countries came to Peres's funeral, including presidents, prime ministers, other heads of state, and senior diplomats. Few people in the 21st century have received such honor. The large gathering symbolized support for Peres—and his stubborn efforts for peace and for humanity—and conveyed a message: The participants want to see progress in the areas Peres pursued most of his life.

"Funeral diplomacy" can be analyzed in various nuances: who came, who spoke, who sat where, who conversed with whom, what occurred in the open and what occurred behind the scenes, and whether it was indeed a global summit meeting. After the death of Nelson Mandela, for example, a similar international summit convened in Johannesburg. Prime Minister Benjamin Netanyahu expressed interest in participating in this important gathering but was compelled to stay home. This was partly due to hints from the South African government that Netanyahu's participation was not desired in light of the history of relations between Israel and South Africa. Peres's funeral can be examined according to similar parameters. As noted, 90 delegations arrived from 70 countries; the main speakers were two U.S. presidents, past and present. Their eulogies focused not only on Shimon Peres, the man and his work in the security and diplomatic fields, but included political messages directed at Israel, the Middle East, and the entire world.

As President Barack Obama said: "Of course, we gather here in the knowledge that Shimon never saw his dream of peace fulfilled. The region is going through a chaotic time. Threats are ever present. And yet, he did not stop dreaming, and he did not stop working . . . Shimon's story—the story of Israel, the experience of the Jewish people—I believe it is universal. It's the story of a people who, over so many centuries in the wilderness, never gave up on that basic human longing to return home. It's the story of a people who suffered the boot of oppression and the shutting of the gas chamber's door and yet never gave up on a belief in goodness."

In his speech, Obama compared Peres to "other giants of the 20th century"—Nelson Mandela and Queen Elizabeth. For Netanyahu, the prime minister of Israel, this was also an important lesson in the extent of international popularity an Israeli figure can enjoy. And unlike the outpouring of international affection for Rabin following his assassination, Peres's global stature had nothing to do with the circumstances of his death (due to natural causes). It is sad to note, but Peres, in his death, momentarily restored the "other Israel"—a democratic Israel, an Israel that dreams, and an Israel that is accepted in the international community. The speeches at his funeral sounded these themes.

The seating arrangement at the event was also significant. Seated in the front row were the king of Spain, the British crown prince, and the president of the Palestinian Authority. Though the Palestinian Authority is not even a state, the participation of the Palestinian president was particularly significant because he does not generally come to Israel and his relations with Netanyahu are strained. As noted, the speakers at the event, their activity during their short stay in Israel, their various meetings, and so on are components of a new angle of public diplomacy.

Bill Clinton, the former U.S. president, eulogized Peres as "a wise champion of our common humanity." He described Peres as "someone who wanted the best for all children. Yes, the Israeli children. But also the children of his neighbors and the larger world."

And a final note. A revolution occurred in late 2016, as eight years of the Obama administration drew to a close. Obama, a Democratic president, an African American, an original and unique thinker, was a great proponent of diplomacy in general and public diplomacy in particular. Elected to replace him was Donald Trump, a Republican, whose views on international relations remain a mystery. During the election campaign, he advocated isolationism and imposing monetary commitments on American allies in return for protecting them. On the other hand, he also spoke of restoring America's "greatness" and of creating respect for the United States in the international community. He harshly criticized the international failures of the outgoing administration and cast some of the blame on his election opponent, Hillary Clinton. The impending denouement of the civil war in Syria in favor of the Assad regime, which relies on Russia's fighter aircraft and the Shi'ite bayonets of Iran and Hezbollah, is the final chord of 2016. This confrontation proved that brutal, unbridled force, bordering on genocide, can triumph. The international community, backed by the United States, cannot stop it through diplomatic means—mediation, negotiation, or political accords.

At Obama's last press conference in December 2016, the president stated that "to be an American involves bearing burdens of meeting obligations to others." However, he had to admit that he was powerless to help the Syrian opposition or even rescue the civilian population: "The challenge was that short of putting large numbers of U.S. troops on the ground, uninvited, without any international law mandate, without sufficient support from Congress, at a time when we still had troops in Afghanistan, and we still had troops in Iraq, and we had just gone through over a decade of war, and spent trillions of dollars, and when the opposition on the ground was not cohesive enough to necessarily govern a country, and you had a military superpower in Russia prepared to do whatever it took to keep its client state involved, and you had a regional military power in Iran, that saw their own vital strategic interests at stake, and were willing to send in as many of their people or proxies to support the regime, in that circumstance unless we were all in, and willing to take over Syria, we were going to have problems, and that everything else was tempting, because we wanted to do something and it sounded like the right thing to do but it was impossible to do this on the cheap."[1]

In practice, Obama was deterred from assuming this burden, and Russia and its partners flooded Syria. Soft power retreated in the face of hard power. And this is how 2016 ended.

Notes

Chapter 1

1. Ron Ben-Yishai, personal interview, August 9, 2007; Channel 1, September 30, 2000.

2. Yom-Tov Samia, personal interview, July 13, 2005.

3. *Maariv*, October 2, 2000, p. 1 (Hebrew).

4. *Haaretz*, October 6, 2000, p. 2 (Hebrew).

5. Henrique Cymerman, *Voices from the Center of the World: The Arab-Israeli Conflict Told by Its Protagonists* (Tel Aviv: Hakibbutz Hameuchad, 2005), p. 160; see also: *Maariv*, October 2, 2000, p. 1 (Hebrew), and *Yedioth Ahronoth*, October 2, 2000, p. 12 (Hebrew).

6. Charles Enderlin, personal interview, August 14, 2007.

7. Yarden Vatikai, personal interview, July 27, 2005.

8. IDF Spokesperson, September 30, 2000.

9. Lenny Ben-David, personal interview, July 4, 2005.

10. Shlomi Eldar, personal interview, April 26, 2006.

11. Gideon Meir, personal interview, July 13, 2005.

12. Giora Eiland, personal interview, August 2, 2005.

13. *Yedioth Ahronoth*, October 4, 2000, p. 9 (Hebrew).

14. Giora Eiland, personal interview, August 15, 2007.

15. *Maariv*, October 3, 2000, p. 10 (Hebrew).

16. Statement by the IDF Spokesperson, October 8, 2000.

17. *Haaretz*, October 6, 2000 (Hebrew).

18. Ron Ben-Yishai, personal interview, August 9, 2007.

19. *Haaretz*, November 1, 2007 (Hebrew).

20. *Haaretz*, November 7, 2000, p. 1A (Hebrew).

21. Giora Eiland, personal interview, August 2, 2005.

22. Ron Katri, personal interview, July 17, 2005.

23. Gadi Eizenkot, personal interview, June 12, 2007.

24. Channel 2, November 27, 2000; Yom-Tov Samia, personal interview, July 13, 2005.

25. Nahum Shahaf, personal interview, July 25, 2005.

26. *NRG-Maariv*, April 1, 2001 (Hebrew).

27. *Liberación*, November 7, 2002; *Kol Ha'ir*, October 11, 2002 (Hebrew).

28. In an interview with Esti Perez, *Reshet Bet*, October 2, 2007.

29. *Jerusalem Post*, November 29, 2007.

30. *Haaretz*, November 1, 2007 (Hebrew).

31. Gérard Huber, *Contre-expertise d'une mise en scène* (Paris: Raphael, 2003) (French).

32. Am-Shalom, personal interview, September 10, 2007; *Makor Rishon*, September 18, 2007 (Hebrew); *Jerusalem Post*, September 17, 2007.

33. *Haaretz*, November 15, 2007 (Hebrew).

34. See https://www.youtube.com/watch?v=bWQcRd_Mg60.

35. Yossi Kuperwasser, personal interview, March 13, 2006.

36. Moshe Yaalon, personal interview, October 6, 2005.

37. Moshe Arens, personal interview, April 4, 2006.

38. Ehud Barak, personal interview, March 2, 2006.

39. Amira Oron, personal interview, August 9, 2005.

40. Meir Klifi, personal interview, August 4, 2005.

Chapter 2

1. Mordechai Yadid, personal interview, June 17, 2007.

2. Alan Baker, personal interview, February 1, 2007; Adi Sheinman, personal interview, April 26, 2007.

3. Michael Melchior, personal interview, February 2, 2007.

4. *Haaretz*, August 5, 2001 (Hebrew).

5. Michael Melchior, personal interview, February 2, 2007.

6. Tova Herzl, personal correspondence, February 21, 2007.

7. Peleg Reshef, personal interview, March 8, 2007.

8. *Haaretz*, September 3, 2001 (Hebrew).

9. Jeremy Jones, "Durban Daze: When Anti-Semitism Becomes 'Anti-Racism,'" *Australia/Israel Review* 26 (October 2001).

10. Peleg Reshef, personal interview, March 8, 2007.

11. Daniel Taub, personal interview, March 8, 2007.

12. Shimon Samuels, personal interview, April 22, 2007.

13. Dina Porat, personal interview, May 1, 2007.

14. Zvi Mazel, personal interview, April 5, 2007.

15. Irwin Cotler, personal interview, February 2, 2007.

16. Daniel Taub, personal interview, March 8, 2007.

17. Eran Lerman, personal interview, February 14, 2007.

18. *Haaretz*, September 4, 2001, p. 1 (Hebrew); Adi Scheinman, personal interview, September 4, 2001.

19. N. Steinberg, World Conference against Racism, Racial Discrimination, Xenophobia and Related Intolerance, World Federalist Movement, November 7, 2001, p. 5.

20. Tova Herzl, personal interview, February 21, 2007.

21. Arad Nir, personal interview, May 21, 2007.

22. Adi Scheinman, personal interview, April 26, 2007.

23. *Haaretz*, September 4, 2001, p. 2 (Hebrew); Jones, "Durban Daze."

24. Mordechai Yadid, personal interview, June 17, 2007.

25. Ibid.

26. Alan Baker, personal interview, February 1, 2007; Michael Melchior, personal interview, January 7, 2007.

27. Noam Katz, personal interview, April 20, 2007.

28. *Haaretz*, September 9, 2001 (Hebrew).

29. From the website of Benjamin Netanyahu, www.netanyahu.org, 2001.

30. *Ynet*, August 31, 2002 (Hebrew).

31. Ibid.

32. Orli Gil, personal interview, March 21, 2007.

33. "The New Anti-Semitism in the Circles of the European Intelligentsia," www.e-mago.co.il, June 24, 2009.

34. Ibid.

35. Amos Hermon, personal interview, January 1, 2007.

36. Patrick Klugman, personal interview, March 3, 2007.

37. *Ynet*, October 16, 2004.

38. Shamir Mozgovia, *Haaretz*, September 22, 2011 (Hebrew).

Chapter 3

1. Joseph Nye, "The Information Revolution and Soft Power," *Current History* 112.759 (2014), pp. 19–22.

2. Joseph S. Nye, "Think Again: Soft Power," *Foreign Policy*, February 23, 2006.

3. Joseph Nye, "Get Smart: Combining Hard and Soft Power," *Foreign Affairs* 88.4 (July/August 2009), pp. 160–163, accessed August 16, 2016; John J. Hamre, Joseph Nye, and Richard Armitage, "Smart Power: Foreign Policy After Bush," *The American Interest* 3.2 (November 1, 2007), https://www.the-american-interest.com/2007/11/01/smart-power/.

4. Joseph Nye, "Hard Decision on Soft Power," *Harvard International Review* (Summer 2009); Joseph Nye, "The Future of Power," *Public Affairs* (2011), p. 84.

5. Joseph Nye, "Smart Power and the 'War on Terror,'" *Asia-Pacific Review* 15.1 (2008), pp. 1–8.

6. Eytan Gilboa, "Public Diplomacy: The Missing Component in Israel's Foreign Policy," *Israel Affairs* 12.4 (October 2006), pp. 715–747.

Chapter 4

1. Basil Henry Liddell Hart, *Strategy: The Indirect Approach* (London: Faber and Faber, 1954), pp. 187–188.

2. Ibid., pp. 187–188.

3. Sun Tzu, *The Art of War* (Oxford: Clarendon Press, 1963), p. 63.

4. Ibid., p. 65.

5. Avi Kober, "Low-Intensity Conflicts: Why the Gap Between Theory and Practice?" in Haggai Golan and Shaul Shay (eds.), *Low-Intensity Conflict* (Tel Aviv: Maarachot, 2004), p. 69 (Hebrew); also see: Martin van Creveld, *The Transformation of War* (New York: The Free Press, 1991), p. 20; Senator William S. Cohen, *Congressional Record*, May 15, 1986.

6. Shmuel Nir, "The Limited Conflict: Collection of Articles," *Zarkor* (IDF: Operations Division-Doctrine and Training, 2002), p. 110 (Hebrew); also see: Shaul Shay, "Limited Conflict and the Concept of Deterrence," in Golan and Shay (eds.), *Low-Intensity Conflict*, p. 168 (Hebrew).

7. Loren B. Thompson, "Low-Intensity Conflict: An Overview," in Loren B. Thompson (ed.), *Low-Intensity Conflict: The Pattern of Warfare in the Modern World* (Lexington: Lexington Books, 1989), pp. 3–4.

8. Yehoshafat Harkavi, *War and Strategy* (Tel Aviv: Maarachot, 1990), p. 193 (Hebrew).

9. Boaz Ganor, *The Counter-Terrorism Puzzle: A Guide for Decision Makers* (Piscataway: Transaction, 2011), p. 17.

10. Thomas G. Mahnken, "Why the Weak Win: Strong Powers, Weak Powers, and the Logic of Strategy," in Bradford A. Lee and Karl F. Walling (eds.), *Strategic Logic and Political Rationality: Essays in Honor of Michael I. Handel* (Portland: Frank Cass, 2003), p. 60; Ben D. Mor, "Strategic Self-Presentation in Public Diplomacy: The Israeli-Palestinian Case," paper presented at the annual conference of the Midwest Political Science Association, Chicago, 2003, p. 29.

11. Nir, "The Limited Conflict," p. 83.

12. Henriete Kunis-Ponta and Rinat Moshe, *On Consciousness and Influence and Their Relations: A Theoretical Model and an Analysis of Case Studies* (Tel Aviv: IDF Center for Consciousness, 2007) (Hebrew).

13. Avi Kober, "Victory and Decision in Modern and Post-Modern Wars," a paper delivered at a seminar held at the University of Haifa on January 28, 2001, p. 14 (Hebrew).

14. Zeev Schiff, private publication, 2007, p. 132.

Chapter 5

1. Jan Aart Scholte, *The Globalization of World Politics* (Oxford: Oxford University Press, 2001), p. 14.

2. Zygmunt Bauman, *Globalization: The Human Consequences* (Cambridge: Polity Press, 1998), p. 59.

3. Other names include the CNN complex, the CNN curve, and the CNN factor.

4. Philip Seib, *The Global Journalist: News and Conscience in a World of Conflict* (Lanham: Rowman & Littlefield, 2002), p. 27.

5. "There is substantial evidence that outlets like Al Jazeera are in fact acting in concert with terrorists to generate overtly false and misleading news reports" (*The Weekly Standard*, April 21, 2004).

6. *New York Times*, February 22, 2011.

7. *New York Times*, November 5, 2011.

8. *Ynet*, January 15, 2011 (Hebrew).

9. *TheMarker*, July 18, 2011 (Hebrew).

10. The April 6th Movement is named for the date in 2008 when a strike was planned in the town of al-Mahalla al-Kobra.

11. Dennis Ross in a speech before J Street on February 28, 2011.

12. *Haaretz*, January 11, 2011 (Hebrew).

13. *Haaretz*, February 19, 2011 (Hebrew).

14. *Yedioth Ahronoth*, January 30, 2011 (Hebrew).

15. *DipNote Bloggers*, February 15, 2011.

16. *New York Times*, February 14, 2011.

17. *Haaretz*, June 13, 2011 (Hebrew).

18. *Haaretz*, February 19, 2011 (Hebrew).

19. *Haaretz*, February 16, 2011 (Hebrew).

20. *Nana 10*, June 4, 2011 (Hebrew); *NRG*, June 4, 2011 (Hebrew).

21. *New York Times*, February 1, 2011.

22. *Haaretz*, February 7, 2011 (Hebrew).

23. *TechRadar*, May 25, 2011.

24. *TheMarker*, May 25, 2011 (Hebrew).

25. *New York Times*, February 12, 2011.

Chapter 6

1. Gershon Agron, *Prisoner of Loyalty* (Tel Aviv: M. Neuman, 1964), p. 45 (Hebrew).

2. *Maariv*, September 24, 1948 (Hebrew).

3. Yaakov Tsur, *An Ambassador's Diary in Paris* (Tel Aviv: Am Oved, 1968) (Hebrew).

4. The decision to establish general television in a full format was made after the war. The rationale was that it was essential to maintain a dialogue with the new Arab population under Israeli control and in the neighboring Arab states.

5. Government Decision 590, July 2, 1967.

6. Government Decision 489, March 25, 1969.

7. Peled Committee Report, 1968, p. 5 (Hebrew).

8. Elad Peled, personal interview, December 1, 2005.

9. Shlomo Gazit, personal interview, December 19, 2005.

10. According to the Gazit Report, "Deployment of the IDF Spokesperson's Unit," 1989, pp. 1–2 (Hebrew), which refers to the report from 1974.

11. Moshe Yegar, *Toward a History of Israel's Hasbara System* (Herzliya: Lahav Publishing with the Israeli Institute for Propaganda Research, 1986), p. 96 (Hebrew).

12. Alouph Hareven, personal interview, January 2, 2008.

13. Moshe Yegar, Yosef Guvrin, and Oded Aryeh (eds.), *The Foreign Ministry: The First 50 Years* (Jerusalem: Keter, 2002), p. 1055 (Hebrew).

14. Shmuel Katz, *No Courage and No Dignity* (Tel Aviv: Dvir, 1981), pp. 48–51 (Hebrew).

15. Azriel Nevo, personal interview, June 11, 2007.

16. Moshe Yegar, personal interview, July 19, 2006.

17. Yegar, Guvrin, and Aryeh, *The Foreign Ministry*, p. 1058.

18. Moshe Tamir, personal interview, July 2, 2006.

19. Zeev Schiff and Ehud Yaari, *Intifada: The Palestinian Uprising* (New York: Simon and Schuster, 1990), p. 45.

20. Eitan Haber, personal interview, July 2, 2006.

21. Yaakov Even, "The Media in the Intifada," in Reuven Gal (ed.), *The Seventh War: The Effects of the Intifada on Israeli Society* (Tel Aviv: Hakibbutz Hameuchad, 1990), p. 134 (Hebrew).

22. Arik Gordin, personal interview, December 25, 2006.

23. Ephraim Lapid, personal interview, November 23, 2006.

24. Tamar Brosh (ed.), *A Speech for Every Occasion* (Tel Aviv: Open University, 1993), p. 139 (Hebrew).

25. Azriel Nevo, personal interview, June 11, 2007.

26. Eyal Arad, personal interview, July 30, 2006.

27. Nachman Shai, *The Media War: Ten Lessons* (Tel Aviv: Maarachot, 2001) (Hebrew).

28. Ralph Shein, personal interview, March 20, 2007.

29. Meron Medzini, personal interview, October 12, 2007.

30. Alon Liel, personal interview, August 3, 2005.

31. Oded Ben-Ami, personal interview, December 27, 2006.

32. Benjamin Netanyahu at the Winograd Commission, January 11, 2007.

Chapter 7

1. Mendy Orr, personal interview, April 6, 2006; Raviv Drucker and Ofer Shelah, *Boomerang: The Failure of Leadership in the Second Intifada* (Jerusalem: Keter, 2005), p. 43 (Hebrew).

2. Gilead Sher, *Within Reach: The Peace Negotiations 1999–2001: Testimony.* (Tel Aviv: Yedioth Ahronoth, 2001), p. 236 (Hebrew).

3. See also David Ziso, personal interview, August 3, 2005.

4. Danny Yatom, personal interview, November 23, 2006.

5. Ehud Barak, personal interview, March 2, 2006; Alon Liel, personal interview, August 3, 2005.

6. Gadi Baltiansky, personal interview, August 4, 2005; Merav Parsi-Zadok, personal interview, December 25, 2006.

7. Amos Harel and Avi Issacharoff, *The Seventh War: How We Won and Why We Lost in the War with the Palestinians* (Tel Aviv: Yedioth Ahronoth and Hemed Books, 2004), p. 17 (Hebrew).

8. Danny Yatom, personal interview, June 11, 2006.

9. Harel and Issacharoff, *The Seventh War*, p. 19.

10. Channel 1, *Mabat*, September 30, 2005; Yom-Tov Samia, personal interview, July 13, 2005.

11. Harel and Issacharoff, *The Seventh War*, p. 17.

12. Shaul Mofaz, personal interview Jul 25, 2007.

13. Harel and Issacharoff, *The Seventh War*, p. 42.

14. Isaac Herzog, personal interview, June 26, 2007.

15. Shlomo Ben-Ami, personal interview, March 29, 2006.

16. Gilead Sher, personal interview, August 8, 2005.

17. IDF, lecture by the commander of Judea and Samaria, 2005.

18. Hanan Shai, "The Intellectual Challenge in the Struggle against Human Terror Bombs and Other Inhuman Terrorism," lecture delivered at the 2nd International Conference on Low-Intensity Warfare, January 31, 2005.

19. Aharon Yaffe, "Targeted Killing: Prospect and Risk," *Nativ* 19.2 (March 2006), p. 109, Ariel Center for Policy Research.

20. Ibid.

21. Mordechai Kremnitzer, "Is Everything Permissible in Countering Terrorism? On Israel's Targeted Killing Policy in the West Bank and Gaza," Israel Democracy Institute, Position Paper 60, 2006, p. 5 (Hebrew).

22. Ron Prosor, personal interview, April 7, 2005.

23. Giora Eiland, personal interview, August 2, 2005.

24. Shimon Peres, personal interview, April 14, 2006.

25. Sharon Feingold, personal interview, June 13, 2006.

26. "Suicide Bombing Terrorism during the Current Israeli-Palestinian Confrontation (September 2000–December 2005)," Meir Amit Intelligence and Terrorism Information Center (MALAM), 2006, p. 17.

27. Ibid.

28. Army Radio and *MSN News*, February 12, 2007.

29. Winograd Report, 2007, p. 38 (Hebrew).

30. Shlomo Breznitz and D. Carmel, *The Effect of Information on the Home Front's Level of Function: Research Project Submitted to the IDF Home Front* (Haifa: University of Haifa, Center for the Study of Psychological Pressure, 1995) (Hebrew); G. Kaplan, "Information for the Public as a Support System," *Collection of Short Articles on Information for the Public* (Tel Aviv: IDF Central Command, 1983) (Hebrew); M. Brender, "The Population's Behavior in Conditions of Stress and Treatment Methods during a Rescue Event," *Emergency*

and Mass Catastrophe (Jerusalem: Labor and Social Welfare Ministry, 1990) (Hebrew); Haim Omer and Nahi Alon, "The Principle of Continuity: Unifying Treatment and Management in Disaster and Trauma," *American Journal of Community Psychology* 22 (April 1994), pp. 273–287; M. Drori, G. Posen, and K. Ginsburg, "A Model for Operating a Public Information Center in a Mass Casualty Event at a Medical Center in Tel Aviv," *Society and Social Welfare* 19.2 (May 1999) (Hebrew), pp. 245–258.

31. A. Carmeli, L. Mevorach, N. Lieberman, A. Taubman, S. Kahanovitz, and D. Navon, "The Gulf War: The Home Front in Time of Crisis," *Human in Battle Project* (Tel Aviv: Defense Ministry, 1992) (Hebrew).

32. Shlomo Ganor, personal interview, June 12, 2006.

33. Philip Seib, "Hegemonic No More: Western Media, the Rise of Al-Jazeera, and the Influence of Diverse Voices," *International Studies Review* 7 (2005), p. 604.

34. Shlomo Ganor, personal interview, June 12, 2006.

35. Zvi Mazel, personal interview, April 5, 2007.

36. Yaakov Orr, *Israel's Arabic Broadcasts* (Defense Ministry, Coordinator of Government Activities in the Territories, November 23, 2000).

37. Reuven Erlich, *The War for Consciousness in the Framework of the Conflict between the Terrorist Organizations and Israel: Hezbollah as a Test Case* (Ramat Hasharon: Meir Amit Intelligence & Terror Information Center, May 2, 2007), p. 11 (Hebrew).

38. Gabriel Weimann, "Public Criticism of the Media during the 2006 War in Lebanon," *The Media in the Lebanon War Series* (Tel Aviv: Tel Aviv University, December 2006), pp. 30–31 (Hebrew).

39. "The International Community Continues Efforts to Stop Broadcasts of Hamas' Al-Manar Television Channel," Meir Amit Intelligence and Terrorism Information Center (MALAM), August 15, 2005 (Hebrew).

40. Yaakov Orr, personal interview, June 21, 2005.

41. Yossi Kuperwasser, personal interview, March 13, 2006.

42. Israel Ziv, personal interview, June 20, 2006.

43. Ibid.; see also the Winograd Report, 2008.

44. *The Limited Conflict* (Tel Aviv: IDF Ground Forces Command, 2005), p. 22 (Hebrew).

45. Colonel (ret.) Ephraim Lavi, head of the central sector in military intelligence, *Maariv-Sofshavua*, December 16, 2005, p. 49 (Hebrew).

46. Israel Ziv, personal interview, June 20, 2006.

47. Ron Schleifer, *Psychological Warfare* (Tel Aviv: IDF–Maarachot and Defense Ministry, 2007), p. 280 (Hebrew).

48. Israel Ziv, personal interview, June 20, 2006.

49. Ruth Yaron, personal interview, February 6, 2006; and State Comptroller's Report 2007A, p. 461 (Hebrew).

50. Amit Livni, personal interview, May 31, 2006.

51. Ruth Yaron, personal interview, August 11, 2005.

52. Gadi Eizenkot, personal interview, June 12, 2007.

53. Kunis-Ponta and Moshe, *On Consciousness*, p. 38.

54. Moshe Tamir, personal interview, July 2, 2006.

55. *Ynet*, January 5, 2006 (Hebrew); *Haaretz*, May 21, 2001 (Hebrew).

56. "Ha'alonka," *Haaretz*, May 3, 2002, p. 3 (Hebrew).

57. Schleifer, *Psychological Warfare*, pp. 283–284.

58. *Haaretz*, February 29, 2008, p. 2 (Hebrew).

59. *Dictionary of IDF Terminology* (Tel Aviv: IDF, 1998), p. 211.

60. Harel and Issacharoff, *The Seventh War*, p. 120.

61. Giora Eiland, personal interview, August 2, 2005.

62. *Haaretz*, April 18, 2001 (Hebrew).

63. Orly Gal, personal interview, February 15, 2006.

64. Moshe Yaalon, *Fifth Session: IDF and the Media in Times of Warfare—Discussion Group on: The Media as a Strategic Consideration in Preparing for Combat*, Army and Society Forum (Jerusalem: Israel Democracy Institute, June 4, 2002), pp. 47–48 (Hebrew).

65. *Yedioth Ahronoth*, July 16, 2001 (Hebrew).

66. Raanan Gissin, personal interview, July 20, 2005.

67. David Ziso, personal interview, August 3, 2005.

68. Elam Kott, personal interview, August 21, 2005.

69. *The Limited Conflict*, IDF, Ground Forces Command, 2005.

70. Alon Gellert, personal interview, April 17, 2007.

71. Eival Gilady, personal interview, May 23, 2006.

Chapter 8

1. Gadi Baltiansky, personal interview, August 4, 2005.

2. Merav Parsi-Zadok, personal interview, December 25, 2006.

3. Raviv Drucker, *Harikari: Ehud Barak in the Test of Results* (Tel Aviv: Yedioth Ahronoth, 2002), pp. 341–342 (Hebrew).

4. Arnon Perlman, personal interview, February 27, 2006.

5. Reuven Adler, personal interview, July 20, 2006.

6. Dov Weissglass, personal interview, February 2, 2007.

7. Reuven Adler, personal interview, July 20, 2006.

8. Asaf Shariv, personal interview, July 19, 2007.

9. Raanan Gissin, personal interview, May 3, 2005.

10. David Baker, personal interview, July 17, 2005.

11. Shai Nitzan, personal interview, December 25, 2007.

12. Remarks at the Winograd Commission hearings, January 11, 2007.

13. Uzi Dayan, personal interview, September 26, 2006.

14. *Yedioth Ahronoth*, May 22, 2007 (Hebrew).

15. Ilan Mizrahi, personal interview, January 1, 2008.

16. State Comptroller's Report, 2006, p. 13 (Hebrew).

17. Charles D. Freilich, "National Security Decision-Making in Israel: Processes, Pathologies, and Strengths," *Middle East Journal* 60.4 (2006), p. 641.

18. Final Report of the Commission to Investigate the Lebanon Campaign in 2006, Vol. A, January 2008, p. 578 (Hebrew).

19. Ibid.

20. *Yedioth Ahronoth*, November 15, 2007, p. 2; December 7, 2007, p. 25 (Hebrew).

21. A. Halfon, "Structure of the Foreign Service of the Jewish State," in Yegar, Guvrin, and Aryeh (eds.), *The Foreign Ministry: The First 50 Years* (Jerusalem: Keter, 2002), p. 9 (Hebrew).

22. Hanan Aynor, *Thirty Years of International Assistance of the State of Israel* (Jerusalem: Haigud Society for Transfer of Technology and The Truman Institute, 1990) (Hebrew).

23. Arthur Avnon, personal interview, August 14, 2007.

24. Ilan Sztulman, personal interview, August 17, 2005.

25. Silvan Shalom, personal interview, May 24, 2006.

26. Nati Tucker, "Israel's New Brand: More High-Tech and Innovation, Less Warfare and Heritage," *TheMarker*, January 3, 2013 (Hebrew).

27. Yarden Vatikai, personal interview, July 27, 2005.

28. Yehiel Horev, personal interview, July 2, 2006.

29. Oded Ben-Ami, *Spokesmanship 2000*, document from IDF spokesperson to Chief of Staff Shaul Mofaz, 2000.

30. Arik Gordin, personal interview, December 25, 2006.

31. Irit Atzmon, personal interview, February 23, 2006.

32. Moshe Yaalon, personal interview, October 6, 2005.

33. Meir Klifi, personal interview, August 4, 2005.

34. Yoni Dahuh-Halevi, personal interview, July 3, 2005.

35. IDF, Grounds Forces Command, *Combat Directives—Media Techniques: IDF and the Media—Integrating Spokesmanship*, 2004 (Hebrew).

36. Ruth Yaron, *IDF Spokesperson's Division: Strategic Summary 2002–2005* (Tel Aviv: IDF Spokesperson's Division, 2005), p. 31 (Hebrew).

37. Avi Benayahu, Army Radio, September 29, 2005.

38. Uzi Dayan, personal interview, September 26, 2006.

39. Hanan Greenberg and Ilan Marciano, *Ynet*, November 20, 2003 (Hebrew).

40. *NRG-Maariv*, October 4, 2004 (Hebrew).

41. Ruth Yaron, personal interview, August 10, 2005.

42. Elam Kott, personal interview, August 21, 2005.

43. Ron Kitri, *Fifth Session: IDF and the Media in Times of Warfare—Open Meeting*, Army and Society Forum (Jerusalem: Israel Democracy Institute, June 4, 2002), p. 12 (Hebrew).

44. Rafik Halabi, personal interview, June 18, 2007.

45. Nachman Shai, *NRG-Maariv*, August 21, 2011 (Hebrew).

Chapter 9

1. Hezi Kalo, personal interview, October 18, 2006.

2. See Alon Navot, *The Shin Bet and the Media*, final project submitted to the National Security College, 1995 (Hebrew).

3. Avraham Shalom, personal interview, February 2, 2007.

4. Moshe Negbi, *Paper Tiger* (Tel Aviv: Sifriyat Hapoalim, 1985), p. 10 (Hebrew).

5. Yechiel Gutman, *A Storm in the GSS* (Tel Aviv: Yedioth Ahronoth, 1995), p. 12 (Hebrew).

6. Hezi Kalo, personal interview, October 18, 2006; see also Yisrael Hasson, personal interview, July 12, 2006.

7. Ehud Yatom, personal interview, November 23, 2006.

8. Yaakov Peri, personal interview, May 22, 2006.

9. Yaakov Peri, personal interview, June 21, 2006.

10. Yehiel Horev, personal interview, July 2, 2006.

11. Carmi Gillon, personal interview, July 23, 2006.

12. Hezi Kalo, personal interview, October 18, 2006.

13. Lior Akerman, personal interview, March 16, 2006.

14. Avi Dichter, personal interview, August 10, 2005.

15. Ofer Dekel, personal interview, July 20, 2005.

16. Yaakov Zigdon, *Studies in the Doctrine of Building Military Force* (Ramat Hasharon: IDF Staff and Command College, 2004), p. 239 (Hebrew).

17. Ron Kitri, personal interview, January 2, 2007.

18. Avi Dichter, personal interview, August 10, 2005.

19. Ibid.

20. Ofer Dekel, personal interview, July 20, 2005.

21. Gideon Ezra, personal interview, July 5, 2006.

22. Ehud Yatom, personal interview, November 23, 2006.

23. Harel and Issacharoff, *The Seventh War*, p. 318 (Hebrew).

24. Alon Ben-David, personal interview, March 21, 2006.

25. Alex Fishman, *Yedioth Ahronoth*, August 19, 2011, p. 1 (Hebrew).

26. Charles Enderlin, personal interview, August 14, 2007.

27. Ofer Dekel, personal interview, July 20, 2005.

28. Amit Livni, personal interview, May 31, 2006.

29. Roni Shaked, personal interview, May 30, 2006.

30. Binyamin Ben-Eliezer, personal interview, July 23, 2006.

Chapter 10

1. Amira Dotan, personal interview, August 14, 2007.

2. Aryeh Green, personal interview, May 9, 2007.

3. Ido Aharoni, personal interview, November 24, 2004.

4. This entailed a fabricated video that ostensibly showed the demolition of the home of the terrorist who murdered students at the Mercaz Harav yeshiva in Jerusalem.

5. Yigal Carmon, personal interview, July 12, 2006.

6. Itamar Marcus, personal interview, July 6, 2006.

7. Phil Blazer, personal interview, June 12, 2006.

8. Joey Low, personal interview, May 28, 2006.

9. Shachar Zahavi, personal interview, October 18, 2006.

Chapter 11

1. *Haaretz*, October 8, 2000; *Yedioth Ahronoth*, October 8, 2000; *Haaretz*, October 11, 2000.

2. Danny Yatom, personal interview, June 11, 2006.

3. Alon Liel, personal interview, August 3, 2005. See also Gadi Baltiansky, personal interview, August 4, 2005; Drucker, *Harikari*, p. 342.

4. Alon Liel, personal interview, August 3, 2005.

5. M. Tuchfeld, *Reshet Bet*, October 22, 2000.

6. *Haaretz*, January 8, 2002; *Jerusalem Post*, October 14, 2001.

7. Israela Oron, personal interview, December 10, 2006.

8. The State Comptroller's Report, 2002, p. 14.

9. Maj. Gen. (ret.) Yaakov Orr, personal interview 2006.

10. Hirsh Goodman, "Israel's Information Policy during the Iraq War," *Strategic Assessment* 6.3 (November 2003), pp. 28–29.

11. Ibid., p. 23.

12. *Haaretz*, March 19, 2003.

13. Report by the Knesset Foreign Affairs and Defense Committee, 2004, p. 31 (Hebrew).

14. Isaac Ben-Israel, *The First Israel-Hezbollah Missile War* (Tel Aviv: Program for Security Studies, College of Policy and Government, Tel Aviv University, May 2007), pp. 7–8 (Hebrew).

15. Meir Elran and Shlomo Brom (eds.), "Introduction," in *The Second Lebanon War: Strategic Dimensions* (Tel Aviv: INSS and Yedioth Ahronoth, 2007) (Hebrew).

16. Israel Maimon, personal interview, July 31, 2007.

17. Tzipi Livni, personal interview, July 23, 2007.

18. Gadi Eizenkot, personal interview, June 12, 2007. (Lt. Gen. Eizenkot, then the head of the Operations Directorate, became IDF chief of staff in 2015.)

19. Colette Avital, personal interview, May 29, 2007.

20. Israel Maimon, personal interview, July 31, 2007.

21. Malcolm Hoenlein, personal interview, January 21, 2007.

22. Silvan Shalom, personal interview, May 24, 2006.

Chapter 12

1. *Yedioth Ahronoth*, October 13, 2000 (Hebrew).

2. *Maariv*, October 13, 2000, p. 3 (Hebrew).

3. *Ynet*, October 12, 2000 (Hebrew).

4. Ibid.

5. Amir Oren, personal interview, June 11, 2007.

6. Ron Kitri, personal interview, July 17, 2005; see also Kitri, *Fifth Session*, p. 20.

7. Dan Meridor, personal interview, May 22, 2006.

8. Ephraim Sneh, personal interview, April 17, 2007.

9. Uzi Dayan, personal interview, September 26, 2006.

10. Yehoshua Mor-Yosef, personal interview, June 18, 2006.

11. Shlomi Eldar, personal interview, April 26, 2006.

12. Drucker and Shelah, *Boomerang*, p. 29.

13. Gadi Baltiansky, personal interview, August 4, 2005.

14. Gadi Eizenkot, personal interview, June 12, 2007.

15. Ron Kitri, personal interview, July 17, 2005.

16. Gideon Meir, personal interview, July 31, 2005; Meir Shlomo, personal interview, July 13, 2005; Avi Dichter, personal interview, August 10, 2005.

17. Amos Harel, personal interview, April 24, 2006.

18. Gilead Sher, personal interview, August 8, 2006; Sher, 2001, pp. 301–302.

19. *Haaretz*, October 13, 2000, p. 1 (Hebrew).

20. Eli Kamir, personal interview, November 22, 2006; see also Meir Klifi, personal interview, August 4, 2005.

21. Avi Dichter, personal interview, August 10, 2005.

22. *Haaretz*, October 13, 2000, p. 2 (Hebrew).

23. Yoni Dahuh-Halevy, personal interview, July 3, 2005.

24. *Haaretz*, October 13, 2000, p. 2 (Hebrew).

25. Ibid.

26. Ibid.

27. Ibid.

28. IDF Spokesperson's Unit, October 12, 2000, A.

29. *Haaretz*, October 14, 2000 (Hebrew).

30. Udi Lebel, "The Legal-Media Complex versus the Political-Security Complex," in Udi Lebel (ed.), *Security and Media: Dynamics of Relations* (Beersheba: Ben-Gurion Research Institute for the Study of Israel & Zionism, 2005), p. 4 (Hebrew).

31. Gadi Eizenkot, personal interview, June 12, 2007.

32. Eti Wieseltier, personal interview, August 4, 2005.

33. *Haaretz*, October 31, 2000 (Hebrew).

34. *Washington Post*, October 19, 2000, p. C1.

35. Charles Enderlin, personal interview, August 14, 2007.

36. Ilan Sztulman, personal interview, August 17, 2005.

37. Nahum Barnea, "The Lynch Test," *The Seventh Eye* (October 31, 2000), pp. 4–5 (Hebrew).

38. Meir Shlomo, personal interview, July 13, 2005.

39. Schleifer, *Psychological Warfare*, p. 258 (Hebrew).

40. Yarden Vatikai, personal interview, July 27, 2005.

41. Eti Wieseltier, personal interview, August 4, 2005.

42. David Baker, personal interview, July 17, 2005.

43. Shlomo Ben-Ami, *Special Edition: Television Broadcasts in Times of Distress* (Tel Aviv: Yedioth Ahronoth, 2006), p. 318 (Hebrew).

44. *New York Times*, October 13, 2000, p. A8.

45. *Washington Post*, October 13, 2000, p. A01.

46. *Yedioth Ahronoth*, October 13, 2000 (Hebrew).

47. *Jerusalem Post*, October 16, 2000.

48. Foreign Ministry website, October 17, 2000. http://mfa.gov.il/MFA/MFA-Archive/2000/Pages/Coverage%20of%20Oct%2012%20Lynch%20in%20Ramallah%20by%20Italian%20TV.aspx#letter

49. Arik Gordin, personal interview, December 25, 2006; Gideon Meir, personal interview, July 31, 2005.

50. Foreign Ministry telegram, October 19, 2000, 4628711, ministerial directive, 10, 42487.

51. Ron Prosor, personal interview, June 25, 2006.

52. Arnon Regular, *Haaretz*, October 13, 2005 (Hebrew); Avi Issacharoff, *Haaretz*, May 21, 2007, p. 4 (Hebrew).

53. Ron Schleifer, *Psychological Warfare in Israel: A Reexamination* (Ramat Gan: BESA Center for Strategic Studies, Bar-Ilan University, 2002), p. 21 (Hebrew).

54. *Yedioth Ahronoth*, October 20, 2000 (Hebrew).

55. Zohar Kampf, "The Lynching in Ramallah and Symbols of the Conflict," *Panim* 23 (February 2003), p. 7 (Hebrew).

56. *News First Class* (NFC), June 29, 2005.

57. A suicide bombing occurred at the Dolphinarium in Tel Aviv on June 1, 2001, killing 21 people.

58. On June 10, 2006, seven members of the Ghalia family were killed on the beach in Gaza from a mine or shelling.

59. Alon Pinkas, personal interview, June 14, 2006.

Chapter 13

1. IDF Spokesperson's Unit, May 2002.

2. Ibid.

3. Statement by the prime minister at the Knesset, April 8, 2002.

4. Giora Eiland, personal interview, August 2, 2005.

5. Gabriel Ben-Dor, Daphna Canetti-Nisim, and Eran Halperin, *The Social Component of National Resilience* (Haifa: National Security Studies Center, University of Haifa, 2003) (Hebrew).

6. Shmuel Nir, "The Nature of Limited Conflict," in Hagai Golan and Shaul Shai (eds.), *The Limited Conflict* (Tel Aviv: Maarachot, 2004), p. 142 (Hebrew).

7. Shaul Mofaz, personal interview, July 25, 2007.

8. Anti-Defamation League, Anatomy of Anti-Israel Incitement: Jenin, World Opinion and the Massacre That Wasn't, Anti-Defamation League, http://www.adl.org/israel/jenin/jenin.pdf, accessed June 10, 2008.

9. Ibid.

10. A. Yavetz, Seminar on "Israel's Media Strategy: Jenin as a Metaphor," July 2, 2002, p. 41 (Hebrew).

11. IDF Spokesperson's Unit, April 7, 2002.

12. *Haaretz*, April 9, 2002, p. 1 (Hebrew).

13. *Haaretz*, April 10, 2002, p. 1. (Hebrew).

14. *Tel Aviv* newspaper, August 2, 2002 (Hebrew).

15. David Eshel, "The Battle of Jenin," *Jane's Intelligence Review* (July 2002), pp. 20–24.

16. *Ynet*, April 11, 2002 (Hebrew); *Haaretz*, April 11, 2002, p. A4 (Hebrew).

17. Adir Haruvi, Seminar on "Israel's Media Strategy: Jenin as a Metaphor," July 2, 2002, p. 26 (Hebrew).

18. *Associated Press*, April 4, 2002.

19. *CNN*, April 6, 2002.

20. *New York Times*, April 7, 2002.

21. F. Halhal, Seminar on "Israel's Media Strategy: Jenin as a Metaphor," July 2, 2002, p. 36 (Hebrew).

22. Ministry of Foreign Affairs, April 9, 2002.

23. *Yedioth Ahronoth*, April 9, 2002 (Hebrew).

24. *Washington Post*, April 13, 2002, p. A1.

25. *Haaretz*, April 10, 2002, p. A5 (Hebrew).

26. *Agence France Presse*.

27. Yehuda Kraut, *Backgrounder: A Study in Palestinian Duplicity and Media Indifference*, Committee for Accuracy in Middle East Reporting (CAMERA), August 1, 2002, http://www.camera.org/index.asp?x_article=217&x_context=7, accessed September 24, 2016; Ricki Hollander, *Study: New York Times Skews Israeli-Palestinian Crisis*, Committee for Accuracy in Middle East Reporting (CAMERA), May 1, 2002. http://www.camera.org/index.asp?x_article=25&x_context=2, accessed September 24, 2016.

28. *Haaretz*, April 11, 2002, p. A4 (Hebrew).

29. L. Yavneh, Seminar on "Israel's Media Strategy: Jenin as a Metaphor," July 2, 2002, p. 20 (Hebrew).

30. Hassan Jabareen, "The Rise of Transnational Lawyering for Human Rights," *Journal of Law and Social Change* 1 (2008), p. 144 (Hebrew).

31. Ibid.

32. Supreme Court website: http://elyon1.court.gov.il/Files_ENG/02/140/031/A02/02031140.A02.pdf, accessed September 28, 2016.

33. *Washington Post*, April 19, 2002, p. A01.

34. Miri Eisen, personal interview, May 28, 2006.

35. *Globes*, April 24, 2002 (Hebrew).

36. *Haaretz*, April 19, 2002, p. A4 (Hebrew).

37. *New York Times*, April 20, 2002, p. 7.

38. Security Council Resolution 1045, April 19, 2002.

39. Shmuel Rosner, *An Outline for Hasbara*, the Jewish Agency, based on a Foreign Ministry briefing, April 21, 2002 (Hebrew).

40. *Haaretz*, April 24, 2002, p. A1 (Hebrew).

41. *Haaretz*, April 25, 2002, p. A1 (Hebrew).

42. *Haaretz*, May 1, 2002, (Hebrew).

43. Zeev Schiff, Seminar on "Israel's Media Strategy: Jenin as a Metaphor," July 2, 2002, p. 10 (Hebrew).

5. *Washington Post*, August 2, 2002, p. A16.

46. *Time*, May 13, 2002.

47. Human Rights Watch, May 3, 2002.

48. Yavneh, Seminar on "Israel's Media Strategy: Jenin as a Metaphor," p. 18.

49. *Yedioth Ahronoth*, March 3, 2003, p. 17 (Hebrew).

50. *Haaretz*, September 19, 2003 (Hebrew).

51. In Levy-Barzilai, *Haaretz*, pp. 30–31 (Hebrew); *Maariv*, November 8, 2002 (Hebrew).

52. HCJ 316/03, ruling issued on November 11, 2003. English translation on Supreme Court website: http://elyon1.court.gov.il/Files_ENG/03/160/003/115/03003160.115.HTM, accessed September 29, 2016.

53. *Maariv*, April 1, 2002, pp. 4–5 (Hebrew).

54. *Haaretz*, April 1, 2002 (Hebrew).

55. *Maariv*, April 1, 2002, pp. 4–5 (Hebrew).

56. Aryeh Mekel, personal interview, July 20, 2005.

57. Dan Harel, personal interview, December 7, 2006.

58. Ron Kitri, personal interview, July 17, 2005.

59. Binyamin Ben-Eliezer, personal interview, July 23, 2006.

60. Eyal Shlein, personal interview, December 7, 2006.

61. Amos Harel, personal interview, April 24, 2006.

62. Charles Enderlin, personal interview, August 25, 2005.

63. Jennifer Griffin, personal interview, April 25, 2006.

64. Amir Oren, personal interview, June 11, 2007.

65. *Haaretz*, April 16, 2002, p. 10 (Hebrew).

66. Rafi Tadhar, personal interview, July 20, 2005.

67. Shlomi Eldar, personal interview, April 26, 2006.

68. Aryeh Mekel, personal interview, July 20, 2005.

69. Meir Klifi, personal interview, August 4, 2005.

70. Miri Eisen, personal interview, May 28, 2006.

71. Dan Harel, personal interview, December 7, 2006.

72. Ron Ben-Yishai, personal interview, August 9, 2007.

73. Ron Kitri, personal interview, January 2, 2007.

74. Yarden Vatikai, personal interview, July 25, 2002.

75. Jacob Dallal, "Bad Information: The Lesson of Jenin," *The New Republic Online*, May 8, 2005, p. 2.

76. *Haaretz*, April 15, 2002, p. A1 (Hebrew).

77. *Washington Post*, August 6, 2002, p. A15.

78. *Haaretz*, July 17, 2002 (Hebrew).

79. Dan Meridor, personal interview, May 22, 2006.

80. *Maariv*, April 21, 2003 (Hebrew).

Chapter 14

1. Decision 1936, July 8, 2007.

2. Israel Maimon, personal interviews, March 23, 2006 and July 31, 2007.

3. Israel Maimon, personal interview, July 31, 2007.

4. Tzipi Livni, personal interview, July 23, 2007.

5. Itzhak Galnoor, quoted in Dan Caspi and Yehiel Limor, *The Mediators: The Mass Media in Israel, 1948–1990* (Tel Aviv: Am Oved, 1986), p. 1 (Hebrew).

6. Wilson P. Dizard Jr., *Inventing Public Diplomacy: The Story of the U.S. Information Agency* (London: Boulder, 2004), p. 34.

7. Zepgoria Digital Marketing, 2016, https://zephoria.com/top-15-valuable-facebook-statistics/, accessed October 17, 2016.

8. *eBizzMBA*, October 2016, http://www.ebizmba.com/articles/social-networking-websites, accessed on October 17, 2016.

9. Danny Naveh, "Government Hasbara Can Be Done Differently," Shalem Center Research Report 9, January 1995, p. 16 (Hebrew).

10. Haim Assa and Yedidia Yaari, *Diffused Warfare: War in the 21st Century* (Tel Aviv: Yedioth Ahronoth, 2005), p. 22 (Hebrew).

11. Ibid., p. 37.

Chapter 15

1. Barak Ravid, "World Sees Israel as a Pariah State, Senior Gov't Official Says," *Haaretz*, August 7, 2016.

2. Pnina Sharvit Baruch and Kobi Michael, "The Delegitimization of Israel: Trends and Responses," in Shlomo Brom and Anat Kurz (eds.), *Strategic Survey for Israel, 2015–2016* (Tel Aviv: Institute for National Security Studies, 2016), p. 85.

3. Yehuda Ben Meir and Owen Alterman, "The Delegitimization Threat: Roots, Manifestations, and Containment," in Anat Kurz and Shlomo Brom (eds.) *Strategic Survey for Israel 2011* (Tel Aviv: Institute for National Security Studies,

2011), pp. 121–137; Pnina Sharvit Baruch, "National Security and International Legitimacy," *INSS Insight* 742 (September 2, 2015), accessed August 16, 2016.

4. Ben Meir and Alterman, "The Delegitimization Threat," p. 110.

5. NGO Monitor, NGO Forum at Durban Conference, 2001.

6. Amir Ofek, personal interview, February 15, 2016.

7. "The Role of the Palestinians in the BDS Campaign," The Meir Amit Intelligence and Terrorism Information Center, July 29, 2015.

8. State Comptroller's Report 66C, "Foreign Ministry: The Diplomatic and Media Struggle against the Boycott Movement and Manifestations of Anti-Semitism Overseas," State Comptroller's Office, 2016 (Hebrew).

9. Tal Schwartzman and Ben Hoffman, "Israel's Economy in the Shadow of the Delegitimization Campaign," Ministry of Finance, February 1, 2015, p. 3 (Hebrew).

10. Naama Teschner, "Initiatives to Boycott Israeli Academic Institutions," Knesset Research and Information Center, December 22, 2013.

11. Chemi Shalev, "The ASA Boycott Could Spark Israel-Centered Brawl Throughout U.S. Campuses," *Haaretz*, December 16, 2013.

12. Michal Hatuel-Radoshitzky, "Israel, BDS, UN: Lowering Volume, Increasing Capacity," INSS "Shorty," April 6, 2016 (Hebrew), http://www.inss.org.

13. "Netanyahu's AIPAC Speech: The Full Transcript," *Haaretz*, March 4, 2014.

14. Ron Dagoni, "Lawmakers and Presidential Candidates in the U.S. Attack BDS," *Globes*, February 7, 2016 (Hebrew).

15. "Adelson and Saban: An Anti-Israel Tsunami is Heading Toward Us," *Haaretz*, June 6, 2015 (Hebrew).

16. State Comptroller's Report 66C (Hebrew).

17. Sara Leibowitz-Dar, "Not So Quick: The Movement to Boycott Israel Is Far from Saying the Last Word," *Maariv*, July 31, 2016 (Hebrew).

18. Nye, "Get Smart."

Epilogue

1. Obama's last press conference, December 2016, http://www.politico.com/story/2016/12/obama-press-conference-transcript-232763, accessed August 16, 2016.

References

English

Bauman, Zygmunt. *Globalization: The Human Consequences.* Cambridge: Polity Press, 1998.

Ben-Meir, Yehuda, and Owen Alterman. "The Delegitimization Threat: Roots, Manifestations, and Containment," in Anat Kurz and Shlomo Brom (eds.), *Strategic Survey for Israel 2011.* Tel Aviv: Institute for National Security Studies, 2011.

Cymerman, Henrique. *Voices from the Center of the World: The Arab-Israeli Conflict told by its Protagonists.* Tel Aviv: Hakibbutz Hameuchad, 2005.

Dallal, Jacob. "Bad Information: The Lesson of Jenin." *The New Republic Online,* May 8, 2005. http://archive.li/b0ohT. Accessed September 24, 2016.

Dizard, Wilson P., Jr. *Inventing Public Diplomacy: The Story of the U.S. Information Agency.* London: Boulder, 2004.

Eshel, David. "The Battle of Jenin." *Jane's Intelligence Review* (July 2002).

Freilich, Charles D. "National Security Decision-Making in Israel: Processes, Pathologies, and Strengths." *Middle East Journal* 60.4 (2006).

Ganor, Boaz. *The Counter-Terrorism Puzzle: A Guide for Decision Makers.* Piscataway: Transaction, 2011.

Gilboa, Eytan. "Public Diplomacy: The Missing Component in Israel's Foreign Policy." *Israel Affairs* 12.4 (October 2006).

Goodman, Hirsh. "Israel's Information Policy during the Iraq War." *Strategic Assessment* 6.3 (November 2003).

Hollander, Ricki. *Study: New York Times Skews Israeli-Palestinian Crisis.* Committee for Accuracy in Middle East Reporting (CAMERA), May 1, 2002. http://www.camera.org/index.asp?x_article=25&x_context=2. Accessed September 24, 2016.

Jones, Jeremy. "Durban Daze: When Anti-Semitism Becomes 'Anti-Racism.'" *Australia/Israel Review* 26 (October 2001).

Kraut, Yehuda. *Backgrounder: A Study in Palestinian Duplicity and Media Indifference.* Committee for Accuracy in Middle East Reporting (CAMERA), August 1, 2002. http://www.camera.org/index.asp?x_article=217&x_context=7. Accessed September 24, 2016.

Liddell Hart, Basil Henry. *Strategy: The Indirect Approach*. London: Faber and Faber, 1954.

Mahnken, Thomas G. "Why the Weak Win: Strong Powers, Weak Powers, and the Logic of Strategy." In Bradford A. Lee and Karl F. Walling (eds.), *Strategic Logic and Political Rationality: Essays in Honor of Michael I. Handel*. Portland: Frank Cass, 2003.

Mor, Ben D. "Strategic Self-Presentation in Public Diplomacy: The Israeli-Palestinian Case." Paper presented at the annual conference of the Midwest Political Science Association, Chicago, 2003.

Nye, Joseph S. "Think Again: Soft Power." *Foreign Policy* (February 23, 2006).

Nye, Joseph, "Get Smart: Combining Hard and Soft Power." *Foreign Affairs* 88.4 (July/August 2009).

Omer, Haim, and Nahi Alon. "The Principle of Continuity: Unifying Treatment and Management in Disaster and Trauma." *American Journal of Community Psychology* 22 (1994).

"The Role of the Palestinians in the BDS Campaign." The Meir Amit Intelligence and Terrorism Information Center. July 29, 2015.

Schiff, Zeev, and Ehud Yaari. *Intifada: The Palestinian Uprising*. New York: Simon and Schuster, 1990.

Scholte, Jan Aart. *The Globalization of World Politics*. Oxford: Oxford University Press, 2001.

Seib, Philip. *The Global Journalist: News and Conscience in a World of Conflict*. Lanham: Rowman & Littlefield, 2002.

Seib, Philip. "Hegemonic No More: Western Media, the Rise of Al-Jazeera, and the Influence of Diverse Voices." *International Studies Review* 7 (2005).

Shai, Hanan. "The Intellectual Challenge in the Struggle against Human Terror Bombs and Other Inhuman Terrorism." Lecture delivered at the 2nd International Conference on Low-Intensity Warfare, January 31, 2005.

Shai, Nachman. *The Spokesperson in the Crossfire: A Decade of Israeli Defense Crisis from an Official Spokesperson's Perspective*. Discussion Paper D-29. Cambridge: Harvard University, 1998.

Sharvit-Baruch, Pnina. "National Security and International Legitimacy." *INSS Insight* 724 (September 2, 2015).

Sharvit-Baruch, Pnina, and Kobi Michael. "The Delegitimization of Israel: Trends and Responses." In Shlomo Brom and Anat Kurz (eds.), *Strategic Survey for Israel 2015–2016*. Tel Aviv: INSS, 2016.

Steinberg, N. World Conference Against Racism, Racial Discrimination, Xenophobia and Related Intolerance, World Federalist Movement, November 7, 2001.

Sun Tzu. *The Art of War*. Oxford: Clarendon Press, 1963.

Thompson, Loren B. "Low-Intensity Conflict: An Overview." In Loren B. Thompson (ed.), *Low-Intensity Conflict: The Pattern of Warfare in the Modern World*. Lexington: Lexington Books, 1989.

van Creveld, Martin. *The Transformation of War*. New York: The Free Press, 1991.

Yaffe, Aharon. "Targeted Killing: Prospect and Risk." *Nativ* 19.2 (March 2006). Ariel Center for Policy Research.

French

Huber, Gérard. *Contre expertise d'une mise en scène*. Paris: Raphael, 2003.

Hebrew

Agron, Gershon. *Prisoner of Loyalty* (Tel Aviv: M. Neuman, 1964).

Assa, Haim, and Yedidia Yaari. *Diffused Warfare: War in the 21st Century*. Tel Aviv: Yedioth Ahronoth, 2005.

Aynor, Hanan. *Thirty Years of International Assistance of the State of Israel*. Jerusalem: Haigud Society for Transfer of Technology and The Truman Institute, 1990.

Barnea, Nahum. "The Lynch Test." *The Seventh Eye*, 2000.

Ben-Ami, Shlomo. *Special Edition: Television Broadcasts in Times of Distress*. Tel Aviv: Yedioth Ahronoth, 2006.

Ben-Dor, Gabriel, Daphna Canetti-Nisim, and Eran Halperin. *The Social Component of National Resilience*. Haifa: National Security Studies Center, University of Haifa, 2003.

Ben-Israel, Isaac. *The First Israel-Hezbollah Missile War*. Tel Aviv: Program for Security Studies, College of Policy and Government, Tel Aviv University, May 2007.

Brender, M. "The Population's Behavior in Conditions of Stress and Treatment Methods during a Rescue Event." *Emergency and Mass Catastrophe*. Jerusalem: Labor and Social Welfare Ministry, 1990.

Breznitz, Shlomo, and D. Carmel. *The Effect of Information on the Home Front's Level of Function—Research Project Submitted to the IDF Home Front*. Haifa: University of Haifa, Center for the Study of Psychological Pressure, 1995.

Brosh, Tamar (ed.). *A Speech for Every Occasion*. Tel Aviv: Open University, 1993.

Carmeli, A., L. Mevorach, N. Lieberman, A. Taubman, S. Kahanovitz, and D. Navon. "The Gulf War: The Home Front in Time of Crisis." *Human in Battle Project*. Tel Aviv: Defense Ministry, 1992.

Caspi, Dan, and Yehiel Limor. *The Mediators: The Mass Media in Israel, 1948–1990*. Tel Aviv: Am Oved, 1986.

Drori, M., G. Posen, and K. Ginsburg. "A Model for Operating a Public Information Center in a Mass Casualty Event at a Medical Center in Tel Aviv." *Society and Social Welfare* 19 (1999).

Drucker, Raviv, and Ofer Shelah. *Boomerang: The Failure of Leadership in the Second Intifada*. Jerusalem: Keter, 2005.

Drucker, Raviv. *Harikari: Ehud Barak in the Test of Results*. Tel Aviv: Yedioth Ahronoth, 2002.

Erlich, Reuven. *The War for Consciousness in the Framework of the Conflict between the Terrorist Organizations and Israel: Hezbollah as a Test Case*. Ramat Hasharon: Meir Amit Intelligence & Terror Information Center, May 2, 2007.

Even, Yaakov. "The Media in the Intifada." In Reuven Gal (ed.), *The Seventh War: The Effects of the Intifada on Israeli Society*. Tel Aviv: Hakibbutz Hameuchad, 1990.

Golan, Hagai, and Shaul Shai (eds.). *The Limited Conflict*. Tel Aviv: Maarachot, 2004.

Gutman, Yechiel. *A Storm in the GSS*. Tel Aviv: Yedioth Ahronoth, 1995.

Halfon, A. "Structure of the Foreign Service of the Jewish State." In Moshe Yegar, Yosef Guvrin, and Oded Aryeh (eds.), *The Foreign Ministry: The First 50 Years*. Jerusalem: Keter, 2002.

Halhal, P. Seminar on "Israel's Media Strategy: Jenin as a Metaphor." July 2, 2002.

Harel, Amos, and Avi Issacharoff. *The Seventh War: How We Won and Why We Lost in the War with the Palestinians*. Tel Aviv: Yedioth Ahronoth and Hemed Books, 2004.

Harkavi, Yehoshafat. *War and Strategy*. Tel Aviv: Maarachot, 1990.

Haruvi, Adir. Seminar on "Israel's Media Strategy: Jenin as a Metaphor." July 2, 2002.

Hatuel-Radoshitzky, Michal. "Israel, BDS, UN: Lowering Volume, Increasing Capacity." INSS "Shorty," April 6, 2016. http://www.inss.org. Accessed September 24, 2016.

Jabareen, Hassan. "The Rise of Transnational Lawyering for Human Rights." *Journal of Law and Social Change* 1 (2008).

Kampf, Zohar. "The Lynching in Ramallah and Symbols of the Conflict." *Panim* 23 (February 2003).

Kaplan, G. "Information for the Public as a Support System." In *Collection of Short Articles on Information for the Public*. Tel Aviv: IDF Central Command, 1983.

Katz, Shmuel. *No Courage and No Dignity*. Tel Aviv: Dvir, 1981.

Kitri, Ron. *Fifth Session: IDF and the Media in Times of Warfare—Open Meeting*. Army and Society Forum. Jerusalem: Israel Democracy Institute, June 4, 2002.

Kober, Avi. "Victory and Decision in Modern and Post-Modern Wars." A paper delivered at a seminar held at the University of Haifa on January 28, 2001.

Kober, Avi. "Low-Intensity Conflicts: Why the Gap Between Theory and Practice?" In Haggai Golan and Shaul Shay (eds.), *The Limited Conflict*. Tel Aviv: Maarachot, 2004.

Kremnitzer, Mordechai. "Is Everything Permissible in Countering Terrorism? On Israel's Targeted Killing Policy in the West Bank and Gaza." Israel Democracy Institute, Position Paper 60, 2006.

Kunis-Ponta, Henriete, and Rinat Moshe. *On Consciousness and Influence and Their Relations: A Theoretical Model and an Analysis of Case Studies*. Tel Aviv: IDF Center for Consciousness, 2007.

Lebel, Udi. "The Legal-Media Complex versus the Political-Security Complex." In Udi Lebel (ed.), *Security and Media: Dynamics of Relations*. Beersheba: Ben-Gurion Research Institute for the Study of Israel & Zionism, 2005.

Naveh, Danny. "Government Hasbara Can Be Done Differently." Shalem Center Research Report 9, January 1995.

Navot, Alon. *The Shin Bet and the Media*. Final project submitted to National Security College, 1995.

Negbi, Moshe. *Paper Tiger*. Tel Aviv: Sifriyat Poalim, 1985.

Nir, Shmuel. "The Limited Conflict: Collection of Articles." *Zarkor*. Tel Aviv: IDF Operations Division-Doctrine and Training, 2002.

Nir, Shmuel. "The Nature of Limited Conflict." In Hagai Golan and Shaul Shai (eds.), *The Limited Conflict*. Tel Aviv: Maarachot, 2004.

Schleifer, Ron. *Psychological Warfare in Israel: A Reexamination*. Ramat Gan: BESA Center for Strategic Studies, Bar-Ilan University, 2002.

Schleifer, Ron. *Psychological Warfare*. Tel Aviv: Maarachot, 2007.

Schiff, Zeev. Seminar on "Israel's Media Strategy: Jenin as a Metaphor," July 2, 2002.

Schwartzman, Tal, and Ben Hoffman. "Israel's Economy in the Shadow of the Delegitimization Campaign." Ministry of Finance, February 1, 2015.

Shai, Nachman. *The Media War: Ten Lessons*. Tel Aviv: Maarachot, 2001.

Shay, Shaul. "Limited Conflict and the Concept of Deterrence." In Golan and Shai (eds.), *The Limited Conflict*.

Sher, Gilead. *Within Reach: The Peace Negotiations, 1999–2001: Testimony*. Tel Aviv: Yedioth Ahronoth, 2001.

State Comptroller's Report 66C. "Foreign Ministry: The Diplomatic and Media Struggle against the Boycott Movement and Manifestations of Anti-Semitism Overseas." State Comptroller's Office, 2016.

Teschner, Naama. "Initiatives to Boycott Israeli Academic Institutions." Knesset Research and Information Center, December 22, 2013.

Weimann, Gabriel. "Public Criticism of the Media during the 2006 War in Lebanon." *The Media in the Lebanon War Series*. Tel Aviv: Tel Aviv University, December 2006.

Yaalon, Moshe. *Fifth Session: IDF and the Media in Times of Warfare—Discussion Group on: The Media as a Strategic Consideration in Preparing for Combat*. Army and Society Forum. Jerusalem: Israel Democracy Institute, June 4, 2002.

Yaron, Ruth. *IDF Spokesperson's Division: Strategic Summary, 2002–2005*. Tel Aviv: IDF Spokesperson's Division, 2005.

Yavetz, A. Seminar on "Israel's Media Strategy: Jenin as a Metaphor." July 2, 2002.

Yavneh, L. Seminar on "Israel's Media Strategy: Jenin as a Metaphor." July 2, 2002.

Yegar, Moshe. *Toward a History of Israel's Hasbara System*. Herzliya: Lahav Publishing with the Israeli Institute for Propaganda Research, 1986.

Yegar, Moshe, Yosef Guvrin, and Oded Aryeh (eds.). *The Foreign Ministry: The First 50 Years*. Jerusalem: Keter, 2002.

Zigdon, Yaakov. *Studies in the Doctrine of Building Military Force*. Ramat Hasharon: IDF Staff and Command College, 2004.

Newspapers

Globes
Haaretz
Maariv
TheMarker
Yedioth Ahronoth

About the Author

Nachman Shai brings his own experience to bear on this issue. He served for many years in central positions in the media and public diplomacy, including press secretary for the Israeli delegation to the United Nations, media advisor to the Israeli embassy in Washington, DC, and to defense ministers Moshe Arens and Yitzhak Rabin, commander and editor-in-chief of Israel Army Radio, IDF spokesperson, national coordinator of *hasbara* at the beginning of the second intifada, CEO of the Second Television and Radio Authority, and chairperson of the Israeli Broadcasting Authority. First elected to the Knesset in 2009, the author has served on the Defense and Foreign Affairs Committee and as deputy speaker. The research for this book included an examination of case studies, best practices of Israeli public diplomacy, and the leading theories in this field.

Index

Note: Page numbers in italics indicate figures; those with a *t* indicate tables.